Columbia University

STUDIES IN ROMANCE PHILOLOGY AND
LITERATURE

MICHELET AND HIS IDEAS
ON SOCIAL REFORM

Columbia University Press

COLUMBIA UNIVERSITY

NEW YORK

SALES AGENTS

LONDON

HUMPHREY MILFORD

Amen Corner, E. C.

SHANGHAI

EDWARD EVANS AND SONS, Ltd.

30 North Szechuen Road

MICHELET AND HIS IDEAS
ON
SOCIAL REFORM

BY

ANNE R. PUGH, PhD.

New York
COLUMBIA UNIVERSITY PRESS
1923

PREFACE

The present study constitutes three Parts of an investigation of Michelet's *Ideas on Social Reform,* which are here published without their complementary Part IV, containing chapters treating of the historian's Ideals of the "Patrie," National Education, and the "Messianic Mission" of the Nation. It is hoped that these three Parts may in themselves give a fairly complete understanding of Michelet's personality and of the fundamental ideas upon which he based his social homilies. They are here published as they were written, save that since the work does not appear in its entirety, the Introduction and the end of the last chapter have been somewhat modified.

In writing these chapters an effort has been made to allow a prophet of interesting personality to speak for himself in so far as he may be said to be able to do so in passages which, whatever attempt they may reveal of a sincere endeavor to render the author's feeling, make no pretence of being literal translation. This effort to leave to the great historian in so far as possible the exposition of his own ideas, is perhaps the only justification for the undertaking of any study of so complex and important a personality as was Michelet, by a writer so far separated from him in all the accidents of time, space, human circumstance, and human environment.

The interesting work of M. E. Seillière (that part at least comprised in the first three volumes of *l'Impérialisme démocratique*), has been full of suggestion to the author. M. Seillière's work on Michelet himself did not come into her hands until her work was ready for publication.

Wherever possible, however, account has been taken of it in notes.

If the names of all those who have been of assistance to the writer were given here, the list would be a long one. Those who are named below are in no way responsible for the character of this work except in this, that they have made it better than it would have been without their help. These chapters have benefited by the wise criticism of Professor J. L. Gerig, of Professor Raymond Weeks, and Professor Dino Bigongiari of Columbia University; and of Professor Henri Chamard of the Sorbonne, Professor Jules Legras of the University of Dijon, and M. Bernard Faÿ of Paris. The manuscript has had the advantage of suggestions from Professor E. A. Ellis, Miss Margaret Landes, and President Kerr Duncan Macmillan of Wells College. Grateful acknowledgment for biographical data is due to Professor H. C. Lancaster of Johns Hopkins University, to Professor André Morize of Harvard University, and to Dr. E. E. Slosson of Washington, D. C. The author's work has been much facilitated by courteous and ready attention to her needs on the part of Librarians of Columbia University, of Cornell University, of the New York Public Library, and of Wells College.

Especial indebtedness is felt, though here quite inadequately expressed, for help and invaluable suggestions from Professor H. A. Todd of Columbia University and from Professor Gilbert Chinard of Johns Hopkins University. Without their friendly advice and aid, these chapters would have lacked much of whatever suggestiveness or usefulness the reader may be generous enough to find in them.

A. R. P.

CONTENTS

INTRODUCTION

MICHELET A PROPHET AMONG PROPHETS

"Une nouvelle ère se prépare, le monde est au travail, tous les esprits sont attentifs."

Ballanche, Palingénésie sociale, 1822, p. 24.

In 1876, two years after Michelet's death, Bersot declared that the great historian had been for his generation a representative man; that in so far as essential matters of belief were concerned, his epoch could see itself reflected in him.[1] In 1848 he had been acclaimed by the university youth as a 'prophet.'[2] It was a title easily earned at that particular moment. However, if one accepts the definition offered by M. Suarès, "a prophet is one who proclaims what all are eager to hear,"[3] Michelet undoubtedly held some claim to it. It was not a paramount claim. The hopes and aspirations of the early nineteenth century were too numerous and varied to allow the message of a

---

[1] Mme. J. Michelet, *La mort et les funérailles de J. Michelet*, 1876. Bersot's statement is: "Sur le fond des choses, notre temps peut se reconnaître en lui." H. de Régnier, *Revue de Paris*, 15 juillet, 1898, pp. 225–246 says: "Personne n'a pénétré plus avant dans l'âme française que Michelet," and (p. 246) "Il fut de l'humanité, de son temps, de sa race, de son pays."

[2] Mme. E. Quinet, *Cinquante ans d'amitié*, 1899, p. 158. "La Révolution de 1848 rendit la parole aux professeurs. C'est Edgar Quinet qui est chargé de prononcer le discours d'ouverture. . . . Quel enthousiasme éclate à la vue des deux frères d'armes. . . . 'Les prophètes! les prophètes!' ce cri retentissait de tous côtés."

[3] A. Suarès, *La nation contre la race*, 1917, p. 1, "Le jeu des prophètes est de clamer au nom du ciel ce que le peuple sent et ce qu'il veut."

single individual to suffice. This epoch of multiple ideals accepted and cherished a multitude of prophets. Men of every class were awaiting a special revelation, and if they did not always accept what was confidently proclaimed to be such, they were at any rate ready to give anyone a fair hearing.[4] Among those offering themselves as bearers of a personal or prophetic message, Michelet came to be for many a well-known and well-loved figure; he obtained a world-wide audience, and his influence still endures in face of the lapse of time and the march of events, and despite the fact that it has never gone wholly unchallenged.

His was a figure of real importance to those who were content with just the combination that he offered,—that of fervid inspiration and reasonable constraint. The recognizedly great Utopians, Saint-Simon and Fourier, the great positivist Comte, even perhaps Leroux and Proudhon, had, by a more or less systematized exposition of their theories organized for themselves either definite adherence or definite opposition. The first three especially had to arouse conviction and ensure submission, in order to recruit proselytes and followers. Since the enthusiasm of this epoch could be (as may indeed that of any epoch) more easily aroused than maintained, their systems as practical solutions of human problems were not long-lived. They very quickly had their day and ceased to be.

The spirit which had inspired them had, nevertheless, passed into the impulses and aspirations of great throngs of thinkers and dreamers who refused to allow themselves to be bound by definitely communistic, socialistic or

[4] M. Ferraz, *Socialisme, naturalisme et positivisme* (1877), ed. 1882, Int., pp. xxxiii–iv, also pp. 77–80, 139, 150, 397–420. P. M. Masson, *La religion de J. J. Rousseau*, 1921; vol. 3, chap. 2; A. Guiard, *La fonction du poète*, 1910. Madame Quinet begins *E. Quinet avant l'exil*, 1899, with: "La vie d'Edgar Quinet fut un apostolat."

F. Strowski, "Le messianisme sous Louis Philippe," *Rev. des cours et des conférences*, 20 Janvier, 1915.

economic theories and ideals; men who refused to be bound, who even refused to face the logical results of such reforms as they themselves advocated. Did not Rousseau himself admit that he would find it unpleasant to live in a newly organized Republic? [5] Their unconquerable individualism had been both strengthened and stranded by the shipwreck of the Revolution. These composed the more prudent, and, on the whole, the more modest of the tribes of those seeking revelation. It is among these that Michelet has his place. Certain traits of his personality and certain facts of his experience had peculiarly fitted him for the rôle he was to play.

Michelet's beginnings were not perhaps more humble or more difficult than those of certain other great men of his day, but they have come to constitute a sort of legend, generally accepted, of triumph over difficulties through unremitting hard work and tenacity of purpose. His autobiographical notes do indeed furnish a touching story of the burden which poverty and a tremendous sense of responsibility had laid upon him. His father, Jean-François Furcy Michelet, was a journeyman printer, and as such had known all the hazards of his trade in the Paris of the great Revolution. His easy optimism had helped him to take his vicissitudes lightly, and at last his success seemed to justify marriage. His wife came of good peasant stock, which had taken on some added dignity through the distinction that some of its scions had gained in the Church. Jules Michelet was born in Paris in 1798.[6] The early

---

[5] J. J. Rousseau, *A Discourse upon the Origin and Foundation of the Inequality of Mankind*, London, MDCCLXI, Dedication (to Geneva): "I should not like to belong to a Republic lately formed, whatever good laws it might be blessed with; for, as the Government of it might be otherwise framed than present Exigencies required, I could not promise myself that it might not be shaken almost at its Birth."

[6] The record of Michelet's childhood is found in *Ma jeunesse*, composed of notes and extracts from his correspondence and his printed

years of the century brought business adversity and imprisonment for debt to his father, want and anxiety to those about him, and finally discouragement and fatal illness to his mother. She died during those years in which every energy was being spent in trying to keep the family fortunes afloat, and to prevent Michelet's education from being interrupted.

When his mother died, Michelet was sixteen years old, just old enough to feel his sorrow like a child and understand it like a man. By dint of substantial sacrifice the boy had been provided with the preparation afforded by the *Collège Charlemagne*, where he had come into contact with Villemain, who was to act for years as one of his counsellors and friends, exchanging this rôle later for that of a somewhat adverse critic.[7] The years spent at the *Collège* were marked with enough triumph to gratify and elate a sensitive spirit which had known the strain of working at high tension; conscious at the same time of

works, compiled and edited (with what care it is at present impossible to determine) by Mme. Michelet. (Cf. G. Monod, *J. M.*, p. 6.) This record extends to the year 1815. It is full of pictures of the sufferings of a highly sensitive, delicate, poorly-clad boy, doubled by the reflections which his own memories aroused in Michelet grown old and accompanied (possibly) by unacknowledged comments by his widow. The record of Michelet's life from 1820–1824 is to be found in his *Journal* written by himself, but edited by Mme. Michelet, *Ma jeunesse*, pp. 175–180. Cf. G. Monod, *J. M.*, p. 6.

[7] *Mon journal*, pp. 12, 218, 367. A hint of Villemain's judgment of Michelet is to be found in his criticism of the second volume of Michelet's *Histoire de France* contained in a letter of Villemain to A. Thierry: "Tu me demandes ce que je pense de l'ouvrage de Michelet. Eh bien! il a beaucoup d'esprit, mais . . . il crée des races, telle que la race celto-hellénique; il jette dans l'histoire des lambeaux de métaphysique allemande, des rêvasseries mystiques, il n'a aucune vue politique, et il est fou en architecture." Cf. *Augustin Thierry d'après sa correspondance et ses papiers de famille*, A. Augustin Thierry, 15 déc., 1921, pp. 863–864, of *R. D. M.* For the opinion of the young Michelet of Villemain's knowledge of philosophy, cf. *Mon journal*, p. 255.

how necessary it was to repay in so far as possible the sacrifices by which it had benefited.

The feeling which animated Michelet's first experience in teaching may be judged by a hope which he recorded in his diary,—the hope that his lessons might "incline a rich young man toward the love of humanity." [8] When opportunity came to test more thoroughly his preparation and to try his fortunes, his progress was steady but not brilliant. His first appointments were just so many disappointments.[9] He refused however to be embittered or discouraged by the difficulty of finding the desired post. He read omnivorously from literature, history and philosophy, studied English, devouring at the same time many of the less serious books which the youth of his day were given to devouring.[10]

While planning to live a solitary life given over to writing useful and exhaustive works, he took upon himself complex and disturbing responsibilities. His *Journal* is, however, a record of the patience and steadiness which held him to the tasks that he had in hand from 1820 to 1824, even while he was beset by the vague longing common to all youth, and tormented by the very definite desire to forge ahead. He bridled his tongue, disciplined his energies, put much eagerness and conscience into his teaching.[10]

Michelet married as soon as his future seemed reasonably assured. He had been living for some years in the rue de la Roquette where he had taken a house in which his father organized a *pension bourgeoise*. Two of its occupants had been fellow employees of M. Furcy Michelet in an institution for the feeble-minded. When this institution

[8] *Ibid.*, p. 59.

[9] *Ibid.*, pp. 247, 252, 258, 272, etc.

[10] The lists of books read by Michelet during these years are appended to his *Journal*. He first gave private lessons, then held the post of *Suppléant* at the *Collège Charlemagne* and became *Répétiteur* at an Institut Briand. In 1822 he received a *Suppléance* at the *Collège Sainte-Barbe*.

went out of existence, these two women came with the Michelets, father and son, to the pension bringing with them charges whom they had been employed to care for. The older of these two associates, Madame Fourcy, spoken of in the *Journal* as "madame Hortense" or "ma marraine," seems to have exercised a real influence upon the young Michelet during the years in which he had lived with his father as a lodger in the *Etablissement Duchemin*. The younger woman, Mlle. Pauline Rousseau, and Michelet were married in 1824.[11]

This year was to be in many ways decisive for Michelet. He met now for the first time Victor Cousin whose acquaintance with German philosophy and whose "metaphysics of history" helped the younger man to systematize his own conception of the Philosophy of History. It was in this same year that he plunged into the study of the work which was to remain a constant inspiration to him. This work was the *Scienza Nuova* of Giambattista Vico. Michelet's translation of portions of Vico's treatise, published with an introduction in 1827, brought him favorable recognition. It likewise renewed knowledge of the great Italian in France.[12]

[11] *Ma jeunesse*, pp. 141–173. Cf. also Part III, chap. 1.

[12] For the difficulties which prevent one from accepting the date given by Mme. Michelet of her husband's acquaintance with Vico's work, cf. G. Lanson, *The Historical Method of J. Michelet*, *International Quarterly*, 1905, April, note on p. 80. M. Lanson's conclusion is that Michelet learned to know Vico's *Scienza Nuova* in 1824. There still remains to be explained the statement of the *Journal*: "Je l'avais entrevu (Vico) l'année même où j'ai pris pour la première fois Dugald-Stewart (1821)." A close examination of Degérando, whom Michelet was reading in the autumn of 1820 and the early winter of 1821, might perhaps reveal some possibility of Michelet's having "glimpsed" Vico through Degérando; for B. Croce states that "an Italian exile, Cuoco, introduced Vico's work to Degérando, then at work on his *Histoire comparée des systèmes philosophiques*." (B. Croce, *The Philosophy of Giambattisto Vico*, translated by R. G. Collingwood, 1913, p. 273.) Croce adds: "Another exile, De Angelis,

Whatever interest Michelet may have felt for another writer who was to influence his work—Herder—must have been greatly increased in 1825,[13] when he made the acquaintance of Edgar Quinet, the young translator of the *Idées* (*les idées sur la philosophie de l'histoire*) of the German writer. From this meeting and the long discussions which followed it, full of the common interests which occupied the minds of these two young men, sprang a life-long friendship which helped from now on to determine the destinies of both Quinet and Michelet. Among other things, it encouraged and facilitated in many ways the efforts of the latter to form a better acquaintance with German learning. In 1828, Michelet joined his friend in Heidelberg, where Quinet was to be held for many years, not alone by his interest in German thought, but by his affection for a young German girl who was to be the wife of his first marriage.[14]

put the *Scienza Nuova* into the hands of Jules Michelet." An appendix in this treatise upon Vico by Croce contains the statement that Vico became so widely known in France that a novel of Balzac contains a passage where Vico is quite naturally mentioned as a name recognizable by the public. G. Monod (*J. M.*, p. 17), states that Michelet's attention was called to Vico by Victor Cousin. M. Lanson comes to the same conclusion. Mme. Michelet denies it.

[13] There is some comment on Herder in the passage which M. Lanson, in the note above mentioned, dates as "subsequent to 1825," and as "connected with the memories of 1821, but not of that epoch." Michelet must in any case have had some knowledge of Herder's work in this year, for there are several mentions made of it in the *Histoire comparée* of Degérando, which Michelet was reading in 1820-1. (Cf. Note 12.)

[14] *Ibid.*, pp. 176–178. The discourse pronounced by Michelet at the funeral of Mme. Mina Moré Quinet (Quinet's first wife), contains this statement: "Chaque nation m'a été révélée par une amitié." (March 13, 1851.)

The six weeks which Michelet spent in Germany during the late summer and early autumn of this year of 1828 were full of feverish activity. In view of all that he undertook, his statement of about a year later that "all the light of Germany, poured suddenly" into

After 1826 honors and distinctions had begun to come more quickly and easily. Guizot among others was quick to recommend a young scholar of brilliant promise and steady purpose. During the earliest years of his teaching, Michelet gave "Catholic instruction," because this was expected of him. The general impression produced by his personality and attainments from 1826 to 1838 was such as to win for him very general approbation and favor.[15]

It was the year 1831 which had brought him the appointment that put into his hands the materials neces-

---

his poor brain, had "wounded" it, is not surprising. He read constantly, took lessons in German, studied the German Bible and discovered that the history of Luther's life revealed certain analogies with experiences of his own. This visit gave him the opportunity of meeting some of the German savants and men of letters whom he had learned to know in their works. It gave him, too, the sense of being able to follow intelligently the movement of German thought. On his return his course on Philosophy in the winter of 1829 included Kant as well as the Scottish philosophers, whom he had early begun to study. In the same year, the names of Fichte and Schelling appear in his reading lists.

One immediately important sequel of this short German sojourn was the translation of a compilation of Luther's *Tischreden*, completed in 1828 but not published until 1835. Soon after his return Quinet had pointed out to him the interest of Grimm's *Deutsche Rechtswissenschaft des Alterthums*. This work and the correspondence between its author and Michelet formed a part of the inspiration to which the latter owed his volume of 1837, *Les Origines du droit français*.

[15] He was appointed to teach history to Mlle. de Berry, the nine year old grand-daughter of Charles X; and later to the Princess Clémentine, daughter of Louis-Philippe, better known perhaps as the mother of Ferdinand of Bulgaria. In 1827 he entered the *Ecole préparatoire* as occupant of the "Chaire d'histoire et de morale." In 1830 he was appointed to the chair of Ancient History, and in the spring of this same year, during a convalescence, he made a rapid journey down the length of Italy as far as Rome. The following autumn, when the *Ecole préparatoire* was reorganized as the *Ecole normale*, Michelet received his appointment to teach Modern History.

sary for an historian of France. He was then made "Chef de section aux archives nationales." The air of reality which his abundant documentation gave to his presentation of history, the opportunity afforded him to make a notable contribution to knowledge, aroused all his enthusiasm and enabled him to communicate it to others. His first volumes, le Moyen-Age, were especially well received.[16] He widened his experience by journeys in France, he visited Great Britain, the Netherlands, and began his acquaintance with Switzerland. By 1840 his work had become increasingly expressive of his convictions, and was already the subject of attack.[17] Whatever final judgment may be passed upon him as an historian (he seems at present to have comparatively few defenders), there can be little doubt that an historian of another type might have furnished a much less interesting human document. Both as a maker and as a writer of history he remains a figure of undeniable significance. His numerous volumes, eloquent of the vivid impressions that he drew from the National Records, written by a spirit of another order would have lacked certain characteristics which may enable Michelet's writings to survive work much more impeccable in some regards than his own.

His teaching has been described by certain of his hearers as an occasion of intellectual awakening. His earlier lectures are said to have offered a rare satisfaction for the historical curiosity that they could hardly have failed to awaken. Michelet acted as Suppléant at the Sorbonne for Guizot in 1834–1836. From 1833 to 1847 he produced volume after volume in quick succession. Having received in 1838 his appointment at the Collège de France, as occupant of the "Chaire d'histoire et de morale," his future seemed to promise quiet and security.[17] He now became closely associated with the great Polish poet, Mickie-

---

[16] G. Monod, J. M., p. 66. E. Biré, Article cited in bibliography.
[17] G. Monod, op. cit., p. 66.

wicz, who was lecturing at the *Collège de France* on Slavic languages and literatures.[18] In 1841 Edgar Quinet came to occupy the "Chaire d'histoire des littératures du midi de l'Europe." [19] Within a year the growing ultramontanism of the Church and the threatened 'invasion' of the University by the Jesuits began to rouse Quinet and Michelet to outspoken resistance.[20] Two indictments of the confessional and of the rôle which Michelet believed that it played in the family life (*Les Jésuites* in 1843, and *Du prêtre, de la femme et de la famille* in 1845) were the beginnings of an agitation which was eventually to cost the historian his university chair. In 1846, he expressed his fervent faith in democracy in *Le peuple*. He set it forth even more eloquently a year later in a series of lectures which, having been interrupted by his suspension from the University, appeared in printed form and received eventually the title *L'étudiant*. Michelet's spirit of conviction and of resistance rode gloriously on the rising waves of discontent, aspiration and revolt which finally broke in the revolution of 1848. The turn which the election of Louis Bonaparte gave to French official affairs was the occasion of the historian's dismissal from the *Collège de France* in 1851. In 1852, having refused to take the oath of allegiance to the Empire, he was deprived also of his post in the Record Office.

From 1840 on, Michelet's faith in liberalism and in scientific enlightenment had spoken more and more elo-

[18] Cf. Part VI, chap. 1. A. Mickiewicz opened his course the 22d Dec., 1840, and closed it in 1844. Cf. Introduction, by L. Mickiewicz to A. Mickiewicz, *Les Slaves*, 1914. In the preface to the same, M. F. Strowski says (p. xi), "The following year (1843–44) the professor . . . is inspired, he is a prophet."

[19] Mme. Quinet, *op. cit.*, pp. 113–114. Quinet's first lesson of 1843. Mme. Quinet describes how "The ardent Mickiewicz, the Prophet-poet of Poland, on leaving the hall threw himself into Quinet's arms."

[20] *Ibid.*, pp. 115–16.

quently in all that he wrote. He married in 1849, ten years after the death of his first wife, a woman twenty-eight years younger than himself. Her tastes and interests and convictions corresponded more or less closely with his own, while her romantic appreciation of nature and her eager desire to establish some means of collaborating with her husband were added inspirations and help for the historian when he began, in 1856, the publication of a series of what today we should call "nature books"—a series of studies more or less popular, full of an enthusiastic, poetical interest in the facts of natural life and in the revelations of science. His second marriage was coincident with a renewed interest on his part in matters pertaining to woman's rôle in society. He lectured on this subject in 1849–1850, and in 1858 and 1859 appeared two books devoted to the consideration of it, *L'amour* and *La femme*. In 1847 the first volume of his *History of the Revolution* appeared. After his dismissal from the *Collège de France*, he completed this work and, in addition, brought down to the outbreak of the Revolution the *History of France* which had been temporarily discontinued with the volume on Louis XI. This long task he finished in 1868. Some years later, he undertook to complete the story of his country in a *History of the Nineteenth Century*, and was engaged in writing it when he died.[21]

[21] Michelet's death occurred in 1874. The Franco-Prussian war had been a crushing blow for the historian. Broken in health he had taken refuge in Italy, where his sympathy for the nationalistic ambitions of the country had created for him numerous friends. Here he wrote his protest against German bad faith and his defence of France, published in 1871 as *La France devant l'Europe*. Michelet's intellectual contact with writers of various countries, his enthusiasm for all political idealism and his faith in patriotic aspirations had made him a notable and much loved figure for 'patriots' and liberals of varying shades of political conviction. When the ceremonies of his final interment took place in 1876, in the cemetery of Père-Lachaise, they were attended by men of

So much for what it is, perhaps, indispensable that one should know of the circumstances of Michelet's life in order to understand the character of the man who began, continued and ended his career with the unfailing and reïterated desire to accomplish a very special service for 'humanity.' This, as has been said, contributed to make him a representative figure in an age of social idealism, which by so many was felt to be a very decisive epoch.

In 1841 Pierre Leroux, in a moment of suggestive reminiscence, described the limitless hopes which the revolution of 1830 had brought to his day and generation. "Ten years ago," he writes, [while] "our souls were still stirred by the downfall of the old political and religious order, we found in our hearts the principles for which we were seeking." [22] It was there—in their "hearts"—that all the disciples of Rousseau were seeking the inspiration of which they felt themselves in need. And even those who remained more or less faithful to traditional beliefs, and kept their faces turned toward the past, felt in their hearts also the hope of some fresh imminent revelation, and faith in the help and healing that it might bring to a generation

many nationalities. The honor paid him by his own country gave this occasion a certain importance. A monument erected in this cemetery to commemorate him was constructed by means of a subscription, which was instituted and carried through in such a way as to give it as nearly as possible the character of an international tribute.

The historian's centenary was marked in 1898 by ceremonies in the schools of France, implying an official recognition of the importance of his work and of his influence. Michelet's desire that well-lived lives should become a part of the democratic legend of his country has had in his own case a definite realization. His life and work continue to command respect and consideration, although they invite attack and criticism from numerous sources.

For Mme. Michelet's account of the work of the committee which collected the funds for Michelet's tomb, cf. A. de Brahm, Les curiosités de Carnavalet, 1920.

[22] P. Leroux, Oeuvres, 1850, vol. i; Avertissement, pp. vi, viii, ix.

still unnerved by violent social changes.[23] Such a faith is apparent in the plaint uttered by Alfred de Musset: "All that has been is no more, and all that shall be is not yet." In the last years of the preceding century Joseph de Maistre had written: "All the universe is striving toward a new order of things in sorrow and in travail," and he called on all true philosophers to choose between two alternative possibilities: one, the formation of a new religion, the other, the rejuvenation of the Church "through some extraordinary means." [24]

In the minds of very divergent categories of thinkers the hopes awakened by the repercussions caused by the downfall of the old régime persisted long, and they took on new vigor at the eve of every fresh revolutionary outbreak. In 1840, Lamennais was all aglow with them:

"The old world is melting into nothingness, the old doctrines are snuffed out. In the midst of seeming disorder, of confused effort, one can make out the glimmer of new lights, of new beliefs; and one can even catch a glimpse of a new organization for the world. The religion of the future casts its first gleams over mankind waiting in expectancy, and over all its future destinies." [25]

And Lamertine in his turn announced, "We have come to one of the sublime halting places of humanity. We

[23] H. Louvancour, *De Saint-Simon à Fourier*, 1913. Preface, pp. 29–38; also, P. Leroux, *op. cit.*

[24] J. de Maistre, *Considérations sur la France* (1796), ed. 1821, pp. 55–61. In his *Soirées de St. Pétersbourg*, in the eleventh *Entretien*, this author writes with even more emotion: "Il faut nous tenir prêts pour un événement immense dans un ordre divin, vers lequel nous marchons avec une vitesse accélérée qui doit frapper tous les observateurs." For further examples of this very general "Messianic state of mind," characteristic of the epoch, cf. H. Louvancour, *op. cit.*, Preface and P. Leroux, *Discours aux politiques* (1832), ed. 1850, vol. i, pp. 91–98.

[25] F. de Lamennais, *Esquisse d'une nouvelle philosophie*, 1840, vol. 3, p. 273.

have arrived at an epoch of transformation like that perhaps of the Gospel age." [26] Ballanche's mystical version of the history of the human race as a prolonged 'initiation' effected by voluntarily accepted 'expiation,' was written with a keen conviction that a very significant moment was at hand in the prolonged test to which humanity was subjected; and that he, Ballanche, was the interpreter of this moment.

Such hopes and predictions are so many added proofs that the Revolution had been no mere political upheaval. For multitudes it had swept away the old props and barriers. It was as if some great tidal wave had passed, leaving behind it surges and eddies, breaking the calm of the most sheltered coves, stirring the farthest inlets.[27] Not all imaginations were touched by these hopes; but on the whole, society at large had awakened to the realization that even what might be most unforeseen was by no means impossible. Hearts were beating with a quickened expectation of new life, and souls sensitive to what was going on about them were awaiting the supreme revelation which their aroused religious sense led them to believe impending.

Prophets of new religions multiplied, proclaiming the passing of the old, for this they considered a necessary part of the preparation for the coming of the new. Such a statement as the following, published by Saint-Simon's disciple as a part of his master's exposition of his religion, presented no unusual claim: "The people of God, who had received revelations before the appearance of Jesus Christ, have always felt that the Christian doctrine founded by the fathers of the Church was incomplete. They have always promised that a new epoch would come, and the adjective that they applied to this hope was 'Messianic.' It was the expectation of an epoch during which the doctrines of religion should be presented with

[26] P. Leroux, *op. cit.*, p. 93.   [27] *Ibid.*, Avertissement, p. xiii.

all the comprehensiveness of which they are susceptible. At last, I hold a complete conception of the Christian doctrine, and I am going to formulate it." [28]

Michelet felt a lively sympathy for all expressions of the consciousness of standing thus poised in the joyful expectancy of a hope just about to be fulfilled. He recognized it as the attitude of his time, and his fellow-feeling for those who held it was in no wise dulled by his realization that men have always stood thus from age to age, nor by his conviction that they will continue so to stand as long as time endures. This expectancy he will preach as one of the powerful factors which may be counted upon to work for the realization of the common hopes and ideals of humanity. In his historical studies, where he had met at every turn man's power to make and cherish ideals, he had seen in every epoch men darkened by misery and troubled by material insecurity, waiting with souls illumined by faith. [29]

He admitted that the fulfillment of hope had never been complete. [30] Indeed, his philosophy of History and Religion precluded the possibility of such fulfillment, for it was based on the conception that life is a sustained and progressive revelation of its own origins and of its own ends. However, no one was more ready than he to give the trumpet call of promise, and he gave it with a courage that was unfailing, if not always serene. It lent the dominant note to his *Introduction* of 1831, [31] and in 1869 he was still writing,—and in a moment of discouragement too,—"I have traversed numberless epochs, I have lived in many ages," then added, after having confessed that every

[28] O. Rodrigues, *Nouveau Christianisme*, 1832, dialogue 7, lettre 11.
[29] *Armagnacs et Bourguignons*, pp. 136–7; *Henri IV et la ligue*, pp. 40–41; *La Régence*, preface, pp. 1–2; *Hist. de la Rév.*, vol. I, pp. 146–7.
[30] *Hist. de la Rév.*, vol. I, p. 179, Ah! le temps n'a pas marché vite, les générations se sont succédées, l'œuvre n'a guère avancé . . .
[31] Cf. Part II, chap. 1.

hope fulfilled brings with it its disappointments: "But a great idea is purifying our lives, a brilliant light is scattering all the mists with which they are heavy. Wait! In a moment you will see that we are better than we seem." [32]

He proclaimed that it is in such hope that men must work; such hope it is that brings the salvation for which men wait. He greeted evidences of it wherever he found them with a sense of kinship for those who had formulated it. He was quick to recognize Dante as the prophet of his age, although he had small sympathy for the content of his prophecy. But the great Florentine had known the dire need of his time, and having felt its sorrow, it had been given to him to see a vision of things divine.

"Deserted by the old world, as yet unable to discern the new; in the darkness of Hell he can make out but dimly the lights of Purgatory. Virgil, who is standing beside him, is fading from his sight, and Beatrice has not yet come. All that he is leaving behind him seems to rest on its pyramidal point. But it is just at this moment that the two worlds touch,—the world of light and the world of shadows. One effort more, and the light will appear! And the poet having reached the last step of the ascent will be able to cry: "The soft light of oriental sapphire floats in the serene air, and its purity comforts my eyes. I have left behind me the deadly vapors which saddened my heart and clouded my vision." [33]

Michelet had this same sensitiveness to what he believed was the dire need of his own time, and it awakened in him the sense of being called to seek and impart important and widely needed revelation. How much of this conviction was due to the influence of Lamennais, and how much of his conception of the prophet's rôle he may

[32] *Nos fils*, 1869, éd. définitive, Flammarion, p. 288.
[33] *Discours d'ouverture*, ed. 1834, p. 260.

have owed to association with the poet-prophet Mickiewicz, especially at one period of his life, are questions
which present a very special interest.

The consciousness of an apostolate having, as has been
seen, come to be a habit of mind during the years closely
following the Revolution, it was to be expected that it
should at times be marked by the manifestations of the
well-known delusion which has been duly classified as
'Messianic,' some phases of which might be noted in
Mickiewicz' conception of his mission. Back of the mode
and the madness lay something indestructible in human
nature,—the power to hope for supreme salvation, and
the faith to feel it near.

That this hope and faith should often have taken on
such exaggerated and abnormal proportions as they did
during these years was due perhaps in part to the liberating sense of opportunity which rapidly succeeding social
changes may so readily impart. Saint-Simon's confidence
in his power to produce a definitive form of the Christian
religion brought him sympathy and support from most
unimpeachable intelligences. Fourier's call to his generation to escape from the limitations of civilization received
a certain response.[34]

---

[34] M. Ferraz, *op. cit.*, pp. 135–151.
The imagination touched by the conviction of being 'the chosen
one,' or a prophet of the chosen, may become the victim of complicated vagaries. M. Strowski, in articles cited in the bibliography,
has characterized some of those of Mickiewicz. An extreme example
of the form that they may take, is afforded by a letter which its
author states he had attempted in 1832 to transmit to the president
of the council of ministers, M. Casimir-Périer. It is characterized
by the desire to place all the hope of humanity in faith in some great
hero whose achievement or whose legend is such as to inspire confidence. The chosen hero in this particular instance is Napoleon.
The writer begins:
"There are epochs in history . . . which no known rule can
govern. However new this truth may be, it is founded on the philo-

Renan in his *Vie de Jésus* has noted some interesting impressions which suggest the different aspects which the 'Messianic' faith of these years assumed, and which help one to feel the sincerity of its hope. They suggest too the

sophical and religious work, the *Prodrome du Messianisme*, that I have the honor to address to your Excellency."

One may judge of the general character of the writer's 'religious' and 'philosophical' ideas by the following extract which has at least a faint contemporary interest:

"It is our duty to enlighten men in spite of themselves, for they stand on the edge of this infinite precipice into which they would otherwise certainly fall. The sole hope of salvation which remains for the moment, lies in the fact that the armed force which fights for the principle of divine right will actually triumph. The hopes of this triumph we have set forth in our *Scientific Predictions*. However, as we announce in these predictions, the principle of human right so strongly revealed today in the conscience of men will assume, by its very suppression, a new energy and will unfailingly triumph in its turn. In the alternative struggle between these two indestructible principles, humanity visibly approaches the abyss in which it will soon be engulfed. At the present time, in order to bring about this terrible epoch, nothing else is necessary than an insurrection among the Slav nations of Russia, in that powerful Empire which Providence seems to have formed in order to preserve the moral order of the world in the midst of its upheavals. It is the knowledge of the future which has led us to treat first its practical side. . . . But we must not forget that this absolute doctrine embraces the entire future of humanity. It is thus that under the name of *Messianism* the practical part of the doctrine bears principally upon THE FINAL DESTINIES OF MAN, and differs in all respects from all practical doctrines which have so far been produced."

The author's 'principle' (an interpretation of "the mysterious ideas" of Napoleon,—since "the moral order is the true spirit of Napoleon,"—and a reform of mathematics are both a part of its exposition), although it may "differ in all respects" from that of the other prophets whom we have so far mentioned, holds something which relates it to whatever 'principle' they may have held. His confused half-mad lucubrations are not for a moment to be compared with the utterances of such thinkers as Saint-Simon or Fourier, but to the casual reader the resemblances might be as touch of madness that often characterized it and the exploitation to which it was perhaps at moments exposed. Renan writes:

"All attempts to form religions, as we have seen them, show an indescribable mingling of the sublime and the bizarre. Read the testimony of the early Saint-Simonists, published with such admirable candor by their survivors. Beside the repulsive rôles, the insipid declamations which they contain, what sincerity as soon as a man or woman of the people enters upon the scene, bringing the naïve confession of a soul that smiles under the first ray of tender light which has ever touched it!" [35]

Something of these varied aspects shows in Michelet's expression of his mystical hope and faith. In his preaching, he was only too prone to mingle the declamatory, the vain, and even sometimes the insipid with much that is touching and sincere, and over it all plays the vivid light that his rare genius could lend to anything that he might choose to say. All this helped to make his message alluring and commanding for a generation which lived closely enough to the Revolution to believe that the making of creeds was properly a layman's task.

Michelet had, moreover, an arresting personality, so arresting as to ensure a respectable hearing for almost any creed that he might proclaim. He is described as having been at the age of twenty-five, "a little thin man with a ruddy face, long hair and a naïve air." Madame

striking as the differences, so identical with theirs is his tone of confident authority,—and he offers the same appeal, the promise of an infinite hope!

This passage is drawn from the translation of an anonymous pamphlet the original of which was published by Didot, Paris, dated March 19, 1843, pub. 1879. For the faith of the Polish friends of Michelet in the legend of Napoleon, cf. Part IV, chaps. 1 and 4 The use of this translation was made possible through the courtesy of Professor J. L. Gerig, of Columbia University.

[35] E. Renan, *La vie de Jésus* (1863), ed. 1867, preface, p. xxii.

Quinet's personal memory helps one to understand more clearly the power of this "little man."

"Nothing more mobile than Michelet's face with its precocious wrinkles, his hair white at thirty, his eyes which appeared quite black and which seemed to scintillate with 'malice.' I have often seen him grave, sometimes deeply moved. His emotion in pronouncing certain sacred words was communicated like an electric shock to those who heard him speak. I still carry in my ears, in my nerves, the voice and accent of Michelet formulating thus an entire event of contemporaneous history: 'Messieurs, le droit est éternel!'" [36]

The testimony of one who was perhaps a less kindly critic than Madame Quinet—Jules Simon—might be cited to show what a wizard's spell this unusual personality was capable of exercising. It is easy to see how readily the French university youth might rise and hail such a man as a 'prophet.' [37]

He was, as has been said, one of a multitude to whom the title was tendered in that impressionable year of 1848; and if he accepted the rôle rather credulously, it was partly because he with all his generation sought for prophets and believed in them. He says himself, in speaking of the delusion which the sense of being divinely chosen had produced in his great Polish friend: "The Messianic delusion is so natural to man that he must be pardoned for feeling the presence of God within him." [38] This "de-

[36] Mme. Quinet, op. cit., pp. 6–7, and 182.

[37] J. Simon, Victor Cousin, 1891, p. 174: "Quand une fois on a pris la main qu'il vous tend, on ne peut plus s'arrêter, c'est une fascination, une magie."

[38] Louis XIV et la Révocation de l'édit de Nantes, p. 50: "Cette illusion messianique, qui revient souvent dans le moyen âge (et que nous avons vue naguère dans l'honnête et très pur Messie polonais) est chose naturelle à l'homme" . . . etc. "The very pure Polish Messiah," here referred to might have been either Mickiewicz, or perhaps the Pole, Towianski, who exercised at a certain moment so great an influence on the well-known Polish poet.

lusion," which even in its mildest form makes one see one's beliefs and convictions as authoritative even for others, is perhaps readily encouraged by the democratic ideal of citizenship. Mr. Santayana implies in his study of Josiah Royce that every American citizen sees himself somewhat in the light of a prophet. It may be that in a society organized on the double basis of anonymous sovereignty and individual liberty, the dividing line between the reasonably useful and the uselessly exaggerated notion of one's personal influence and importance may be difficult to trace. It may be entirely obliterated when an ideal is upheld and cherished in the face of discouragement or persecution.

The idealists of the early nineteenth century lightly disregarded this dividing line when they felt that they had caught a glimpse of things unseen, or had grasped some portion of the hoped for. We have seen that there were inflammable imaginations to which the vision of the 'City' had become a fairly everyday possession, and that even the man in the street might be given to vaticination.[39] When this natural tendency toward belief in the ideal, characteristic of the democratic imagination, is turned toward a vague and incurable Utopianism, the conviction that the proper principle on which to base society has been discovered will resist any number of disastrous manifestations of the difficulty of applying the principle. Thus the Utopian vision may have alternately its Ezekiel and its Jeremiah,—often in the same prophet. We shall have occasion to study Michelet himself in this double impersonation of the prophetic spirit.

He could draw to himself a sympathy and even a certain following from those who maintained an unshaken faith in the Revolution as a manifestation of great social principles, and from those of a large group who had no clearly

[39] G. Richard, *La question sociale et le mouvement philosophique au XIXe siècle*, 1914, pp. 108–119, 143–5.

outlined formulas of social beliefs, but who contented
themselves with a conception too vague to either encourage or justify great daring,—the conception of human life
as a great triumphant march, proceeding toward a distant
and dimly seen consummation of ideals not too clearly
formulated,—one which could not, therefore, too greatly
jeopardize the security of the present. This warning of
Sainte-Beuve was not needed by Michelet:

"If humanity has not yet chosen its place of shelter, it is
not because it is not invited every morning to do so, and each
time in some untried enclosure. However, although incontest-
ably in need of succour, exposed to all the hardships due to
nature and to the carelessness of its guides, this poor humanity
does not seem over anxious to betake itself to any one particular
terrestrial paradise of all those which are offered to it. It is
waiting to be sure, it feels its need and would accept with gratitude any positive help. But in order to be convincing one must
refrain from promising too much. It has outgrown the illusions
of its childhood." [40]

This was where Michelet's temperamental prudence
and grounded good sense stood him in good stead. He
did not seem to promise too much. His demands are in
fact more numerous at first glance than his promises.
Through his settled faith in the Revolution as a consummation of social hopes, he was in a sense—not indeed the
usual one—a prophet of the past, and through his adherence to the Revolutionary principle in general he was
the prophet of a never attainable, ever receding, social
goal.

His 'religion,' which he gradually formulated in accordance with his revolutionary faith, was never really
systematized. He marshalled its arguments mainly for
his war upon the Church. This religion was a revolutionary social faith [41] which he believed would enter into the

[40] Sainte-Beuve, *Portraits contemporains*, vol. 2, p. 504.
[41] Mme. Quinet, *op. cit.*, p. 217, letter of Michelet to Quinet

moral structure of the future 'City.' This 'City of Providence,' for him and others a substitute for a longed for and distant heaven, was very emphatically a City of Man, and in his proclamation of it Michelet appropriated aspirations and ideals wherever he found them. Christianity furnished at moments the wherewithal to found his 'temple' and lay the foundations of his 'City.' [42]

These methods were not unusual in the tactics of the prophets of the day, but Michelet's personality lent him an unusual success in the use of them. His character in its large outlines was admirable, and his private life was, on the whole, estimable. His public life had borne the sanction of official approbation. He spoke, moreover, with the authority that a comparatively safe conservatism may bestow. When banished from his university chair and after falling heir to a modified martyrdom and the mild lustre of a dim halo, he was too reasonable to exploit unduly the comparative hardship which his deprivation of office brought him: and much too sincere and simple to pose as a martyr.[43]

His combination of daring and reserve made him a model for the race of prophets whose program does not in actual practice go much beyond unremitting effort in some social cause and a ceaseless proclamation of the personal message. His was an incarnation of the modern prophetic type, which displayed no gross exaggerations, no immediately recognizable or radical vagaries. More-

(1854): "J'ai écrit sur l'unité latente mais croissante de l'Eglise (socialiste révolutionnaire)."

[42] Michelet formulated his ambition thus: "reëstablish the tradition of France, . . . reconstruct the corner stone of the Temple and of the City," in an unedited note communicated by G. Monod to R. van der Elst and published by the latter in *Michelet Naturaliste*, p. 67.

[43] Mme. Quinet, *op. cit.*, pp. 243, 257–8. There is a point of bitterness in these contrasts between the exile of Quinet, and the life that Michelet led in Paris under the Second Empire.

over, by distinguished effort, he had attained to an enviable success, such as only good hard work, put to the service of undeniable genius, could bring with it. And although success was by no means a necessary stamp of approval to a prophet's message, it could but lend it prestige.

But Michelet's work, even apart from its success, offers much which might make it worthy of consideration. It was, for one thing, the achievement of a life lived in accordance with his religion. One great principle of the historian's faith was the belief in personal effort. He did not always devote much consideration to the purely external character of achievement. "Great nations," he had written, "judge as God himself and with his own equity, valuing work not so much according to the result, as to the effort and the strength of will." [44] An ideal common to his time had been bequeathed to it by the Rousseau of the *Confessions*, according to which the moral character of the life, and even the moral character of the accomplishment to which the life is devoted, become, in some degree, negligible considerations. Thus, as will be seen, Satan himself may become quite naturally a romantic hero, with a mission of his own.

If the value of human life be thus computed, regardless of what might seem to constitute its moral worth or to detract from it, there is no one of us so mean but that he may rise and testify from the midst of his uncertainty and discontent; and self-confession may come to partake of the nature of an evangel. In the measure that Michelet's worship of life as an aspiration and an effort became a definitely accepted faith, his own life and his own personality assumed for him increasing worth and importance. The records of his life had always held for him a real value. In the end, they came to be one of his preoccupations.

His *History of France* became in many respects a per-

[44] *Louis XIV et la révocation de l'édit de Nantes*, p. 246; *Moyen Age*, vol. 2, p. 109.

sonal message and, as such, a fragment of the dreamed of 'Bible' which should bring new enlightenment. The autobiographical note had always been sufficiently obtrusive in his work.[45] It ended by becoming predominant. The preface to the last volume closes with a confession which formulates his standard of the value of effort. There breathes in it the hope that his work might be looked upon, not as a product to be judged and evaluated impersonally, but rather as a personal achievement. It had been for him, he says, an individual revelation of himself,—"I would above all else tell of that which went on within myself during this long journey. My work has been more to me than a work. It is the pathway in which my soul has walked. It has made me and made my life."[46]

Michelet was justified as to the importance which he attached to his own personality. His message, one can but repeat, could never have carried so far nor have struck so deep but for the force that this personality lent to it. It is generally admitted that one great secret of its power lay in his emotionalism, which shaped and colored all his convictions and all his judgments, both glorifying their force and at the same time distorting it. The form of emotion which he claimed with greatest pride as the one which had most strongly dominated him, and which has indeed been conceded to him as something of a distinctive possession, is his *emotion of pity*. The use that he made

[45] Prefaces, especially that of 1869. Michelet in his letter of congratulation to A. Thierry, after the publication of the latter's *Dix ans d'études historiques*, wrote: "Il eût été bien à souhaiter que tous les hommes de génie nous fassent ainsi connaître le progrès de leurs idées." A. Augustin Thierry, "Augustin Thierry, etc." *R. D. M.*, 15 déc. 1921, p. 865. This Michelet seems conscientiously to have tried to do. Madame Michelet in the preface to *Mon journal* tells with what care Michelet classified the notes to be used in writing of him.

[46] *Louis XVI*, Preface, 1869.

of this emotion has been variously dilated upon both by his friends and by his enemies, "each in his own tongue." An examination of some of its sources and of some of its manifestations cannot but have a real interest, for it helped to model all of Michelet's conceptions of God and nature, it played a paramount rôle in determining his ideas in regard to woman, and determined the form of his humanitarian idealism, which made him look on man as the supreme expression of the divine impulse of the universe, thus leading him naturally to give to all human effort a profound reverence.

The following chapters are those portions of a general review of Michelet's *Ideas on Social Reform* which were inspired by the reverence which he felt for his own characteristic conception of God, of man, and of woman. They are here published separately, in the hope that they may furnish a picture (not totally inadequate perhaps, although necessarily partial because incomplete) of Michelet himself. For whatever interest may be afforded by the historian's Ideas is to be attributed above all else to the personality of which they were the expression,—the personality of Michelet himself.

PART I

MICHELET'S TEMPERAMENT

Le don que Saint Louis demande et n'obtient pas, je l'eus: "Le don des larmes."

Michelet, Preface of 1869.

CHAPTER I

MICHELET'S TEMPERAMENT AS MOULDER OF HIS IDEAS

"Le don des larmes"

"O plaindre, c'est déjà comprendre."
Victor Hugo, "A ma fille," *les Contemplations.*

It was Michelet's immense capacity for emotional compassion which did so much to ensure him a wide hearing. This compassion took on the colors of a very complex personality, the contradictions of which it often masks without ever completely concealing them.

Like the famous sadness of Shakespeare's melancholy Jacques, Michelet's ever ready pity was "compounded of many simples." It was an emotion cultivated with especial predilection in his day. It helped to frame and fashion the language of an entire generation. But by Michelet this language was spoken with all the vigorous individuality that his vigorous genius could lend it. With him pity often had the grace of a rare tenderness and yet again it might show an explosive force which was disconcertingly devoid of tenderness. It has been said of George Sand that she had all the defects of her time, of her hour, of her minute and of her sex.[1] Michelet likewise had many of these defects (he was given to saying that his was a "génie maternel"),[2] and besides he had

---

[1] J. Moréas, *Esquisses et souvenirs*, 1908, p. 102.

[2] G. Monod, *J. M.*, p. 138: "J'ai eu le GÉNIE MATERNEL . . . mille enfants dispersés dans le temps et dans l'espace; also, *ibid.*, p. 181. Madame Quinet, *op. cit.*, calls Michelet's counsels "maternal." Cf. p. 8.

those particular to his own sex. His sympathetic sensibility held a curious compound of what is known as " a man's brutality and a woman's gentleness." His History has been described as "dripping with pity." It must be promptly added that it bristles as well with asperities.

The readiness of Michelet's compassion had been bequeathed to him by a long national tradition which may be considered later. But his inheritance was immediate as well, his father's tears had come easily and there had been much in his life to summon them. From the first, the historian's sense of pity had been fostered by the experience of hardship and the sight of suffering. It had taken deep root in his boyhood, and his *Journal* shows it growing through the difficult years of his early manhood, flowering then with a grace and delicacy that were later to lose some of their charm. But even at this time one finds it lightly touched at moments by self-consciousness. For Michelet was early given to self-examination, and was not displeased at what his introspection revealed to him. In his *Journal* he writes:

I am moved by the sight of the deformed, the infirm, the weak, and even by the sight of animals. They are so akin to us in feeling. I wish that every one about me could be happy. Sometimes this feeling for humanity is so strong that it becomes a form of suffering.[3]

It is curious to note how different is the effect produced today by so conscious an expression of self-admiration from the impression that it would probably have left upon the imaginations of Michelet's own day. For, as has been said, his sense of pity was in part the emotional trademark of his " time, of his hour and of his minute." This was very largely,—to quote Hugo's little Gavroche,— "the fault of Voltaire, the fault of Rousseau." The historian had studied appreciatively the power of compassion

[3] *Mon journal*, p. 82.

displayed by both these men. Voltaire's humanitarianism seemed to him the noblest form of belligerency. It was to him in any case a surprising revelation of what forceful weapons of attack and defence may be forged in the white heat of pity. Brilliant indeed was Voltaire's exhibition of all the possible uses of these weapons in the polemic wherein he was forced to parry the attacks which his religious and political scepticism invited. One of his cleverest feints was his deft handling of telling contrasts between commonly accepted conceptions of human and divine pity, contrasts in which the former showed to every advantage. His *Poème de Lisbonne* is an example of his triumphant skill:

> "C'est l'orgueil, dîtes-vous,—l'orgueil séditieux,
> Qui prétend qu'étant mal nous pouvons être mieux.
> Allez interroger les rivages du Tage,
> Fouillez dans les débris de ce sanglant rivage;
> Demandez aux mourants dans ce séjour d'effroi,
> Si c'est l'orgueil qui crie: "O ciel, secourez-moi,
> O ciel, ayez pitié de l'humaine misère!"

In his *Dictionnaire* Voltaire wrote under the rubric *Pitié*, "O merciful God, if any human face were like that of the wrongdoer whom they so constantly show us busy in destroying thy works, would it not be the face of a persecutor?" Michelet, it will be seen, never attained to the conscious mastery displayed by Voltaire in his polemic. He had comparatively little of the cool hypocrisy and hard cynicism which the latter could use upon occasion. His were seldom nicely studied feints. He was given, in moments of excitement, to striking out hotly and unguardedly, rendering thus his adversary's counter-thrust only too effective.

In Rousseau, the preacher and pedagogue had always been unpleasantly obtrusive in the mind of his disciple. Michelet took however from his master whatever might be of use to him. Among other things he borrowed precisely that authoritative attitude of exhorter and preacher which he so resented in the great apostle of sentiment,— one phase of what he was wont to call Rousseau's '*papisme.*'

Now the use that Rousseau had made of pity as a means of creating and promoting class distinctions had penetrated too deeply into all social conceptions for anyone to be able to free himself easily and immediately from an inclination to make the most of what can be done with it. The Revolutionary leaders had quickly discovered what valuable distinctions could be established between those who are pitiless and those who are to be pitied, and had applied these distinctions with discrimination, according to the exigencies of the moment and of the party who ruled it.[4] This use of the appeal to pity for the marking out of social and party lines was one of the reproaches which Michelet will frequently urge against Robespierre,[4] with no apparent consciousness of being himself at times an unconscionable fellow sinner.

Revolutionary emotionalism, as he had personally known it and was later to study it in great popular outbreaks, constituted for the historian a soul-stirring manifestation of what a force human pity may become. It will be very natural for him when he comes to write the history of the great Revolution to treat it as a vast "explosion de pitié,"[5] most admirable when it flaunted its violence on all the street corners. Although he will be at

[4] Cf. *Hist. de la Rév.*, vol. 1, pp. 76, 115. Some of Michelet's disapproval of Robespierre seems partly inspired by the latter's power to maintain a cool command over his emotions, while stirring to the utmost the feelings of others. ("Ses attendrissements calculés, de fréquents retours pleureurs sur lui-même" . . .), vol. 7, pp. 66, 137–141.

[5] Literally: "Chez les hommes de '93 (et non de '94) une maladie éclata,—la furie de la pitié." (*Hist. de la Rév.*, preface of 1869 to vol. 7, p. xxxv.

moments a stern critic of its exaggerations, he will find it
easy at others to make of himself an ardent interpreter of
its frenzies. The episode of Charlotte Corday will afford
him an excellent opportunity for sagely deploring Revolutionary violence even while manifesting in his deprecation
of it much of its sinister exaltation. Such an occasion is
to be found in his account of the girl's execution:

A religion is inaugurated by the shedding of Charlotte's
blood,—the religion of the poignard. André Chénier writes a
hymn to the new divinity:

> O vertu! le poignard, seul espoir de la terre,
> Est ton arme sacrée.

What does a young man see henceforth while he is meditating
some great act? Is it Brutus as a phantom appearing to him in
his dreams? No, it is Charlotte, beautiful in the sinister splendor
of her red mantle, her head crowned with the halo in which were
mingled the blood-red July sunlight and the purple of the night-
fall.[6]

Some diluted 'purple' of this new religion, it must be said,
splashes many a page not only of Michelet's *History of
the Revolution*, but other pages of his work as well, mingled
with every tint that compassion could lend to it.

The Revolutionary tribunal had apparently striven to
compensate for whatever dignity it had lost, by the use of
such means as it could find for appealing to the emotions.
Among these, the appeal to pity had been found to insure
quick and easy returns. In the world of letters likewise,
the emotion soon gained in power and had lost in dignity.
In tragedy it was no longer the noble force which purges
and purifies the human soul, and had become in the
melodrama a source of sentimental self-indulgence both
for the author and the audience. In verse the elegiac
calm of a Millevoye did not perhaps invite such widespread

[6] *Ibid.*, vol. 7, pp. 340-341. Cf. also note 4.

admiration as did the polemic note which sounded at moments in the neatly turned Alexandrines of the worthy Jacques Delille, who made an unsparing use of the demagogic appeal to pity in his long poem *Malheur et Pitié.* His admiring commentator, M. Michaud "de l'Académie," gives an illuminating appreciation of the ways in which the emotion may be exploited. He was right in finding them to be one of the most cherished heritages which the Revolution had bequeathed to oncoming generations.

> I know,—says M. Michaud,—that pity still made itself heard in those unhappy times. But it was no longer the natural benevolence which goes out to all men. Only too often it had its source in a spirit of faction. Tears were shed not over the ills of humanity, but rather over the misfortunes of a party. Men were touched by your misfortunes not because you were a man, but because you defended an opinion.[7]

Michelet will often hold his gift of tears at the disposition of party interests, and approve or disapprove a like use of it by others according to his personal sympathies. He had admired it in the Classical and Revolutionary tribunal, but he will deplore what Robespierre had done with it. In Jean-Jacques and the lay preachers who were Rousseau's direct descendants, he will be prone to treat, unless his prejudices interfere, what seems now to be the mere power to summon at will and nicely to regulate emotional capacity, as an uncontrollable force and as the noblest form of human self-expression. Danton, whom he himself was to call "the greatest of comedians," will

---

[7] J. Delille (Londres, 1802), ed. 1824, *Malheur et Pitié*, pp. 20–21, 157–159, shows interesting comparisons with Michelet's use of pity in narrative.

The citation is from *Le printemps d'un proscrit, suivi de plusieurs lettres à M. Delille sur la pitié,* par M. Michaud de l'Académie, 1803, p. 171. M. Michaud adds: "Il n'est pas rare de voir les hommes se menacer de leur pitié, comme ils se menaceraient de leur colère et de leur mépris."

be pictured by him as a direct exponent of its force and dignity.

As a literary medium he was destined to find it invaluable. He played with the fancy that pity was one of the forces which had modified and modeled literary types. The Indian legend which made of a man's quickened heartbeats the source of rhythmic verse had all his sympathy. Here is his comment:

India was well rewarded for her gentleness of nature. Her genius lay in her gift for pity. The first Indian poet saw two doves hovering in the air, and while he was admiring their grace one of them fell pierced by an arrow. He wept. His sobs measured by the pulsing of his heart took on a rhythmic motion, and poetry was born.[8]

Wherever he found this emotion's appeal he responded immediately to it, and his *Journal* shows that as a young man he could find it in unexpected places. When, to avoid choking too abjectly over *Paul et Virginie*, *Manon Lescaut*, and *La nouvelle Héloïse*, he stretched out his hand toward his bookshelves and (having bravely passed over *Clarisse Harlowe*) took down *Tom Jones*, he found it full of "touching situations." Byron's orgies of self-pity left him with a delicious sense of horror, he felt as if he had spent a night dreaming of crime. He cried out against the attraction that novels exercised upon him; he says however, "In spite of myself I keep coming back to them." This Michelet continued to do all his life. He confesses that with all the rest of his generation, he had been touched by Romanticism. Many of his pages would be quite in place in one of those novels of Walter Scott's which he early devoured. Over and over again, he will use fiction as his vehicle of expression, coloring what he has to say with emotion instead of making it sober with fact.[9]

[8] *Le peuple* (1846), p. 250.   [9] Cf. Part III, chap. 2, note 31.

In the earlier volumes of his *Histoire de France*, the historian easily found life noblest when it had been most completely a failure. The tragedy of human destiny held for him in his young manhood so high a significance that, with all those of his day, he was prone to linger over the poetry of its sadness,—and this in spite of the fact that he had already begun to constitute himself a sort of official preacher of the joy and vigor of action.[10] Indeed the beauty of the pathos of life was a mystery which helped him to accept in his general conception of all life an unquestioning belief in effort and action. He could thus look on life as a continual triumph over a continual defeat. In his youth the moral beauty of the defeated soul touched him most deeply. He found here the revelation of the meaning of life: "To attain to the fulness of selfhood, the self must cease to be, it must perish and undergo transformation."

From this conviction that it is the portion of the human soul to find itself overborne, his earlier work derived some of its most significant passages, and his tenderness and compassion lent to his style its supreme literary touch, making of it the direct expression of his emotional power. He created occasions for the use of it. When he imagined Jeanne d'Arc facing the certainty of death he felt that she must have felt herself forsaken by her faith. His need to indulge his pity brought to him this conviction, and this conviction in its turn afforded him the climax that seemed to him both true and telling for a tragic tale of temptation and suffering. Did Jeanne express a doubt? He could find no record of it, "C'est chose incertaine."

---

[10] Michelet's *Journal* bears witness to his precocious taste for preaching. Cf. p. 59: "Je viens d'avoir un moment de bonheur bien vif. . . . J'ai parlé peut-être trop; ce serait une précieuse conquête que d'incliner à l'amour de l'humanité un homme riche." Also p. 92: "Je venais de jeter sur le papier le plan d'un beau livre, *Exhortations à mes contemporains*."

But since he felt that otherwise the tragedy of her death would be incomplete, he adds: "I affirm that this was true." It was not only the "sense of the majesty of human suffering" which Michelet's telling touch translated, but also a desire to "affirm" a belief in human equality established by a common lot of sorrow. He could pity himself in the sympathy which he gave to past suffering and thus divine the unspoken word, supply perhaps the thought, and make, as here, "the silences of history speak." [11]

Such appeals on the part of the historian to his own sense of pity brought him sympathetic response. The power which he claimed was conceded to him. A vast reading public admitted that the strength of his sympathy supplied them with the ability to participate vicariously in the past. His readers and hearers conceded to him the accomplishment of his endeavor, and it was proclaimed that he had made of History a "Resurrection," which, logically enough, he strove to complete by a work of "Redemption." This too his admirers saw as a part of his achievement and this too was wrought by his imaginative pity.[12]

His power of compassion furnished him a portion of the evidence upon which he based his contention that the chain of existence was absolutely unbroken. His haunting sense of the profound unity of life, which he felt most surely through his sense that so much of life was suffering, revealed to him the meaning of existence, its continuity and its identity throughout all the ages. And since the power of pity is most apparent when it disregards the limitations laid upon it by ordinary tradition, he seemed to feel a personal gratification at the discovery

[11] *Jeanne d'Arc*, p. 282. P. Lasserre, *Le Romantisme*, 1907, uses this to show the method of interpretation which Michelet so instinctively uses. M. Lasserre "affirms" as a counter argument to Michelet's "J'affirme qu'elle a douté," that Jeanne did not doubt.

[12] Cf. note 28.

that his pity went out spontaneously to the most elemental, often to the most brutal manifestations of human violence. Thus he was glad to date the expression *un bon Français* back to the epoch of the peasant uprisings, the great brutal outbreaks of the fourteenth century. His sympathy gave him a sense of solidarity with those desperate famished men, bent on pillage and murder,—"These peasants are Frenchmen, do not be ashamed of it! They are you yourself, O France!" This sentiment (one might almost say this sensation) that he had of feeling himself shaken by the throes of the self-creative life of his country served him often in lieu of the historical sense. He was its victim and he yielded helplessly to its power:

Suddenly when I least expected it, the figure of Jacques rose there before me, rose from the furrow, a monstrous and terrible figure! Great God, this was my father, this man of the Middle Ages! For this is what they have done to me! Look at what they have done to me, look at these marks of a thousand years. I felt his sorrow surging up within me from the farthest and remotest past.[13]

Even later, when Michelet sought really discriminating and penetrating psychological comprehension, he looked to pity to supply it, and naturally he was not disappointed. To him Molière was the most tragic figure of the court of the great Louis and he found the explanation of the tragedy of this figure in his compassion for the poet who could not find it in his heart to despise the king as he, Michelet, could and did despise him. "Misery," he exclaimed, "profound misery! not to be able to despise force which is unjust!" [14]

Other writers of history, notably Thierry, may have helped to suggest to him the uses that may be made of compassion in the development of historical theory.

[13] *Etienne Marcel*, p. 299.
[14] *Louis XIV et la révocation de l'édit de Nantes*, p. 109.

Michelet carried it much further in tracing the development of national life and came at times to make of his historical investigation a sort of search after moral suffering. Even where he could find no sure trace of it he supplied it, as we have just seen, from a sort of vicarious self-pity,—by the conviction that if he had been the person that he was studying, he would have been sorry for himself.

No one questions Chateaubriand's contention that all modern writers owe an enormous debt to Christian sentiment for whatever grace of tenderness and gentleness may have touched the strength of their emotion. Michelet surely betrays unnumbered evidences of its influence upon him. From his childhood he had felt its beauty. But he did not long yield unreservedly to it. His *Journal* records that after hours spent in the study of Saint John he would plunge into the reading of Greek tragedy in order to harden himself. We shall find later in what way he had first discerned its grace in the *Imitation*. His reminiscent tenderness for this book, given to the French "in their hour of greatest need," will always tremble on his lips. "These dialogues between God and a soul in sickness touched me with a feeling of profound tenderness. I listened as if a soft and loving voice had been speaking to me."

This arch-enemy of Christian 'mysticism' consented at moments to go further in his sympathetic appreciation of the mystic's rapture than the Church tradition itself consented to lead. He could follow the mystic ecstacy of Madame Guyon's *Torrents* with a poetical understanding which enabled him to fill page after page with eloquent sympathy for her yearnings for communion with God. His reflections on the barrenness of the Alpine heights unfed by those waters moving toward the sea are less convincing than the poetic beauty which he lent to his description of their music and their murmur.[15] And yet

[15] Cf. Part III, chap. iv; E. Seillière, articles cited in bibliography.

he was the professed adversary of mysticism of any type![16]
He was the professed adversary of Christianity itself,
yet Christianity had lent to his voice poignant accents
for his wordy battles against her. All the nostalgia of
limitless regrets alternated with his ruthless onslaughts
on the faith and all that Christian consolations can give
to deepen sympathetic understanding had passed into his
imagination.[17]

It is evident that the sources which fed the emotional
force of this apostle of pity were rich and varied. All his
vast intellectual effort and all his learning served to deepen
and enrich it. It had been colored by the turbid violence
of the great social battles which had stirred his sympathies
and by the political polemic of the early century; it was
alive with the quivering intensity of the Romantic metaphysical anguish, and we shall see that a fresh ardor will
be imparted to it by Michelet's increasing interest in
scientific discovery.

Despite all this and although the surrender to pity of
any kind was delicious to him, there was that in him which
rose up against self abandonment to any emotion. Something there was which spurred him to try to resist (not
always with success) the tendency to allow his strength of
sentiment to degenerate into mere sentimentality. He
had the strength and weakness which capacity for emotion
can give, and when he was conscious of the weakness, he
fought it with vigor. Under all the waves of self-pity
which beat over his soul the "vieille roche cornélienne"
stood fast and firm, showing a sturdy edge in some of

[16] Cf. Part II, chap. i, also Part III, chap. iv.

[17] *Jeanne d'Arc*, pp. 128–142. This analysis of the spirit of the
Consolation, forms one of Michelet's famous chapters. Cf. Part II,
chap. i, and Part III, chap. iv.

Michelet says of Christianity (*Tableau de France*, p. 110), "Il a
laissé de lui un si poignant souvenir, que toutes les joies, toutes
les grandeurs des âges modernes ne suffiront pas à nous consoler."

his softest moods. In moments of Romantic revery, meditating on the "sadness of nature," he found himself led on to reflections of quite another sort. Tempted by the melancholy which one may feel before a stretch of ocean, he would reach out instinctively in search of support for resistance:

There is sadness and sadness. There is the sadness of women and of strong men; that of sensitive souls which weep over their sorrows, and that of generous hearts which accept their fate and can bless nature even while they feel all the wrongs of the world. These can draw from their very sadness the strength to act and to work. How much our countrymen need to steep their souls anew in heroic melancholy.[18]

His power to draw fresh courage from such reactions against self-surrender determined some of the important moral crises of his life. The much quoted picture of him as a mere boy, rising at a hard moment to stoical resolutions, catches him in a characteristic attitude in which there is no pose whatsoever.[19]

It is clear that Michelet's self-confidence might possibly borrow strength both from his consciousness of capacity for sympathy, and from his sense of being able to resist the temptations which this capacity offered. This faith in himself gave him unbounded confidence in his mission and confirmed him in his belief that he had that in him which could help the world to discover the revelation of which he thought it to stand in need. The condemnation

[18] *La mer*, ed. '85, pp. 25–26.

[19] *Ma jeunesse*, p. 99: "Dans ce malheur accompli, privations du présent, crainte de l'avenir, l'ennemi étant à deux pas, mes ennemis à moi se moquant de moi tous les jours; un jour, un jeudi matin, je me ramassai sur moi-même; sans feu, ne sachant trop si le pain viendrait le soir, tout semblait fini pour moi. . . . J'eus en moi, sans nul mélange d'espérance religieuse, un pur sentiment stoïcien, je frappai de ma main crevée de froid sur la table de chêne, et je sentis une joie virile de jeunesse et d'espérance."

which he poured out upon the Christian dogma of Redemption and on the doctrine of divine grace were but one form of the passionate demands that he made for the recognition of the efficacy of the strength of human pity, which, he seemed to maintain, would be the great agent of self-redemption, the means by which might be inaugurated the beginning of the redemption of the social world.[20]

This sense of the efficacy of his compassion, as he grew older fed increasingly his sense of power. His capacity for pity in the meantime borrowed strength from every phase of his emotional life. "When, in order to be reasonable," Michelet had written in his youth, "I think I have buried my heart alive, all the power I have to love turns into philanthropy." [21] This power was later to enable him to feel sufficiently strong to dispense with all existing forms of faith, and to attack them all from the solid ground which the consciousness of his strength lent to him.

Chateaubriand's analysis of charity would have found supporting evidence for some of its assertions in a study of Michelet's personality.

Religion,—he says in his *Génie du Christianisme*,—being bent on reforming the human heart and on using our affections and tenderness in such a way as to help our virtues profit by them, invented a new passion. She did not use for it the name of love (it was not severe enough), nor that of pity, which stands too close to pride.[22]

In Michelet's love and pity there was indeed, often enough, too little severity, and oftener still there was to be found at the heart of it, like a closely wound spring, a vigorous strain of pride.

[20] Preface of 1847 to *l'Hist. de la Rév.* The same conviction fills certain chapters of *Le peuple*, of '46.

[21] *Mon journal*, p. 11.

[22] R. de Chateaubriand, *Le génie du Christianisme* (1802), ed. 1859, p. 50.

Pride there was in Michelet's pity, and other unexpected ingredients were added to it as life brought conflict with it. Some of them he would have found disturbing had he been fully conscious of their presence. Sceptical critics of pity could find matter for argument in many of the manifestations of the emotion which Michelet was so glad to feel stirring within him,—manifestations which reveal traces of the egoism and selfishness which La Rochefoucauld, Helvétius and Nietsche have studied as the most subtly revealing proofs of man's power to cherish illusions in regard to himself. Whether this egoism be inherent or not in the emotion of pity, anyone malicious enough to probe the depths of Michelet's motives in order to discover what may be brought to the surface, could find traces of it.

"Pity is often a sense of our own ills felt in those of others; it is a wise foresight in respect to misfortunes into which we may fall; we help others in order to oblige them to help us in like occasion." [23] In this sceptical analysis of our incapacity for participating profoundly in the sorrow of another, La Rochefoucauld is delicately reserved and critical, implying vaguely a certain sense of deprecatory regret, something self-condemnatory in the human insincerity of pity. The other two critics are frankly scornful of pride in the emotion and of the humanitarianism which may be its expression. Thus speaks the author of Zarathustra:

Wherever pity is preached today, it is the only religion. Let the Psychologist open his ears! Through all the vain and useless noises which these preachers are making (as preachers always do), he will hear a hoarse sobbing note of self-depreciation. It is a part of all that has been spoiling Europe and making it hideous for the last century, if indeed it be not the only source of it. This creature of modern life, this proud ape, is infinitely dis-

[23] "La pitié est souvent un sentiment de nos propres maux dans les maux d'autrui; c'est une habile prévoyance des malheurs où nous pouvons tomber. *Maximes*, CCLXIV.

satisfied with himself and his vanity demands that everybody share his suffering.[24]

"This proud ape," whom Nietsche saw flaunting himself in all the humanitarianism of the century is perhaps not more apparent in Michelet's over use of pity than in Zarathustra's haughty refusal to yield to the temptations of the emotion.   For although the historian's readiness of emotion did reveal an interesting mingling of all the elements which went to make up the definition of pity upon which Nietsche is said to have pondered (a definition by Helvétius),[25] although there was to be found in it not only the traits of unconscious egoism posited by Helvétius as components of pity, instinctive altruism, self-surrender, and respect for social justice went with these to make up the generous compassion of this "little man."   If he sometimes overestimated the value of its influence, it was not because he did not try, and try with all sincerity, to use this influence with reason and a sense of measure.

Even in his moments of egoistical self-contemplation, Michelet the man seems to have sought to exercise his capacity for self-discipline and for self-criticism and this desire seems to have availed to keep him more or less modest as a writer, even in his haughtiest moods.   We have seen that it gave him strength to offset his gravest weaknesses.   He wrote, to be sure, such passages as the following:

Sad destiny of the historian, to lose so many things; to live over again the loves, the griefs of humanity.   Since all men must die, let us begin by loving death.   In following the progress of

[24] Nietsche, *Jenseits von Gut und Böse*, Werken, Leipzig, 1899, vol. vii, pp. 173–74.

[25] Analysis of Helvétius' definition cited by M. E. Seillière (*La philosophie de l'impérialisme*) 1905, vol. 2, p. 127.   Cf. also Helvétius, *De l'homme*, Londres, 1792, p. 104.

the human race and its course from one ideal to another, we
will place our own high enough to make all reality henceforward
fill us with a sense of pity.[26]

But even here the historian hardly seems to merit the gibe:
"O la vile chose et abjecte que l'homme, s'il ne se lève pas
au dessus de l'humanité!" He could and did rise above
the 'abject' moods of his humanitarianism. In a closely
following sentence he wrote, seemingly with buoyant hope,
"Let our soul come to feel the strength of her wings and
our next journey will be more lightly made." His power,
which has already been noted, to create courage out of
discouragement rarely failed him.

But one would find oneself quite in the wrong if one
sought to depict Michelet's temperament as consistently
admirable. It had certain defects, those of his qualities
being perhaps the most evident. He allowed the generosity
of his temperament to color unduly his public utterances,
and he seems to have allowed it to complicate unneces-
sarily his private existence. Thus his lyric power of self-
expression serves to reveal, sometimes with disconcerting
clearness, certain weaknesses. In spite of his undeniable
moral strength, he appears to have been capable of some
suggestion of intellectual irresponsibility, and in spite of
his ready generosity a tinge of unconscious selfishness
comes to the surface just at those moments when he seems
surest of revealing his unselfishness. Did he suspect
what one might be tempted to read into the following
confession, to be found in Monod's *Jules Michelet?*
(The italics are mine.) "What influenced me in all
my passions rose from certain moral forces, from a
keen compassion which made me believe that *arriving as
a consoler, I would have greater certainty of being loved."*
The next sentence shows indeed, that this confession was
intended as a tribute! "By one woman, then another

[26] G. Monod, *J. M.*, p. 91.

(all of them so good!), I was cherished, reserved for great things: I kept my *sursum corda*."

This hope of gratitude however, after all, is natural enough in those who give love and compassion. But it is not only here that Michelet's expression of his need to pity takes on something of an air of self-centered assurance as to himself. Such sureness reveals sometimes certain symptoms of that need to dominate which M. Ernest Seillière has analyzed so penetratingly in its many manifestations as "la volonté de la puissance." [27] We would not insist further upon its presence in his conception of the historian's mission were it not that it gives an opportunity to quote at length one of his most poetical interpretations of this mission as one compounded of pitying consideration and sympathetic understanding. He prefaced this note (published comparatively recently by G. Monod) with the three words: "*Moi, histoire, nature.*" Here it is, almost in full:

Plutarch tells that Cæsar, while journeying by water, fell asleep and dreamed that he saw an army all in tears, a throng of men who wept and stretched their arms toward him. When he awoke, he wrote in his tablets: "Corinth and Carthage." And he rebuilt these two cities.

His grandson, Claudius, did more. He did not rebuild cities, but he essayed to restore the peoples themselves, to renew them through their history. Leaving Rome and the Empire to his slaves, he made himself emperor of the dead. He patiently gathered up within his fingers whatever dust remained of Etruria, Tyre, and Carthage. He warmed as best he might these pitiful ashes and, desiring that their name at least might live on, he founded a chair in the museum of Alexandria. . . .

The historian is neither Cæsar nor Claudius, but he is one who sees in his dreams a throng lamenting and in tears; those who have not lived out their full lives. This throng is everyman,—humanity itself. Tomorrow we shall be there, a part of it.

Men of a hundred years, nations of a thousand years ago, and

[27] E. Seillière, *Apollôn ou Dionysos*, 1905, passim.

babes long dead, all say that they had not yet begun to live or that they had but begun to live; that like Jephtha's daughter they had been given but a month to weep before that they should die.

They say that if they had known themselves and could have learned resignation, they would have accepted their lot and would not still be here wandering among us; that they would have allowed their urns to close gently over them.

But when you were alive in the warm light, when you had your moment, if you lived, loved, suffered, as we do now, why did you make no effort to lend endurance to what you loved, to give to your short infinity an infinite eternity?

We died while as yet we could only stammer. Our sad chronicles show it plainly. We had not attained to the sovereign attribute of man,—a voice articulate, distinct, which, through expression, would have brought us consolation. Even if we had had a voice, could we have told our lives? But we had none!

Let someone come who can tell them, as we cannot, to whom God has given a heart and ear to hear from beneath the earth the thin voice and the faint breath (*triste et acutum*), someone who loves the dead and who can find for them, and speak for them, the words that they could never say, words which remain unspoken and weigh yet on their dead lips.

It is not only an urn that they implore with tears and sighs. It is not a mourner, it is a divine *vates*,

> Sed non ante datur telluris operta subire
> Auricomos quam quis decerpserit operta fetus.

And he must bear the golden bough! Whence shall he pluck it? From his own heart!

It is from his own griefs that the historian reproduces the sorrows of the nations. He renews them to console them. But the dead ask more than an urn and tears. It does not suffice to renew their sighs. They must have the divine *vates*. So long as they have not this interpreter they wander about their tombs and know no rest.

They must have even more. They must hear uttered the words they did not speak. (Look in your hearts and you will find them there.) We must make the silences of History speak. . . .

Then only will the dead consent to burial. The shades are quieted and find rest. They go away, cradled by loving hands. The Pontiffs of History bear them on, with what tender care! As they would bear the ashes of their fathers, of their sons! [28]

The conception of the historian's mission revealed by this note is fundamentally characteristic of him at all periods of his life, but was most apparent in the younger Michelet, the author of the *Moyen Age*. This "moon mild Michelet" (as Heine somewhat mistakenly called him), with no well defined faith in accepted creeds but with a deep reverence for life, felt an especial pitying regard for the past as evidence of the value of life which to him—so far as its individual form was concerned—had but its one short span on earth. The projection of the past into the future constituted what in his eyes was the only assured form of immortality granted to man,—not the immortality of the individual personal life save as this individual personal life still lived on and made itself felt in the general life of humanity.

Hence the peculiar conception of the sacred office of the historian. He granted to the dead the resurrection in hope of which many of them had lived, which all merited in any case, through the interest which in Michelet's eyes was inseparable from every human destiny. Such a conception lent him a compassionate reverence for life and death. It was full of a poignancy not necessarily present in the regard felt for the individual life by those whose firm faith in a personal immortality might discount somewhat the value of human existence upon earth.

But in time it became apparent that to write history as a "Resurrection" could not fulfill the entire mission to

[28] G. Monod, "Note inédite," of 1842, cited *Bibliothèque universelle et Revue suisse*, "La place de Michelet parmi les historiens," juin, 1910, pp. 468–470.

which Michelet felt himself called as "Pontiff of History!"
The time soon came when it seemed imperative to him to
make of his "Resurrection" a work of "Redemption."
Moreover, this redemption had to be accomplished at such
times as he rather arbitrarily willed. The self-consciousness of his power grew upon him and led him to use his
authority with a shade of caprice. He was indeed the
bearer of the golden bough! But instead of bearing it in
all humility into the realms of the past which it opened
to him, he came to use it as an emblem of authority which
gave him especial rights and privileges there.

His political and social opinions and his exposition of
them were dominated, as has already been suggested, by
his sense of pity. It justified for him as well his political
dreams and ideals. Democracy as he foresaw it was to
be such a social order as his sense of pity would lead him
to comprehend—an order of society created and unified
by human pity. As time went on he conceived that this
pity could only be instilled into it by those who held it
as they would a peculiar and superior gift and who bestowed it as they might a personal possession. Thus
through all of Michelet's teaching the tacit confession of
the inferiority of what he most idealized—Women and
le Peuple [29]—became gradually more clearly discernible.

What is this great anonymous force, the "People," of
which Michelet constituted himself the priest, prophet
and chronicler? In the last analysis, it is most often those
whom one may pity. The title "the People" is granted
or withheld by Michelet according as he could or could
not, might or might not, pity those who should put in a
claim to it,—"All those who sigh and suffer in silence, all
those who aspire and mount toward life,—these are the
people, these are my people." [30] The full magic of this
power of pity, sometimes so capriciously bestowed, lifted

[29] Cf. Parts III and IV.   [30] *Le peuple*, ed. 1885, p. 217.

or abased whole social orders in his eyes. Kings, the clergy and the peasants in his first volumes held an inalienable right to respect and esteem, for Michelet in writing this portion of his work felt sympathy for them and detected in them a capacity for sympathy. In his *Révolution*, group after group rises for a moment as the historian's pity or his sympathy touches first one and then another of them with irregularly varying force.[31]

He came also to have subtler uses for emotion. As the more gentle and romantic spirit of his youth gave way to the belligerency of a spirit sharpened and slightly hardened by polemic battles, and as Michelet began to seek for argument wherever he could find it (among other places in the evidence of medical records), he masked at times his insatiable curiosity under the gracious panoply of pity. This disguise for the indiscretion which he manifested sometimes in the presentation of his solution of physiological and psychological problems and puzzles, hid from him perhaps, if not from others, a tendency to dwell somewhat unduly on the physical and moral defects of his victims. He filled many pages with the discoveries which he believed that he had made in probing the miseries of the wicked or of the unfortunate, showing a trace of that spirit defined by the philosopher of pity as "the hypocritical substitute for compassion," that *Schadenfreude* which has been described as "an excuse to get near enough to Job's dunghill to feast one's eyes on his suffering." [32]

[31] *Hist. de la Rév.*, vol. 1, pp. 198–200; vol. 3, pp. 310–311; vol. 4, pp. 345–346. "Non, cette foule . . . n'était pas une bande de brigands, c'était le peuple tout entier. Une scène pathétique eut lieu dans l'Assemblée nationale. Qu'elle passe à la postérité pour témoigner à jamais de la magnanimité du 10 août, du noble génie de la France." Also *ibid.*, pp. 348–367.

[32] Schopenhauer, *The World as Will and Idea*, Translation, London, R. B. Haldane, and J. Kemp, 1907–1909, vol. i, p. 485. Cf. also E. Seillière, 1905, *Apollôn ou Dionysos*, p. 137; and Schopenhauer, *On Human Nature*, M. A. Saunders, 1902, p. 23.

Michelet's sense of compassion did not, indeed, at
any period of his life yield habitually to this its hypocritical substitute. He was however often frankly ironical
in manipulating it for the undoing of those whom he would
confound. But even on such occasions, even while trying
to exploit his pity with calculated skill, his sympathetic
sensibility swayed him and produced mingled and unexpected effects. These might well be studied in the
picture which he composed of Richelieu as a sort of seven-
teenth century Job, beset by ills both physical and moral,
with all his comforters at hand in the shape of malevolent
foreign and court influences. In this uncomfortable en-
tourage the great Cardinal is brought to his end, worn
out by his own bad faith and that of others, prone on
what seems indeed to have been for Michelet a sort of
national dunghill,—the France about to pass into the
hands of the Queen and Mazarin.[33]

That he understood to the full what an effective force
was to be found in the passionate expression of social pity
may be seen from the fact that he imputed it to his enemies as one of their unpardonable sins.[34] "Pas de pitié
pour la pitié," seems to have been one of his battle cries,—
No pity for any save his own brand! His use of it was at
moments so exaggeratedly passionate that it seemed fully
to justify a definition cited by M. E. Seillière, which makes
of humanitarianism "a timid and undeveloped form of

[33] *Richelieu et la Fronde*, pp. 226, 237, 244. *Ibid.*, p. 200: "La
France du XVIIᵉ siècle procède de deux caducités, de la vide es-
pagnole et de la pourriture italienne." On p. 233, Michelet shows
Richelieu wearing all the dignity of an afflicted Job.

[34] *Hist. de France, La Régence*, p. 370.
Somewhere in *Henri IV et la ligue* there is the following observation: "C'est ainsi qu'avec la pitié on fait tant qu'on veut de la rage,
et que l'amour peut devenir l'aiguillon de l'assassinat." Also *ibid.*,
p. 248: "Pour donner l'impression de vengeance et de cruauté, rien
n'est meilleur que d'entamer les choses par l'attendrissement; un
peuple attendri est terrible; les larmes sont près du sang."

desire for military conquest." [35] Michelet came to glory
more and more, as he grew older, in the force which this
humanitarian appropriation of the sense of pity could
lend to the violence of social battles. It has been seen
that Voltaire, armed with it, was for him a hero supremely
noble. He commented on the fact that one of Voltaire's
critics had been surprised to find that in spite of the bitter
lines about the great satirist's mouth, the eyes above this
mouth shone with a great gentleness and tenderness.
Michelet himself saw no contradiction there:

> A great contrast? not in the least. Tenderness and compassion
> and the satirical spirit, war, are not opposed to each other.
> Kindness and pity in some souls are full of a spirit of combat.
> They make one pitiless for all forms of cruelty, for all barbaric
> ideals, for every inhuman doctrine. [36]

Plainly it is here a matter of definition. Michelet's def-
initions were quickly and passionately formulated, his
pity and sympathy were indeed often stimulated by an
intense "spirit of combat." His unreasoning emotionalism
was a force which makes it very hard to gauge and judge
his influence. It has tempted his critics to show much of
the same spirit of partisanship and partiality that at
certain moments of his life he showed in pronouncing upon
others. It lifted his passions into domains of ardent mysticism, threw its heat into bitter controversy, betrayed
him into regrettable exaggerations, frequently into manifestations of questionable taste, sometimes of unkindliness,
but it gave him undeniable power!

It was a force indeed! It could make him as unreason-
ingly tender at times as it made him irrationably bitter
at others. But a wonderful grace was his through this

[35] Cited by E. Seillière, *Apollôn ou Dionysos*, p. 137. "La pitié
donnerait l'impression la plus agréable à ceux qui n'ont pas de chance
de faire de grandes conquêtes."

[36] *La Régence*, p. 371.

vivid sympathy, which made him quick to divine the beauty of humble moral aspiration and of defeated effort. It inspired him with a deep respect for life and made his belief in endeavor very sincere. It lent him, too, an admirable regard—sometimes poorly regulated—for human personality. This unfailing respect for life demanded of him such interest in all its manifestations that the 'natural rights' of man could not have been for him a matter of supreme importance, had he not been able from the affirmation of them, to go on and posit for all life the right to full and free development. He posited for it likewise beauty and dignity.

It is easy to divine that when he came to study the world of nature, he could find there fresh revelation of the rôle that universal sympathy might play. Many men of his epoch found moral inspiration in the discoveries of science. The historian eagerly examined what those discoveries could offer to him, and his power of pity warmed itself at the "religious spark" which gleamed for him in all the new facts that he could cull from the scientific activities of his day.[37] By its light he caught the most convincing revelations of the unity of life, and its moral energy seemed to him to find its realization in pity. He felt it pulsing strongly enough in his own veins to inspire him with the following naturalistic and materialistic account of the genesis of the emotion:

The force of the higher forms of life is in the blood. By it a fresh youthfulness has its beginnings in nature, in desire, love, love of family, which as it comes to man will give to life its divine crown of pity.[37]

After 1852, his deepening interest in the study of nature led him to complete his humanitarianism by what one

[37] R. Van der Elst, *op. cit.*, pp. 96–102; 80–81. Citations are taken from *La mer* (ed. 1861), chap. xii, p. 259; *Le peuple* (ed. 1885), p. 179.

may call a sort of *animalism*, of which his *Journal* gave early promise and which later was more succinctly expressed in such passages of *Le peuple* as this: "Animals, what a somber mystery, an immense world of mute dreams and suffering! But signs reveal their grief as well as language." [37]

Plants also came finally to play a touching rôle in the great system of mutual service constituted by nature. Michelet found them the more touching because he was forced to doubt that they could have any knowledge of the value of their contribution to the scheme of life. But if plants were without knowledge, it was not so sure that they were without feeling. And for Michelet a "roseau pensant" could have little superiority over a possible *roseau sentant!* It was community of sentiment which established for him the great community of life of all kinds. Sentiment was the crowning title to the "droit de cité" which he claimed for all existence, and with sentiment went capacity for sacrifice. He saw flowers tender with human feeling, touched as if with human sadness: "The water-lily gives out her sweet treasure of love; the forget-me-not dreams and sheds a honeyed dew of tears." [38] What he said of another is quite what he would have wished one to say of him:

Penetrating the secret of life by this untiring effort, he only increased his sympathy for life. The minute detail of the infinitely small had revealed to him the keen sensibility which life has hidden everywhere in nature. He found it in the lowest scale of life and this discovery taught him a respect for all life. [39]

However, the reserve here indicated was impossible for Michelet. Unable to limit himself to a reasonable respect

[38] *L'insecte*, ed. 1857, p. 483. The author hopes to publish soon a note on "Michelet and Erasmus Darwin," too long to have a place here.

[39] *L'insecte* (ed. Flammarion, without date), p. 283.

for all life, his sense of pity plunged him into an emotional interpretation of all life.

"The struggle for existence" was not the form in which he desired to conceive of the plan of universal life. He chose rather to look on it as a system of vast responsibility laid upon beings whose equipment for life is complete, since all existence constituted a solidarity of sentiment and of effort. He implied that if the paternal instinct could not be completely expressed by certain sea creatures, this but laid a heavier burden on other forms of life better fitted for self-expression. The fish was for him something like a pathetic merman with all the feelings of a father and nothing but fins for service! "It is pitiful to behold such an effort of the heart incapable of attaining its goal; pitiful that this creature should be limited by the fatality of nature to a mere initial impulse toward perfection." [40]

When an effort of nature failed at some point along the line, Michelet found it incumbent on those whose "art" was more perfected to "carry on" at whatever point they might find themselves. "The Great Community" was for him nothing short of the universe itself, seen with a vision rendered so keen by the desire to sympathize with all sense and sentiment that the whole scheme of things might seem the power of love grown visible:

The abyss of life would have seemed to me empty, desolate and sterile without God;—if I could not feel the all-pervading warmth and tenderness of universal love in the universality of the soul. [40]

Thus with the power of his imagination drawing its strength from a conviction of the universality of sympathy (the supreme proof of its existence being that he felt it in himself), Michelet formed a conception of love infinitely increased, grown strong enough to govern all life. Instinctive activities and rational loving sacrifice would both

[40] *La mer*, p. 253. *L'insecte*, p. 515.

be guided by it and all the great social forces would be coördinated.[41] This was the dominating conception of the personality of which it was declared that in all essential matters of belief, it might be said to be representative of the generation to which it belonged.

Whether Michelet was or was not this representative man is perhaps a debatable question. But in any case, no one will deny that in spite of all that he may have had in common with his day, there was in him something very unusual. His simplicity—something surprisingly naïve and childlike in his nature—made him a being somewhat apart. Therefore in spite of his violence and his virility; in spite of his irrational emotionalism (or perhaps because of it), he remains very disarming to one's severer judgment. His was a sincerity which seems at times to justify the strength of his feeling, even the exuberance of its expression. All this until such time as one finds it too strongly tinged with partisanship, and at moments dishonored, as he grew older, by gross exaggeration and by what seems a morbid intensity.[42]

Despite all that weakened his power, he remained one who could make others feel the force which he felt within himself; and on the whole it is probable that his power to love has made itself more strongly felt than his power to hate. Toward personal devotion and social harmony he cherished profound aspirations. And the sincerity with which he expressed them, even when he seemed to be working against them, lent him great personal dignity. All this imparts to his character a naïve gentleness and an

[41] *Le peuple*, 2e partie, *l'Affranchissement par l'amour*, passim.

[42] Cf. Part II, chap. 3.

For an example, in the preface of *la Bible de l'humanité:* "Revenant des ombrages de l'Inde . . . ici j'avoue, j'ai soif. J'apprécie Nazareth, les petits lacs de Galilée. Mais franchement j'ai soif . . . je les boirais d'un coup." His *Bible* seems to the present-day reader full of such examples. For its influence on his contemporaries, cf. article by Grace King cited in the bibliography.

effect of harmony which a closer examination, it may have been seen, somewhat discomposes. He retained always a desire to sympathize with every type of social effort and he expressed so convincingly this desire that it is not surprising that friends and enemies have alike testified to the extent of his influence upon themselves or upon others.

Among the influences which he himself most freely acknowledged as having been potent in his own life and as having entered most deeply into his sense of social pity he often cited his association with his two friends Quinet and Mickiewicz, who with him composed what he called "la triple chaire d'unité," in which was taught international unity as the social goal toward which a 'chosen' Messianic race was guiding the whole world.[43] In Quinet, Michelet seems to have found one who shared not only many of the same sources of inspiration with him, but also one who was animated by a like spirit of combat. He was accustomed to say of Mickiewicz that he had studied in him a charitableness which could not cherish rancor. It must have been the Polish prophet too who had encouraged in Michelet a mystical conception of the efficacy of suffering. Of these two men, there will be occasion to speak more at length later on. Here it may not be amiss to try to discover somewhat more clearly what ideal Michelet beheld in his own mind when he was most inclined to look favorably on himself and his influence.

It may perhaps be found in his enthusiastic celebration of an influence that seemed to him worthy of all the praise which century after century had bestowed upon it. Michelet claimed even more eloquently than Sainte-Beuve, Lamartine or Hugo, that he owed a great debt to Vergil. This wizard of the ages had touched his imagination from the first. In him the historian found the poetry and beauty which he seems to have tried to carry over into

[43] Cf. Part IV, chap. 1. Also art. by F. Strowski cited in bibliography; and Mme. Quinet, *Cinquante ans d'amitié*, passim.

his conception of his own mission, and the poetry and beauty which the mission of his own race held for him. Does he not seem to believe that the whole gamut of Vergil's inspiration was consonant with his?

Tender and profound Vergil, I who have been nourished by him, upon his knees, am glad that this gift of pity should be his; his gift of pity and his nobleness of heart. This peasant of Mantua with his virgin-like timidity and his long peasant locks was and is, without knowing it, the true priest and prophet, who stands between two worlds, between two ages, at a mid-point of history. Indian in his feeling for nature, Christian in his love for man, this simple-hearted man reconstructs the universal City, which shall not be closed to any living thing. . . .[44]

Here we may well have Michelet's idealized vision of the personality fitted to perform such a social mission as he believed his own to be. He often spoke of Vergil as if he were another self:

His influence was all the more penetrating because he talked to me in his low subdued tones, almost without words. Sometimes it came to pass that I forgot the invisible friend who was speaking to me, imagining his voice to be my own and that it rose out of my own heart like an almost inaudible plaint.[44]

It was not unnatural that Michelet should see himself in this Mantuan of humble birth,[45] one of the simple of

[44] *Ma jeunesse*, p. 200; G. Monod, *J. M.*, pp. 17–18; *Le peuple*, p. 183.

[45] *Le banquet* (*Un hiver en Italie*) under the title of Chapter IX, has a subheading, "Virgile," followed by: "Il a été l'ami de mon enfance et de toute ma vie. Pourqoui cette préférence? Tout y est contenu. Il est la voix des proscrits. Il est le monde." Michelet's friend Poinset, for whom the writing of the *Journal* was undertaken, writes him in June, 1820: "Je te félicite de t'essayer à prendre pour exemple et pour modèle, Virgile, Rousseau, Bernardin de St. Pierre." Michelet quotes J. Delille's translation of Vergil in *l'Oiseau*. Delille's expression of admiration for Vergil is almost as ardent as that of Michelet.

the earth who spoke with prophetic power born of his instinctive tenderness for life of all kinds. To Vergil too it had been given to foretell the reign of peace, to him had been divinely granted the Messianic accent. Vergil moreover had made the story of the founding of a City a chronicle of personal grief and of human love. *Tantœ molis erat!* He could strike all the chords of the great lyre of human pity. And was it not through pity for a woman's passion that his great national epic had threatened for a moment to lose its coherence and its harmony? At that moment at least he had come very near to admitting what Emile Faguet has declared was always true of Michelet,—that "for him, the humblest soul weighed infinitely more than a realm."

Vergil had offered to his disciple much from which to build his idea of citizenship. From him and from other and varied sources whence he drew inspiration for his admirable effort and achievement, Michelet seems to have learned some of the secrets of piety, as Vergil understood it and as Dante characterized it:

Wherefore Vergil in speaking of Aeneas attributes to him Piety as his greatest praise! But Piety is not only pity taken in the vulgar sense. . . . That is, it is not an emotion which consists in grieving over the ills of others. . . . It is rather a noble disposition of mind, prepared to feel compassion, love and other charitable emotions.[46]

Michelet's personality certainly showed many of the noblest lines of the Vergilian Piety. He caught from his great master a certain grace which was not indeed always efficacious, for the historian had no unquestioning obedience to tender to the gods. But the invocation that he had offered to his master seems to have been a not entirely idle prayer—"Holy Vergil, pray for me!" [47]

[46] *Convivio*, Tractate II, xi.
[47] *La Renaissance*, p. 292.

In spite of Michelet's belief in emotion and its power, in spite of a certain rebelliousness, he showed in his own life respect for authority, a gentle reasonableness in face of the hard facts of experience. Temperance and prudence he cultivated so far as in him lay, as well as what other modest virtues he found at hand.[48] Along with his cherished possession, the famous "don des larmes,"[49]—"the sense of tears in human things,"—he kept a sense of measure and a power of self-repression which gave him real dignity as a lay preacher (one of the few such preachers, according to M. Lanson, whose homilies are not such as to excite ridicule),[50] and which helped to compose in him something of "that noble disposition of mind which is prepared to feel compassion, love and other charitable emotions."

We shall find that he believed that life, instead of stifling emotion, should deepen and strengthen it and constitute for it effective self-discipline. And he seems to have tried to make of his own life a manifestation of the strength of human emotion and of its natural capacity for accepting what life imposes of needed discipline. It was in his own experience that he sought much of the matter from which were made the doctrines which he preached. And however much one may feel inclined to criticize his sense of having received a personal call to preach, one cannot question the honesty of his purpose or the sincerity of the emotion which gave his utterances their power and assured them their hearing. Nor can

[48] A. Fouillée, *Rev. philosophique*, 1899. *La Psychologie religieuse de Michelet*, pp. 259–275.

Mme. Michelet in her preface to the *Journal* quotes Jules Ferry's discourse at the inauguration of Michelet's monument at Père–Lachaise, 1883: "La plus humaine [personality] de ce siècle, qui fut incommensurablement bonne."

[49] For Michelet's gratitude for this gift, cf. Preface of 1869 to *Hist. de France.*

[50] *Histoire de la littérature française*, art. J. Michelet.

one deny, moreover, the earnestness of his effort to use his emotional power in the service of social pity, whatever may be one's judgment of his characteristic manifestations of pity or of his particular conceptions of society.

These conceptions were presented with all the persuasive force which personal conviction and lyric intensity could lend them, in Michelet's preaching of his personal trust in some divine source of life and love, in the urging of the cause of women according to his notions of what woman should be, and in the setting forth of what he believed should be the rôle of France in the final unification of international life—proclaimed by him to be the actual and visible "City of Providence" which in time all men would make their own.

The succeeding chapters will be devoted to some examination of Michelet's ideas on the problems involved in the foregoing considerations.

PART II

ANTICLERICALISM

Michelet's 'Satan' and His Revolutionary Idealism

All' aura il vigile
grido mandate:
s'innova il secolo,
piena è l'estate.

Gittò la tonaca
Martin Lutero;
gitta i tuoi vincoli,
uman pensiero,

e splendi e folgora
di fiamme cinto;
materia, inalzati;
Satana ha vinto.

Inno a Satana, Carducci, 1863.

CHAPTER I

THE "NEGATIVE WAY" BY WHICH MICHELET APPROACHED HIS CONVICTIONS

'SATAN'

Salute, o Satana,
o ribellione,
o forza vindice
della ragione! [1]

All hail to thee, Satan!
Rebellion all hail!
Hail power of reason,
Avenge and prevail!
(Translation by Miss Emily Tribe.)

Some knowledge of the stages of doubt and rebellion through which Michelet passed in trying to formulate his social and religious faith helps one to understand somewhat why his credo held what it held, and why it lacked some of the articles which one might have expected to find in it. The promise of it, such at least as it was openly confessed from 1830 to 1840, may be found in the vague and generous idealism which filled his *Introduction* of 1831. The note of challenge is tempered here as yet by a certain reserve and sense of reverence for tradition; but one can detect in it, as early as this date, clear indications of the spirit of battle which the author was later to reveal. After the end of this decade he was to

[1] This long *Hymn to Satan* was with Carducci the occasion for a paradoxical play on the name of Satan as a bizarre and symbolic expression of revolt against belief in anything that might create fear of life and progress. Michelet's use of the word reveals numberless contradictions, because he sometimes reverts to the more ordinary acceptation of the adjective "satanic." But on the whole,

declare that he had come to know himself by "a purely negative method,"—"Je ne me suis connu que par voie négative." [2] Nothing could be more natural; for, as the product of a revolutionary age, in spite of his prudence he found himself drawn into rebellion. And here, at a very significant moment in his career, he invoked the name of 'Satan.'

For every name there is supposed to exist some corresponding thing, "il y a le nom et la chose." This is only partly true of Michelet's 'Satan' which, more than anything else a mere name, was used at various stages of his development in order to avoid the use of other terms more usual and more conventionally decorous. Resonant and vague, it had been enriched by all the connotations which the Romantic admirers of Milton, Byron, Klopstock and Goethe could lend it.

One might enlarge indefinitely upon the origins and the development of the types of rebelliousness and resignation which were furnished by the Romantic 'Satan.' Here one can do little more than indicate that if Michelet's Satan type was an individual and characteristic one it

both he and Carducci use the term *Satan* in such a way as to indicate a direct attack upon any tendency toward "Satanism" as it is to be studied in Barbey d'Aurevilly or in Huysmans.

Carducci's poem has been rather generously quoted here because he admits that it was to some degree inspired by Michelet (*Polemiche Sataniche*, G. Carducci, 1882). The poem was written, the author states, in December, 1863. Michelet's *Sorcière* appeared in November, 1862. The *Popolo* of Bologna republished the *Inno* in 1869, causing thereby a vigorous attack upon its author. In reply to a critic who accused Carducci of having borrowed from "one Michelet," the poet replied confessing that he had found inspiration for his *Satana* not only in "one Michelet," but in Quinet and Heine. He also remarked in passing that "one Michelet" was no less a person than the author of the *Histoire de France!*

It is a well recognized fact that Satan's "chariot" is the familiar and prosaic railroad locomotive.

[2] *Le peuple*, p. 115.

was also one of a numerous clan, all of them complex in their significance.

They all might furnish an occasion for playing with paradox, for satisfying a love for antithesis, a need of mystery, and a taste for horripilation. But there were other things in 'Satan' beyond all this. The name constituted a plea for a certain relativity in ethical judgments. It was a bizarre symbol affording a sensational approach to the problem constituted by the presence of the capricious and illogical forces of evil in a world God-made. 'Satan' furnished the means for studying the conception of the divine from an unaccustomed angle, an occasion for the plea that stereoptyped judgments might be modified. Above all, he stood for the protest against the too easy acceptance of flaws in the order of social justice. He was a poetical and dramatic version of Voltaire's contrast between divine and human pity. The world was a place

> Où tout était heureux excepté Prométhée
> Frère aîné de Satan qui tomba comme lui.[3]

This elder brother (it was quickly pointed out), with his ill-requited zeal, was by no means an empty conception of rebelliousness. And Satan was not always the incarnation of the affirmation of evil and the denial of good. As a matter of fact, he came, in time, to be the exact contrary. He ended by losing all suggestion of intellectual arrogance. He was a different being from the types offered by Faust and his shadow, or by a hero of Byron. Or if he resembled these his prototypes, his symbolic significance was different. Alfred de Vigny's fallen spirit in *Eloa* had a Byronian splendor grown flimsy in the borrowing. But his kinship with the more characteristically French romantic Satan is apparent in that he seems quite as much

[3] J. Giraud, *Rev. bl.*, 18 déc., 1910, p. 758, has studied these lines of *Rolla* as evidence of Michelet's influence on A. de Musset. Cf. note 12.

to represent the power to test the strength of pity as the power to bring ruin.

The French romantic and neo-romantic Satan usually expressed very clearly defined socialistic or humanitarian tendencies. He had borrowed from Milton much of his somber and Luciferian majesty, in which the last touch of the clear-cut grotesqueness of the devil had been lost. He added to the picturesque and mysterious dignity of his exterior a corresponding nobility of sentiment. If he had the pride of the humiliated, he had also boundless compassion and sympathy with humility. Thus Satan came to connote the need to feel compassion for the outcast. He was the symbol of instinctive sympathy for those for whom pity is forbidden. When he put on a show of Titanism it was that of the humanitarian anarchist or socialist. His latent appeal and his profoundest significance lay in the fact that he was the incarnation of "la majesté des souffrances humaines."

The humanitarian glorification of the, defeated soul took numberless forms. Eugène Sue's *Juif errant* was a rather pretentious poor relation of the great outcast. Jean Valjean shows closer kinship to his real spirit—symbol as he was of the indestructibility of human aspiration. He was an eloquent justification for the inexhaustibility of pity, and he constituted a plea for unlimited respect as the due of the human individual. He represented in its every phase the dignity of human compassion and the great human need of mercy. Some such sense Pierre Leroux puts into his interpretation of Milton's Lucifer. The name of Satan on Leroux's lips (and on those of George Sand) came to wear the hint of a hard-won salvation. In a certain sense Satan's expiatory suffering might constitute him a good citizen, in the making, of Ballanche's *Cité des Expiations*. He showed usually the proud self-consciousness of the Romantic soul, but he showed the generous impulses of Romantic humanitarianism in that

his suffering self-consciousness was devoted to an effort
to penetrate by sympathy and understanding of anguish
the great common consciousness. It is this effort that
Nietsche imagined as accompanied by "a hoarse sobbing
note of self-depreciation." [4]

Dostoyevski studied very cleverly the 'Satanic'-roman-
tic vaingloriousness, its ethical confusion, and the pathos
of its baffled aspirations in the hallucinations of one of
the brothers Karamazov, touching off the analysis with
malicious irony when he makes his discreet Satan say:
"*Satan sum et nihil humanum a me alienum puto.*" [4a]

Such, stripped of all irony, might have been the self-
characterization of the French Romantic Satan. He was
supposed to be profoundly human and thus naturally
became profoundly humane. He was not the sceptical
self-effacing spirit depicted by the Russian novelist. He
was, as has been said, an embodied protest against resignation to sentence of condemnation passed by powers
constituted as a final court from which there could be no
appeal.

The tragedy of defeat, instinctive defiance, and the
will to assert a sense of personal dignity, the rancor
born of disproportionate suffering and of the pride which
stiffens in the face of insult, make of Leconte de Lisle's
Qaïn the supreme type of the Titanism of anguish, the
'Satanism' of suffering and of compassion. The prayer
of a like symbolic figure of hopeless humanity in *La fin de
l'homme* shows that it is not only resentment against

---

[4] Quinet's *Ahasvérus* is vaguely related to this type of symbol, in
spite of its autobiographical character. His poem *Prométhée* naturally conforms to the tradition which we are trying to interpret
more or less imperfectly. Mickiewicz's Konrad in the *Dziady* depicts
the rebelliousness of suppressed patriotism. One of his most characteristic lines is: "I bear in my heart the love of a whole nation."

[4a] The original (Terence, I, i, 25) reads:

Homo sum: humani nihil a me alienum puto.

divine injustice that he cherishes; the sense of the need
to pity has deadened his power to remember wrong—
it is a sense of fellowship with all human anguish:

> Grâce, j'ai tant souffert, j'ai pleuré tant de larmes,
> Seigneur, j'ai tant meurtri mes pieds et mes genoux.
> Elohim! Elohim! de moi souvenez-vous!
> J'ai tant saigné de l'âme et du corps sous vos armes
> Que me voici bientôt insensible à vos coups.

In the poem *Qaïn*, the victim prays for suffering:

> . . . le sanglot des vents, l'horreur des longues veilles,
> Le râle de la soif et celui de la faim,
> L'amertume d'hier et celle de demain.
> Que l'angoisse du monde emplisse mes oreilles,
> Et hurle dans mon cœur comme un torrent sans frein.

This is not the Titanism of pure defiance. It is not
the mere arrogance of egotism. It is the power to suffer
from which springs the impulse to help. Qaïn in a spirit
of prophecy foretells the triumph of this impulse,—

> Je ressusciterai les cités submergées
> Et celles dont le sable a couvert le monceaux,
> Dans leurs lits écumeux, j'enfermerai les eaux,
> Et les petits enfants des nations vengées
> Ne sachant plus ton nom, riront dans leurs berceaux!

It is the Titanism which refuses to accept sorrow sub-
missively as a part of the 'common lot'—the 'common
lot' of which Victor Hugo gives so significant a picture
in *Les malheureux*, where he shows Cain's deed as having
entered into the fabric of human existence and the "ancestors of the human race" as being dumb before the
tragedy of it:

> Ils songeaient, et rêveurs sans entendre, sans voir,
> Sourds aux rumeurs des mers d'où l'ouragan s'élance
> Toute la nuit dans l'ombre; ils pleurèrent en silence,

Ils pleuraient tous les deux, aïeux du genre humain,
Le père sur Abel, la mère sur Caïn.

Out of numerous and divergent impulses of protest
against rigid interpretations of good and evil, from the
instinct which urges to the defense of the defenseless,
from belief in the inalienable dignity of the human individual was evolved a Satan of a positively humanitarian
content. To this content of social pity and a sense of
personal value certain conceptions were added, taken from
some notion of the German metaphysical 'absolute' and
its strivings, and into all this there were fused ideas more
or less vague drawn from evolutionary science. The
resultant 'Satan' was naturally quite different from the
revolutionary anarchistic spirit whose final condemnation
implied to certain imaginations a condemnation of God,
and suggested to them that the accomplishment of the
salvation of humanity must be taken out of the hands
of God. Satan became rather an evolutionary and struggling 'Satan,' a useful and necessary complement to an
evolutionary and struggling God,—both working together
in the interests of humanity.

Such a conception is antipodal to the Satanic type
of Huysmans or of Barbey d'Aurevilly. There is in it
little or no trace of the glorification of evil which is supposed to breathe in Baudelaire's famous *Litanies*. And
even Baudelaire's apparent sacrilege is partly affected,
partly symbolical. His are not prayers for alliance and
aid addressed to powers of the occult and of evil. They
are the paradoxical expression of the need of the sense
of solidarity which common experience may establish;
they are entreaties for the solace of fellowship. They express much the same state of soul which Michelet depicted
in the first pages of *La sorcière*, characterized by such abandonment and hopelessness as drove the debased ignorance
of the middle ages into faith in the powers of the occult.

It is precisely freedom from the least trace of the occult which characterizes the nineteenth century *Satana* of Carducci and the last pages of Michelet's *Sorcière*, where the Italian poet seems to have found some inspiration for his famous *Inno*. Here Satan is thoroughly modernized. He is a democratic spirit, who having an allotted job, has accomplished it with a success totally unromantic in the accepted sense of the early century. He has lost all his poetic charm of vague mystery, all the aristocratic charm of *la belle âme*, all the pathos of the defeated soul.

Such was the historian's Satan-Science—a spirit of enlightenment. He stood for modern progress. It was a sense of the inevitable triumph of the beneficent forces of life which lent to him the Titanism which characterized him. The historian, it has been noted, was the possessor of a temperament to which pity suggested protest as well as protection. Compassion produced in him strong reactions. His power to understand suffering and the possible helplessness of wrong was combined with a determined optimism which refused to believe in the necessary existence of evil. And this he proclaimed with some belligerency. Believing in the unity of life, the solidarity of effort and the triumph of science and understanding, Satan came to be for him a paradoxical symbol for his sense of social pity, and for his faith in the dignity of humanity. Michelet's God, his 'Providence' embraced in the end all that went to make up life, it embraced all the struggles which accompanied Progress and Perfectibility, where 'Satan' had his allotted place.

In 1831, the young historian's Satan, whom he apologetically proffered as a symbol of the individual sense of freedom and belief in liberty, was a name for the glad spirit of challenge which all the world read just then into the promise of the future. It connoted the same assurance of ultimate triumph as did the 'Satan' of the more uncompromising spirits of Proudhon and Bakounine,—but not the same defiance. Admitting that he owed to Byron his impulse to use this symbol, Michelet used it from the beginning with a meaning un-Byronic. In his *Introduction* inspired by the hopes of 1830, he defined his 'Satan' thus: "The heroic principle of the world, so long confused with fatality under the name of Satan has now been revealed, and we may now call him by his true name of Liberty!" [5]

For most beholders there was indeed something both diabolical and divine in the unrest of this moment.[6] For Michelet it was an outward sign of a force which he felt within himself. "As for myself," so he affirmed, "there is that within me which will yield neither to the yoke of Nature nor to that of man." [7] Years later he was to invoke even more ardently and resolutely the same spirit. But it was no longer with the same sense of its easy and predestined triumph.

This moment came in 1842, when, facing the necessity of recognizing and announcing grave decisions, he had fully resolved to disavow all respect for the authority of

---

[5] *Introduction à l'histoire universelle*, p. 34 (ed. 1900). For Michelet's own contrast between Cain and Abel, cf. *La bible de l'humanité*, p. 374.

[6] On the other side of the channel, Carlyle had echoed in the same key the excitement born of this revolution. He too proclaimed Satan the author of its unrest. But to him if it was a hope, it was a desperate one. To those who had thought the French Revolution a madness, he cried that it was a "Truth clad in Hell-fire," and he greeted this fresh outburst of it with fear and reverence:

"A true Apocalypse though a terrible one, that nature is preternatural; if not divine then diabolic." . . .

And he wrote for those who had thought it a "madness and a nonentity":

"To such comfortable philosophers, these three days of 1830 must have been a surprising phenomenon. Here is this same French nation out shooting and being shot to make that same French Revolution good." Centenary ed., vol. 5, p. 201.

[7] *Introduction à l'histoire universelle* (ed. cit.), p. 4.

the Church, and he registered in his private notes his vow of attack and resistance. He wrote: "Are you not young? Is it not the dawn, the spring-time and the rebirth of the year? Does not the morning hour give hope of carrying off the lion's hide?"[8] Then with a backward glance over his life (for he was then quite past the middle point of life that his paraphrase of Dante's well-known passage might seem to suggest), he hailed the future and proclaimed his faith in his own strength. "There still remains," he continued, "the unconquerable will!" This "unconquerable will" was, in his opinion, the essential manifestation of the force which dominated and sustained the onward struggle of humanity. And he saw the power of social life in the process of development as a power which breaks and shatters, if need be, in order to hold its way. He had written in 1837:

> This is the source of the suffering, of the sublime sadness of the world. Man, nature, all existence is being wrought upon by a captive infinity which strives to reveal itself by action and by art. It makes and unmakes its symbols, languorous now from the effort of creation, now from a sense of death.[9]

In 1843, Michelet had fulfilled his resolve and had openly proclaimed his resolution to constitute himself a liberator for this divine and captive "infinite" by attacking what had been worshipped as divine in certain elements of society which he had come to look upon as "dead." Resistance to what he felt that man had outgrown, now came to mean to him the natural expression of individual dignity. It was merely a normal evidence of life. The name which he impenitently—however apologetically—continued to give to the imprisoned life-force was that of the great spirit of rebellion,—'Satan.' With all his revolutionary generation he used it as a

[8] G. Monod, *J. M.*, p. 127.
[9] *Origines du droit*, Introduction, p. xlv.

symbol of the protest of the present and of the future against the past, and of reason against unreasoning submission. "A bizarre name for liberty," he wrote in his old age, "young and militant at first . . . but destined to grow more creative, more fecund." [10] But in spite of Michelet's instinctive respect for the spirit of rebellion, despite all that his revolutionary sympathies owed not only to temperament but to association, for more than half a century he curbed his militant spirit.

Events had indeed strengthened in him whatever revolutionary instincts were naturally his. Through his father's memories his sympathies held a very living contact with the great Revolution in which Joseph de Maistre as well as others had seen something of the "Satanic." [11] Michelet's resentment against the Napoleonic régime could only have been reinforced by the way in which every movement of the great Emperor had ended by upsetting the fortunes of the Michelet family throughout his entire boyhood. When the comparative calm which had followed Napoleon's final downfall was broken anew by the June days of 1820, he thrilled with awe and enthusiasm. His own spirit rose to meet the call which he always heard in "the voice of the People." He wrote in his diary:

I hear coming from the Tuileries an immense uproar. It is as if the cry were uttered by twenty thousand throats. It is not terrible save in its grandeur. This voice to my imagination is the revelation of the people rising as a single man, angered at the loss of its liberties. I feel keenly the need of handling a gun. [12]

[10] Preface of 1869, p. xi.

[11] For Michelet's close association with his father, cf. G. Monod, *J. M.*, pp. 218 ff. The historian's preface of '47 to the *Hist. de la Rév.* contains an invocation to his father, and Michelet quotes him in vol. 6, p. 152, of this same work. Joseph de Maistre characterizes thus the Revolution in the opening sentences of his *Considérations sur la France.*

[12] *Mon journal*, p. 37. The occasion was an insurrection caused by the violation of the Charter.

Michelet's battles were, however, never to be fought with guns; his were quite other arms. And when he returned from Italy in 1830, just in time to hail in the July revolution what he believed was a great onward movement toward the "City of Providence," he displayed a fine mastery of his proper weapons,—a flame of feeling and a fire of eloquence unusual even at that moment when eloquence was by no means unusual. The following year he proclaimed, from what he called "the burning pavements of Paris," that all history had been the struggle of "liberty against fatality, . . . in short, an eternal July!" And to his countrymen he cried: "Forward then, child of Providence! It is the will of God! the will of God! This was the crusader's cry!" In the great modern crusade to be waged by whatsoever means men could find, he read his own meaning into the ancient rallying cry, "Dieus le vuelt!" and offered himself as the chosen type of warrior. He had that in him, so he said, which "refused to yield either to the yoke of nature or to that of man," and which was meant to carry on "the struggle begun with the profanation of the tree of science" and destined to go forward by means of the heroic principle of the world "so long confused with fatality and called by the name of Satan until its true name shall be revealed." [13]

[13] *Introduction à l'hist. universelle*, pp. 28, 34, 94, and short introduction to same, dated 1st April, 1831. The passage cited at the end of the succeeding paragraph has been compared to certain lines of *Rolla*, cf. *Rev. bl.*, 10 déc. 1910, p. 758, art. by J. Giraud, *Michelet inspirateur de Musset*. (Cf. note 3.) The following lines are there cited:

> Je ne suis pas de ceux qui vont à ton calvaire
> En se frappant le cœur, baiser tes pieds saignants;
>
> . . . .
>
> Et je reste debout sous tes saints portiques,
> Quand ton peuple fidèle autour des noirs arceaux
> Se courbe en murmurant sous le vent des cantiques.

What was its true name? Not, in the end at any rate, as has been suggested, the name offered by Michelet at this moment—'liberty,' in the ordinary sense of the word. The historian's whole life was to be an unflinching endeavor to learn its true meaning; since this "heroic principle of the world" seemed to him to be the manifestation of the will of God, and he always longed to believe that the will of man and the will of God were identical. For the time being however, Michelet's 'Satan' was the symbol of the affirmation of man's inherent moral dignity as manifested and maintained by struggle. This implied for him at first no violent rejection of generally accepted sanctions and belief. In 1831 he was still able to remember with reverence that, standing in the Coliseum, he had kissed the cross, the presence of which marked there the triumph of Christianity, "The cross that every day stands more and more alone." He reverenced it because it seemed to him the unique refuge of the religious soul. He saw, however, its altars unhonored, and he asked, seemingly without hope of an answer: "But tell me, I pray you, tell me whether another altar has yet risen?" [13]

Since his early childhood, Michelet had been looking for the altar of his worship. As a boy he had hovered about the newly opened churches of Paris, where great crowds entered as if with a common sense of brotherhood. His complete ignorance of what these gathering throngs went in to seek behind those mysterious portals did not deaden, but quickened rather, his wistful sense that they were in quest of something marvelous: "I was eager for those mysteries, without having any real image of what they might be." A chance, a vague desire, led him to open the *Imitation*, and he felt that it was written for a seeking heart like his. He caught "a sudden glimpse beyond this dull world, of another life more full of hope, or of a deliverance through death," and the vision, he said, never left him:

Religion received in this way without an intermediary was very strong in me. It remained with me as something entirely mine, something alive and free, mingled with my life so closely that it strengthened all that went to make up my life in a multitude of tender holy things, borrowed from art and poetry which are wrongly considered to be foreign to it.[14]

It is clear, however, that this vision remained with him merely as a peculiarly precious personal experience, bringing him little nearer to any ultimate understanding or association with those for whom the book had been written, for he adds:

I can still see the vast unfurnished room, and it seemed to be illumined with a mysterious light. I could not go far in this book, because I did not comprehend the Christ, but I felt in it the presence of God.[14]

Was it still some uneasy haunting sense of having been deprived of something needful and beneficent, of some right, which led him to have himself baptized when he was eighteen years old? Madame Michelet represents her husband as having so remembered it. M. Lanson sees it as an act at once "adroit and sincere." Its sincerity is thus characterized in *Ma jeunesse*, in what might be an elaboration and development of a passage to be found in Michelet's private notes of 1846: "At eighteen years of age, my heart was sensitive and tender (it is an age of love and imagination), and I suffered from not being

[14] *Ma jeunesse*, pp. 38, 58. For a discussion of Michelet's formal connection with the Church as a teacher, giving Catholic instruction and a subscriber to *la Société des bons livres*, cf. G. Monod, *Michelet à l'Ecole Normale*, and article cited, by G. Lanson; *International Rev.*, April, 1905, pp. 71–101. "Michelet took his children to mass in 1840," when, as M. Lanson says, "policy no longer prompted it, but rather the contrary." In 1841, at the beginning of a course on the Reformation, he is said to have publicly declared himself a Catholic. *Ibid.*, p. 77.

affiliated with the great association of Christians, the
only association which as yet exists." With baptism
began Michelet's personal connection with the Church,
the character of which it is impossible to define. It ended
in 1842. His public rupture with the Church tradition in
1842 came later than might have been expected and was,
when it came, coincident and complicated with matters
which were not altogether matters of personal belief.
Long delayed, however, as it was, this rupture was early
to be foreseen; but inevitable as it seems, it was not accomplished without real moral suffering. How inevitable
it was is plainly indicated by this passage of his *Journal*,
written in 1820:

This morning Madame Hortense came in to say that she was
going to mass and to ask me for a Mabillon. This excess of
devotion surprised and hurt me at first. What errors, I said to
myself, she is going to accept without questioning! Under the
sway of this reflection, I asked her gently if she were not con-
demning herself to ignorance of the truth by examining only
one side of the question. I urged her to re-read the *Profession
de foi du vicaire savoyard*, and to make her religion a matter of
choice. When she had gone, I examined myself and seemed to
discern that my pain sprang, not only from my interest in her,
but from my vanity, hurt at seeing her turn away from my
opinions. *Tu te fais centre, encore si c'était ligne*, I reflected; and
I believe that I was foolish to advise her to begin to question. . . .
Natural religion, which presents neither moving ceremonies nor
fixed practices to nourish her at certain fixed times, would not
touch her deeply and would mean little to her.

However, in thinking of her I feel the more strongly the
necessity of a book which should be an habitual nourishment
for a soul which has known such suffering as hers. I have always
been surprised that in this order of ideas nothing has been drawn
from the ancient philosophers and especially from the books of
the Orient, which brings us light on every subject. There the
idea of God is fused with that of action. Greece, Persia, these
are the sources from which I should like to draw. The religion

of these peoples, instead of lulling the mind to sleep, urges it
on in the direction of progress.

It seems to me that desiring to go forward is a proof of being
in the friendship of God.[15]

This citation has been given at length because there is
in it a suggestion of the entire evolution which Michelet's
attitude toward religion was to undergo. And it holds,
besides, so much of Michelet himself! His easily aroused
suspicion of all forms of submission as evidence of moral
and mental languor, his innate tendency to impose his
own beliefs on others, are all here;—this last in spite of
his delicate and scrupulous respect for the feelings and
needs of others. Already this passage, written at the age
of twenty-two, shows that he had measured the whole
road that he was to travel. But he had in no wise gauged
its difficulties. The Vicaire Savoyard, perhaps his profoundest source of inspiration, is thus early under suspicion of "lulling the intelligence to sleep," the conviction
that inspiration for heroic activity must be sought in the
books of the Orient and in the models offered by Greece,
the conviction that religion should be a matter of personal
choice,—all this is here. What is absent from the revelation offered by this bit of self-examination, is all sense of
how hard it might prove for him to carry the world forward
with him in a progressive advance in the "friendship of
God." This carrying on of others was for Michelet a
paramount consideration, for he was imperious by nature,
he craved sympathy and association, and with his apostolic
temperament it seemed to him essential that he should
make his influence felt.

Therefore it was bitter for him to reflect, almost three
decades later, in the strain and disquiet of the social and
religious conflicts in which he had been more or less engaged since he had in 1842 taken his stand against "the

[15] *Mon journal,* p. 47.

religion of the Middle Ages," that the consolation he had dreamed of for the soul that suffers was still undiscovered, the religion of action was as yet unrevealed, and the association of those who should worship together in its faith had not yet been formed. After his father's death in 1846, he faced afresh the problem of the tacit acceptance of ecclesiastical tradition in the question of his father's burial, and he was shaken by a feeling of violent resentment and tormented by his yearning for some faith in which he could satisfy, by worshipping with others, his desire for a religion that could lend him a satisfied sense of fraternal association.

He recalled at this moment that years before he had refused all faith in the Saint-Simonists when they were promising the world some surer revelation. He had then been alienated by their violence against the Church, for this violence had produced in him a revulsion of feeling. An orator in one of their meetings had exclaimed: "Crosses, fall from your temples!" [16] Then in his heart he had answered "No!" He had plainly discerned that the new sect was not prepared to erect the new altar which could replace the one that they were banded to destroy. But in 1846 the moment had come when he could echo their cry from his heart:

If the old altar, crumbling and defiled, prevents for all time a new altar from rising, then let the old one perish! What if its close alliance with all tyrannies should make of it the altar of the devil instead of the altar of God! [16]

[16] G. Monod, *J. M.*, p. 230. It is to be noted that although Michelet's feelings of revolt were always exceedingly strong when the burial of some member of his family forced him to reflect upon the ceremonials of burial, he was never unyielding. His first wife, his father, and his son Charles were buried with the rites of the Church, without public protest on his part save that he did not attend his son's funeral. The second Mme. Michelet was cremated when she died, after twenty-five years of widowhood.

At this moment it is apparent that Michelet's symbolic use of the word 'devil' made of it the exact antithesis of his symbol 'Satan,' and that he felt himself impelled to enlist under the banner of the latter to scatter all the 'tyrannical' forces of the former; which, he implied, had in every age made compacts with the organized spiritual and temporal authority of the Church. And his accusations of this authority are eloquent of the bitterness that his agitation against the Jesuits and his feeling of disaffection toward the Orleanist régime had roused in him. Here he insists as well upon his conviction that the dogma of the Redemption as taught by the Church had fostered social injustice. He worded his indictment thus:

The world has been given over to you for fifteen hundred years. What have you done with it? You have been in league with Roman imperialism, with feudalism, and today with capitalism. What have you become yourself? A government of Jesuits allied with a government of kings who are bankers and of bankers who are kings. Religion of slaves, of what tyranny have you not been the accomplice? A religion of grace, of privilege, you have engendered, justified, exalted government founded on Grace, that is, upon favor and injustice.[17]

It has been said of Michelet's work that, like that of Lamennais, it was composed of two parts, of which the first said "Yes," and the second "No!" Does it not seem more exact to say that the historian began by proffering something much more like "Not yet," and ended by stoutly proclaiming "Now for it!" In his preface to *Luther* of 1835 he is merely hesitating:

Midway in my Roman history, I found Christianity newborn. Midway in my history of France I found her grown old and weak. Wherever I turn she stands before me, bars my way and forbids me to pass!

[17] *Ibid.*, p. 228.

Should I lay hands on her? Only those who do not know her
would not hesitate. As for myself I remember the nights spent
in watching by my sick mother. Her immobility gave her pain
and she besought us to help her change her position. She begged
to be moved, but my filial hand hesitated to touch her body in
pain.

These are the thoughts which have assailed me for years. In
these stormy times they have comforted my solitary revery.
It is a revery which I find grateful, and I am not eager to tear
myself from ancient thoughts which are dear to me.

For a temperament strongly swayed by both sentiment
and conviction, the conflict here hinted at must have
been profound, even in the face of the fact that the deci-
sion which aroused such hesitation had undoubtedly already been tacitly made. But once acknowledged, and
the consequences thereof accepted, such revision of opinion and of statement ensued as to expose Michelet to
accusations not only of inconsistency, but of lack of
measure and of logic. One of the most frequently noted
examples of his inconsequence is the attitude which the
historian took before and after 1840 toward Gothic art.
In his *Moyen Age*, in 1833, he had pictured with fervid
sympathy (believing that it had lost all availing strength)
the strivings of the force which had wrought out the com-
plexities and intricacies of the medieval Gothic structures
—evidence to him of an undeniable communion of social
effort and of the solidarity of human impulse.[18] All the
wonder and beauty of it inspired him with the same lyric
tenderness that he was later to display in describing the
delicate veining of flower petals or the "dainty curve of
some small animal's intestine."

[18] *Eclaircissements*, 1833 (published as an appendix of vol. iii),
p. 302. Et si puissant était la respiration, si fortement battait ce
cœur du genre humain, qu'il fit jour de toutes parts dans son en-
veloppe; Preface, 1869, p. xvi: "Celui-ci aborda la morte chose
avec un sens humain."

In his general preface of 1869, the historian denied to the Church the right to claim any of this tenderness as respect for herself. He asserted that he had found his inspiration merely in his pity for a faith which men had felt for symbols that they themselves had made, and which he had thought them ready to cast aside. He denied that his interpretation of the inspiration which had wafted the airy spires so far aloft and had so delicately carved the slender arches might have something of the profoundly religious character that he had seemed to lend it. He protested that others might not read into his lyric phrases what he had not meant to express in them. He himself was divided between mockery and gratification for what he had done. His last word was that it had been from no sympathy with the Christian faith as a religious faith but from simple love and pity for human effort that he had caught the magic to waken all this Gothic beauty and make it live again. He had "dropped a tear" amid the patient tracery and something living had sprung from it,—

The living blood which feeds the life of old legends, and carried upward by this vital stream, all mounted toward heaven . . . within, without, all burst into bloom,—flowers of stone? no, flowers of life! A tear, a single tear dropped at the foundations of the Gothic cathedral had sufficed to waken all this life.[19]

An examination of Michelet's chapters on the art and ritual of the medieval Church shows much justification for his claim that his respect and reverence for them was largely based on their significance as purely social manifestations. It is thus the more surprising that he should not have been willing to allow his testimony to stand as he had given it, without protest. But he no longer trusted himself to keep any tenderness for the Gothic. He denounced it as impractical and unscientific, comparing it

[19] Preface of 1869, pp. xvii–xviii.

disadvantageously with Brunelleschi's art.[20] Could one find a better example of the uncertainties to which 'Resurrection' as a method of historical interpretation may give rise when the interpreter assumes not only something of the rôle of a prophet, but that of a polemic writer as well! As the historian's endeavor to formulate his faith engrossed him more and more, he felt himself impelled to uncompromising attack on all that might tempt him to hesitate; and thus he ruthlessly sacrificed associations and traditions which he had cherished. Michelet gave as follows his own outline of the progress of his anticlericalism:

In translating Vico, I still hoped to find some accord between science and religion; but in 1833 I posited the death of Christianity, and in 1848 of all religions. I passed ten years, 1830–1840, in recreating the traditions of the Middle Ages, and this revealed to me their emptiness. I spent ten years, in creating an anti-Christian, an anti-Messianic tradition.[21]

It did indeed come to be Michelet's constant contention that all compromise and compact with the Christian tradition jeopardized the entire social fabric. He formulated this belief in his lectures in 1842, and developed it in that year in what became finally the preface of his *Renaissance*. He marshalled arguments for it in his *Peuple* of 1846, and in his preface to his history of the Revolution in 1847. These arguments were largely concerned with his conviction that society had so far failed to insure the freest possible individual development, with the statement of his tender pity and regard for children, and with his passionate demand for respect for all life. All this gave to his polemic a character such that, filled as it was at moments with rancor and revolt, one cannot

[20] Introduction of *La Renaissance*, p. 85: "Voilà donc la forte pierre de la Renaissance fondée, la permanente objection à l'art boiteux du moyen âge."
[21] G. Monod, *J. M.*, p. 16.

fail to feel at all times a sympathy for the ardor which he lent to his endeavor to frame positive and efficacious ideals for the reinvigoration of social faith and social education.

He found himself, however, involved in a polemic which formed part of the annals of an age during which the sharp battles that were waged about the question of the authority of the Church were complicated by the conviction that their outcome would have a decisive influence upon the future of French republicanism and upon a variety of political issues. Therefore, all these matters of politics and of public opinion have the effect of obscuring our appreciation of the moral conviction which entered into these battles, and of confusing our sense of where their real importance lay for those who were involved in them. Furthermore, during the years just preceding and just following the Revolution of 1848, champions of the Revolutionary tradition found themselves faced by the fact that ecclesiastical initiative was vastly increased in France and popularly welcomed. Therefore this initiative, whether it revealed adherence to all that ecclesiastical tradition would have led its adversaries to expect, or whether it showed a tendency to encourage movements that seemed to run counter to such tradition, awakened distrust in such uncompromising spirits as were those of Quinet and Michelet. The consecration by the clergy of a "Tree of Liberty" on the morrow of the February days, in Paris, and the proclamation at Rome of the dogma of the Immaculate Conception might arouse in them equally violent resentment.

Such battles, moreover, as those in which these two comrades were engaged, are seldom studied with real impartiality and thus the outcome of them remains necessarily far from clear. In them, victories and losses are incalculable in their results, the apparent losers often gaining as much as, if not more than, their victors; while the victors themselves endeavor in vain to count accurately their gains. Neither today nor tomorrow will enable one to decide just what Michelet's rôle in these conflicts may ultimately prove to have been. Hence whether or not he was one of the influences (it has been claimed that he was) which contributed through the sheer force of his opposition to reinstate the Jesuit order in France, is a matter of minor importance compared with the fact that he fought this order in such a fashion as to perpetuate and disseminate certain beliefs, opinions, and ideas in regard to important social questions.

For he fought untiringly when he found himself forced into open belligerency by the turn that the tides of popular and official opinion had taken. He had in his youth believed these tides to be oriented quite as he would have desired. They were not. Therefore "the going forward" of the world in "the friendship of God" had not proved the simple, natural thing that he had dreamed, and there were moments when he felt himself thwarted on finding himself accounted a spirit of opposition, however numerous his comrades in revolt might be, and he more than once recorded his regret.

No one [he wrote] more than myself has resisted the idea (of attack), no one has prayed more than I for a quiet, gentle transformation which would permit what is innocent in form to live on. Weakness and error! New life is more exacting. It demands the sacrifice, the death of what has gone before. The form protests in vain when the substance is impeded at the moment when it is ready to create the form.[22]

This "moment for the 'creation of the form'" he believed to be the moment in which he was living. "New life" was being revealed by science and was evident in the changing ideals of humanity. Michelet refused to believe that the Church could ever favor or further the changes which promised so much to him. Therefore he

[22] *Ibid.*, pp. 231 and 228.

accused the Church of being the creator of evil, in that she saw evil in what to him was supremely good. "You hate verdure," so ran his indictment, "you see a devil in the nightingale's song." She was, he added, compact of "a bizarre asceticism," having in her no trace of "Naturalism" or "Heroism." It was in the name of "Naturalism and Heroism" that Michelet proclaimed that the Church must die, so that another order of things might be inaugurated.[22] This new order would bring the Revelation of which he had found the promise in science. What matter if there were those who saw it clothed in "hell-fire"!

For Michelet it wore the promise of a divine radiance. It portended fulness of life, and if it demanded that the past should die, well and good! "Men having learned to doubt, without having learned to regard truth as innocent," he was ready to attack all that insinuated a doubt as to the innocence of the human right to doubt, or as to the innocence of instinct. Was he not ready to proclaim with Bakounine, with Proudhon, and with other adversaries of the existing order: "For God is foolishness and cowardice, God is hypocrisy and misery, God is evil!" [23] If he was not thus ready, it was largely because he had never conceived of God as a being whom one could assail with such hatred. His synonym for the fitting object of such vituperation was the organized authority of the Church. And even against this authority he had held no such bitterness until he had met it at certain turning points in history and in certain crises in the life of his own time and in his own personal experience, where it had seemed to him pitted against the progressive and Revolutionary tendencies which he cherished. The authority of the Church was guilty in his eyes because it seemed to him to be distrustful of what might ensure the emancipa-

[23] P.-J. Proudhon, *De la justice dans la Révolution* (1858), ed. 1883, p. 449; M. Bakounine, *God and the State*, Free Society Library, 1900, p. 2.

tion of human impulse and that of the forces of natural instinct.

The historian did not, however, find these forces to have been everywhere and in every age a power which could be easily symbolized by the radiant ideal which he proclaimed to be the source of such promises as were offered by the "sunlit" days of the July Revolution of 1830. This modern and comparatively respectable spirit of freedom had then behind him a long struggle, in which he had conquered—and had been conquered—by unworthy means. He had often been trodden underfoot and had not failed to sting the heel that had bruised him.

It was in the power of life and a perverted sense of its beauty—perverted through the hatred which springs from ignorance and repression—that Michelet explained the wretched image which haunted the starved imagination of the believers in sorcery in the Middle Ages. From the degradation of suppressed and thwarted impulse had sprung a strange fantastic Satan, a *Satan-Peuple*, with something of the meanness and maliciousness of both Pathelin and Agnelet, and he had pitted his base impishness against all restraint. With a force grown furtive, he could impose his power in places where the Church was helpless. The haunting longings of the downtrodden peasants found expression in this their ideal of the spirit of rancor and revolt.

A strange ancestor surely for the resplendent ideal of the revolutionary aspirations of the nineteenth century! But the historian seemed to insist that there was back of them a common origin, that the medieval Satan was a grotesque manifestation of man's instinctive craving for liberty and life; and Michelet saw in him the beginning of an ideal, just as he had seen his own soul looking out from the degraded faces of the peasants, distorted by the murderous violence of the fourteenth century Jacquerie.[24]

[24] Cf. Part I, note 13.

This 'Satan,' it must be admitted, betrays at moments vague suggestions of the occult, for Michelet pictured him as the creation of an age in which instinct found freedom by hidden ways. He was the ally of spirits which had not known or felt the power of Love. But belief in him, so Michelet seemed to wish to show, held for men a hint of faith in their own strength. He was without dignity because he was the creature of an environment where human life was without dignity. He was most especially the refuge of the woman who guessed in him a power which could enable her to show her own strength, help her impose her own will. Woman bound to the soil was worse than an outcast, and yet she was the sacred depositary of life. Having been forced into hatred of life because she knew it only as defiled and unworthy, she had made common cause with the spirit of revolt and rebellion to which, as well as to herself, the right of individual existence was disputed. With him she exalted and glorified degradation. She had found her cause to be one with that of the eternal outcast. The almost unreadable history of their alliance fills those chapters of the *Sorcière* of 1862 in which Michelet traced the horrors which he was pleased to represent as having sprung from the enforced alliance of Woman and Satan—enforced through scorn of woman's human dignity and through scorn of life, making in the end of woman a perverted force and converting Satan to malicious devilishness.

In the unsavory Satan of the *Messe noire* Michelet found then some trace of the justifiable craving for personal power; Satan was a distorted expression of the claim for personal dignity. When the historian depicted, in his account of the annals of witchcraft, in what manner a debased conception of the power of instinct had, through ignorance, degraded and defiled the imagination of woman and had exploited both her weakness and her power, he seems to have attempted to make of all the degradation that he found in these annals, a sort of inverted plea for a sane and scientific evaluation of the legitimacy of human impulse as the basis of the education of the future. The safeguarding of woman's dignity, her education, and the education of sentiment in regard to her influence, constituted the beginning of wisdom in so far as the future of social well-being was concerned.

Such social well-being would result from faith in God as revealed in "Nature" and in humanity. It was in this faith that the education of woman was to be undertaken. Such a conception of God constituted the satisfaction for the profound need that Michelet expressed when, in the heat of his battles against accepted beliefs, he ended by proclaiming, "je ne puis me passer de Dieu."

CHAPTER II

"NATURALISM AND HEROISM"

Au fond d'une mélodie, au calice d'une fleur, vous rêvez nature
et vous rencontrez Dieu.
Michelet, *Journal Intime*, July 26, 1850.

Michelet, it seems apparent, had felt at every moment
of his life that his task of negation was subordinated to
the necessity of bringing some positive faith out of his
questionings and unbelief. For him, God could not be
"evil"; for to him God came to be life itself. It is plain
that the blows which the historian struck were not aimed
merely to destroy. We have just seen that he could not
exalt for worship quite the same spirit of revolt as that
to which so many of his revolutionary contemporaries
gave the name of Satan and which they called "the eternal
rebel, the first free-thinker and emancipator of worlds." [1]
What "Titanism" there was in him was put to the service
of the hope in which he wrote,—that of stimulating society to formulate positive beliefs, rather than violent
negations; and although he was actuated in part by an
unconquerable individualism, he could not relinquish the
conviction that some new faith would serve as the basis
of a social solidarity greater than that which had so far
been realized.

Such aspiration had seemed to fill the resolutions which
he confided to his notes in that decisive year of 1842.

---

[1] See Chap. I, note 22. Matthew Arnold has written interestingly
of the possible Celtic origins of the "Titanism" in English literature.
Cf. *Culture and Anarchy*.

He evidently formulated them with mingled sentiments of hope and regret as he wrote: "Farewell to the Church. . . . I am setting out for an unknown infinite, for somber depths in which I feel without perceiving him, the God of the future." [2] Let us follow Michelet through some stages of this search for "the God of the future," as he sought him in some vague philosophical conception, in the revelations of 'Nature,' by means of a symbolic interpretation of historical tradition, and especially in a single manifestation which it seemed to him had been the full revelation towards which all modern history had tended,—the French Revolution.

He ended by believing that he had found this God. He came to see "the unknown infinite" as a great realm of being, palpitant with energy and life. He had little difficulty in assigning to man the rôle which he must play there. As an official and responsible member of the French University, he found himself forced, on taking up the discussion of the relation of man to the universe,[3] to

[2] Cf. Monod, *J. M.*, p. 130.

[3] Michelet's work does not show, properly speaking, any systematic discussion of philosophical problems as such. He wrote to Quinet soon after his return from Germany that his course in philosophy would "inspire him with pity," and that he needed to go over the whole ground dialectically. (Mme. Quinet, *op. cit.*) G. Monod states that in the Ecole Normale Michelet's courses were concerned largely with psychology. M. R. Van der Elst has discussed in detail the entire philosophical and scientific content of Michelet's work, suggesting in one of his comments a comparison between Michelet and Bergson, (This might prove more suggestive perhaps than any other possible survey of the historian's metaphysics.), intimating too at the same time the reason why any detailed study of the philosophical side of the historian's work might prove more or less futile: "In such a metaphysical conception a process of becoming is substituted for being, as in the Hegelian metaphysics; and God himself would not escape being a part of the general process. It would be something like Bergson's *Creative Evolution*, were it not for *the fact that Michelet's system is rather insinuated than expressed*, throughout his whole work. *One has to look for it in order to construct*

consider the problem of man's freedom.[4] Or rather, he would have had to consider it if he had ever looked upon it as a problem. But since he felt rather than saw problems, and since this was one of which he felt the solution rather more distinctly than he felt the problem itself, he found the solution ready for him in his own personality. There was that in him, so he said, "which refuses to yield either to the law of man or of nature."

"Every system," Nietsche has somewhere said, "is the result of a temperament." We have seen what abundant reason there is to believe that this would be true of whatever system Michelet might elaborate. His way of feeling having always largely determined for him his way of thinking, it produced for him many of his metaphysical ideas. One can hardly say his metaphysical conclusions, for strictly speaking, he reached but few and he admits himself that he felt very little in need of them.[5] He found

it." *Michelet naturaliste*, 1914, p. 160. Cf. also note 3. (The italics are mine.)

M. Van der Elst's treatment of Michelet is to a certain degree 'controversial.'

[4] For some statement of the French philosophical tradition in regard to 'liberty,' cf. D. Parodi, *La philosophie contemporaine en France*, 1920, chap. I, p. 17.

[5] For Michelet's statement that certain metaphysical problems were for himself personally non-essential, cf. note of 1871 published by G. Monod in the *Bibliothèque universelle*, 1910 (article cited in bibliography): "Je définis l'histoire dans cette Introduction: la victoire successive de la liberté humaine sur la fatalité de la nature. Un esprit plus systématique eût suivi exclusivement cette tendance qui donne tout à la liberté. Moi, au contraire, j'accordai une place égale aux deux principes dans le mouvement alterné des choses humaines. Et au prix d'une inconséquence apparente, je marchai (comme le monde marche) par cette voie géminée, sur deux rails." M. Lanson sees in Michelet's antithesis of 'Freedom' and 'Fatality' (or nature), poetic symbols which take account of well recognized facts and forces which history must reckon with in the study of the development of society. Cf. article cited, *International Rev.* It must, however, be confessed that the evolution of his symbols ended

it perfectly natural to uphold, so far as in him lay, the great French philosophical tradition. He proclaimed to the end of his days 'man's freedom,' but his emphasis in affirming it was very different at different moments of his life. From 1828 to 1850, as a Professor of History, he had been inclined to place man over against 'Nature' as an eternal combatant. After this date he was more inclined to study him as one of the participants in the universal impulses of 'Nature.' [3]

The historian had drawn from many sources the conception that human life and effort are the manifestations of God's continuous acts of self creation. "Man is his own Prometheus" was the formula which he had borrowed from the thinker who had been his guide in his efforts to establish some governing conception for his philosophy of history. "Man is his own Prometheus," and in his artistry Michelet saw God's own activity. By his self creation in life and history God was increasingly revealed. Until 1848 Michelet had studied the manifestation of the 'divine activity,' mainly in human society and in the world of men. And he had studied it more or less under the guidance of the author of the *Scienza Nuova*. Italy had, so he said, given him Vico "for nourishment" in his maturity, as Vergil had been given to his youth, "potent cordials both which have many times renewed my strength." In Vico he had found a spirit after his own heart; one, it has been said, who could "compress into one sentence more lyrical feeling than may be found in an ode"; one too who had maintained

by admitting the possibility of lending to his work a naturalistic and monistic conception of the universe. This did not, so he insisted, impose upon him any belief which would jeopardize faith in human 'liberty.' Mr. Woodbridge Riley discusses in a recent number of *La Rev. philosophique*, jan.–juin, 1921, vol. 91, pp. 234–271, how large a rôle Bergson may have left to liberty and intelligence. A master of Bergson, Ravaisson, was one of Michelet's students. Cf. H. Hauser, *art. cit.* in note 7.

that religions were due not "to someone else's imposture but to one's own credulity." This had been at first Michelet's own attitude toward the religions of the past, which he had regarded as precursors of the religion of the future, and as such to be respected, until he chose to disregard much of what Croce has called "the wisdom of ignorance"; having laid aside much of that reverence which is due to "all religions as truth." [6]

But Vico's more purely intellectual conception of the unfolding of history and of life was soon blurred in Miche-

---

[6] In Vico Michelet had found, too, so he maintained, his own conception of history. This was but partly true, for naturally he did not try to carry over into his system of historical treatment certain inconsistencies by which Vico could distinguish between sacred and profane history, nor did he long show any trace of Vico's devout desire to reconcile his philosophical conception of history with Roman Catholic dogma and belief. In spite of this desire, Vico himself seems to have tacitly posited the immanence of God in the march of history. He had maintained that "it is intelligence that gives its impulse to the world of nations. . . . The creator of this world was mind, since men made it by their own intelligences; it was not Fate, since they made it by their free choice, nor yet chance since to all eternity the self-same activity produces the same result." It was this conception of the human mind gaining vigor through its eternally renewed contact with all the conditions, the obstacles and the opportunities of the natural world that Michelet called the civilizing "struggle against Nature" or "Fatality." Cf. B. Croce, *The Philosophy of Giambattista Vico*, translated by R. G. Collingwood, 1913, pp. 71, 72.

B. Croce, *ibid.*, pp. 116–119, and on page 143: "But the conception of an immanent providence is no less irreconcilable [than the notion of progress which "dates from the Reformation"], yet Vico is saturated with this idea. Progress deduced from the immanent providence would have accentuated the difference within the uniformity, the origin at every moment of something new. . . . It would have changed history from an orderly traversing and retraversing of the line drawn by God under the eye of God to a drama whose *ratio essendi* is contained within itself. . . . In face of this vision Vico paused in apprehension and stubbornly refused to proceed: the philosopher in him had yielded to the Catholic."

let's imagination by his reading of Herder, by his sympathy with what he himself interpreted as "pantheistic" in German philosophy, and by his study of science and the revelation which he thought that science had brought of the unity of life. Michelet claimed that Herder had "taken his stand in nature to view man's activity," while he, Michelet, was convinced that he maintained his stand in the world of intelligence and of man. His reading of German philosophy seems to have encouraged his tacit acceptance of a monistic conception of the universe, but his reading does not seem to have been finely critical. He was probably "influenced by Schelling but he characterized Schelling's philosophy as "Pantheism." Whatever may have been his knowledge of Kant and Fichte, and whatever the debt which he owed to them, he does not seem to have been willing to accept their conception of "freedom." He was wont to complain that they "threatened" his *moi*. Michelet seems to have carried into his idea of universal life some conception of the strivings of the Hegelian 'absolute.' [3] He came finally to conceive of life as one great divine impulse, of which he posited the source to be love; he maintained, nevertheless, that in this ever-impeded but never interrupted 'becoming,' man 'freely' worked out his own ends and 'freely' directed his own activities.[7] Man was the moulder of his destiny,

[7] For possible establishment of interesting analogies between Bergson and Michelet, cf. notes 3, 5, 26. *L'insecte*, ed. 1859, p. 128: "Il faut rappeler les grandes et nécessaires réactions de la nature. Elle n'a pas marché avec l'ordre d'un flot continu, mais avec des retours, des reculs sur elle-même qui lui permettent de s'harmoniser. Notre vue myope qui s'arrête sur ces mouvements, s'alarme et s'effraye, méconnaît l'ensemble. C'est le propre de l'amour infini qui va créant toujours."

Ibid., p. 260: "Nothing will perish, I am sure of this, no soul of man nor lesser soul. We go on living more and more; acquiring originality, stronger and more powerful. God will not permit us to lose ourselves in him."

Cf. *Le peuple*, p. 204: "Reflection knows that it is superior in that

carrying within himself not only the consciousness of his
individual artistry, but as well, a vital sense of his solidarity with the medium in which and by which his individual
energy found expression. This was Michelet's claim for
human liberty. Upon a continuous stream of feeling and
consciousness man worked by means of his reflective reason and by his considered acts. Out of a great fund of
intuitive consciousness there came to humanity common
sympathies and a capacity for sympathetic penetration
into what is divine in all forms and manifestations of life.[7]
That this vaguely defined conception of man as an
agent participating 'freely' in universal energy could be
interpreted as Pantheism—that he himself should ever
be called a Pantheist, was always inexplicable to Michelet.
If a Pantheist is one who easily allows himself to be absorbed by nature, then he, so he insisted, was not that
man. He did not indeed lightly consent. To the end he
resisted absorption. He never relinquished the claim to
man's autonomy.[8] He conceived of himself and of all

it is enlightened; it is nevertheless inferior to instinct. The genius
accepts with joy and gladness the feeble essays of instinct. From
them something springs forth. Whence does it come? Impossible
to say, but it will live and grow in him as in nature." (This is in
some degree almost a paraphrase of certain sayings of Mickiewicz.)

L'oiseau, ed. 56: "Do not speak of blind instinct. One will see in
certain facts how this clear-sighted instinct is modified according
to circumstances, in other terms, how little this reason in its origins
differs in its nature from lofty human reason.

For Michelet's acquaintance with German thought through Leib-
nitz, Kant, Schelling, Fichte, Niebuhr, Creutzer, etc., cf. G. Monod,
Michelet et L'Allemagne. For Michelet's interest in the relation of
Vico's theory of knowledge to the philosophy of Leibnitz, cf. H.
Hauser, "*Michelet naturaliste*, et l'âme française d'aujourd'hui,"
Rev. du mois, 10 jan. 1919.

[8] G. Monod, *J. M.*, p. 88: "If a pantheist is he who easily allows
himself to be absorbed by nature, I am not that man." For the
indiscriminate use of the term "Pantheist," and for the stigma
attached to it, cf. H. Taine, *L'idéalisme anglais*, 1864, p. 118, "ce

"heroic creators" in social activity as direct manifestations of divine effort, gaining energy by the expenditure of energy. He looked upon them as artists in whom intuitive spontaneous consciousness and creative power found direct expression in just the measure that these creators had learned to love life and respect it. Scientific knowledge of life would inevitably awaken love and sympathy for all forms of life, and sympathy for life enlightened by science would redouble human effort." [9]

But however great the emphasis that Michelet put upon the glory of effort and its achievement, his insistence upon the beauty of the humblest forms of energy was inspired by his belief that all life was sacrifice, and that by it the power of love became visible. The inconspicuous manifestations of this power touched him, simply because they were destined to pass unperceived. Thus despite the fact that life seemed to him beautiful and good, he pitied it. Transformation was necessary to it, and this made him sad, because his sympathy for the individual was not dwarfed by his joy in the great sum of achievement made up of the sum of universal sacrifice. [10]

It was about such conceptions as these that the historian wove the themes in which he expounded for public admonition his mingled sentiments of pity, trust and optimism. After he had been deprived of his university chair and dismissed from his post in the National Record

qui signifie fou ou scélérat," is his rendering of the popular estimate of a Pantheist.

[9] *Le peuple*, pp. 210–213, Here the genius is shown as the guide in the "social arts" and described at length as excelling and as comprehending everything because of his sympathy and love. *Ibid.*, p. 176: "Le cœur a vaincu, la miséricorde a vaincu, l'humanité va s'éloignant de l'antique injustice."

[10] *Ibid.*, p. 209: "Le fond de l'art comme celui de la société, ne l'oubliez pas, c'est le sacrifice." This is the theme of *L'étudiant*, of *Le peuple* as well as of the "nature books" (and of *L'amour* and *La femme*, in a certain sense). Cf. also *Nos fils*, Part IV, chap. I.

Office, he seems to have felt more strongly than ever the
call to an apostolate. A successful preacher may speak
either from absolute conviction or from an instinctive
sense of what may carry conviction. Michelet always
spoke so far as possible from both. He now resolved to
reach a wider audience and if possible to speak more
clearly. He was henceforth cut loose from whatever
anchorage had held him responsible to the demands of
professorial dignity and of official opinion. In 1852, as
he was leaving the house in which he had lived since his
second marriage, he asked himself what his life was henceforth to be, and the reflection which he recorded is the
following one: "What I had most to fear was the sterility
of routine and the overburdening weight of erudition.
For whatever has come about has come about through
ignorance. This is a call from God to a better and more
popular science." [11]

Such his science became, if a more popular science may
be called a better science. It was at this period of his
life that he wrote pamphlets in defence of nationalities
which he believed to be threatened. His volumes of
history began to express more frankly his sympathies.
His historical presentation had always been vivid. He
now lent it an added heat of controversial energy and a
note of earnest exhortation. He recruited all the artists
of the ages to his cause and in his volumes on the Reformation and the Renaissance, he represents Michael-Angelo
as having made the Sistine Chapel ring with his denuncia-
tions of all that may dare to cast a doubt on the dignity
of the impulses and forces of life. [12]

Art he depicted as the conscious or unconscious revela-

[11] G. Monod, *Bibliothèque universelle et Revue suisse*, 1910, vol. 60,
pp. 449–470, "la place de Michelet dans l'histoire de son temps,"
quotes this note of 1852.

[12] *La Renaissance*, pp. 317 ff.; *La Réforme*, pp. 89–913. G. Monod,
J. M., p. 142.

tion of the strength of such forces. They were the sources
of the artist's inspiration whether he was aware of it or
not, and his interpretation of his inspiration was most
often a prophecy of their triumph. Sometimes such
prophecy was like a secret sign. It was so with the work
of Leonardo de Vinci, but with all its secrecy it was un-
mistakable. Through the face of the Saint John of this
"Italian brother of Faust" there lurked the face of
Bacchus, or if you will, in the eyes of his Bacchus there
looked out something of the saint,—"art, nature, the
genius of mystery and discovery"—and Michelet quoted
Quinet's interpretation of his mysterious gaze:

The same curiosity of good and evil in the gaze of the precursor, dazzling, bearing in it light and laughter at the obscurity
of the time and of things; the infinite avidity of the spirit which
seeks knowledge and cries: 'I have found it!' [13]

The prophecy of Michael-Angelo, on the other hand,
was like a trumpet blast, calling all the world to judgment.
That the Pope did not know what terrible things his
painter was saying was only because he was a creature of
the past, and therefore deaf to the voice of the future.
The Titanic Michael-Angelo and his Herculean figures
seemed to Michelet to be shaken by the fervor of the
proclamation of a future illumined by an understanding
of human justice, and of the destruction of the kingdom
of a God whose reign had been upheld by "grace." This
grace of God was henceforth to be condemned because
it had been "a scourge and a flagellation," whereas the
future was to be "Justice and Judgment." And the historian describes the prophecy thus: "Intense suspense in
the face of a terrible future, that is what fills the Sistine
Chapel and trembles in its walls and vaults." All this
stir of life so prescient of threat and menace, Michelet
saw gathered in the figure of the prophet Ezekiel, whose

[13] *La Renaissance*, preface, p. 89.

prophecy was the supreme vindication of life and its
liberation from the Biblical curse which had been laid
upon it.

> His furious cynical utterance contains the final revelation
> which destroys the impious doctrine of the vengeance of God,
> damning the world for the sin of one man.[12]

Ezekiel spoke of the day when judgment should be given
into the hands of man. These hands, so Michelet believed, held sufficient strength to accomplish man's salvation, each man being the savior of himself through his
service to others.

Ezekiel's prophecy was of the reign of "Heroism" and
it was spoken with the accumulated violence of resentment
which our historian felt for a world that had heeded neither
the Renaissance nor the Reformation as harbingers of
this reign. He had found an instinctive reaching out
toward it in the very beginnings of modern art:

> The need of creating, of making over his God and himself was
> not lacking to the man of the Middle Ages. This effort appeared
> in drawing and in the arts of imitation. The day when Giotto
> and Van Eyck delivered the holy images from Byzantine fixity,
> every man desired a god for himself and tormented the painter
> or the sculptor until he gave it to him. But on the morrow,
> having received it and carried it away, each said: "This is not
> yet my dream." [14]

The dream had been passed on from age to age, however,
and at last a means was found for seeking, no longer "each
man for himself" but together by means of music, which
seemed to Michelet preëminently a social art.

Luther had made all Germany sing, and song might
have renewed the Church herself. "Harmony, song in
parts, the accord of voices which are free and yet fraternal, that fine mystery of modern art, sought and missed

[14] *La Réforme*, p. 91.

by the Middle Ages, had been found by the Protestant Goudimel. . . . Toward 1549 he passed some time at Rome and formed some students, among others Palestrina. Admirable nature, with all the Italian sensibility which vibrated to every echo." That this impulse toward fraternal association in song had been lost, was a source of grave regret to the historian, but he insisted that it had been lost. Palestrina "could not evoke new victorious chants which could inspire a great mass of men." The next effort of song which Michelet could celebrate unreservedly will not come until the outburst of the Marseillaise. The "Catholic Marseillaise" had not been found, the music of the Church remained "buried" under the weight of ecclesiastical tradition. But to the historian its cadences translated a dream of escape from this tradition. He describes it as "full of tears, touching tears, which tell of the death of Italy under the name of Jerusalem," and he shows his Ezekiel, thundering out his prophecy of the future, but sheltering with compassion in the meanwhile this faint song and "sighing at hearing so little hope in the moans of Italy." [15]

Does not this Ezekiel bear a strange resemblance to Michelet himself? and does not the historian interpret his history of the Renaissance much in his Ezekiel's own manner? "Sacred forces of life and generation, you are from God alone and *le néant* shall not usurp you!"

In the cathedral of Strasbourg Michelet had found his definition of the art that had made it: "The work of God passing through man. God in the second power, creation of creation." That the artist's impulse had always been shackled or hampered, was due to the fact that man had not known how to seek the complete revelation of the God who "worked through him." History told of the ever-renewed defeat of man's quest, Michelet had early felt a sense of where man might find his needed guidance. He

[15] *Ibid.*, pp. 89 ff.

believed that science held the revelation of what the final triumph of life and all its forces should be. Therefore when, after his second marriage, he set himself to the study of books of science, he summoned all his keen interest and his sensitive appreciation of natural beauty to testify to this his faith in the power of science to reveal ultimate truth. He eloquently evoked what he believed to be the significance of all the facts that he encountered; but he dictated, as might be expected, what this significance should be.[16]

As he bent over his microscope or as he walked abroad, he discovered in the simple facts of the mutation and transformation attendant upon the processes of life, comforting and explicit evidence of the solidarity of all the life of the universe. Upon this evidence he based his claim for what he called the universal 'heroism' of life, which consisted apparently in the fullest possible participation in whatever constituted the tasks imposed by these processes. The moral evaluation of such effort remains problematic. Michelet's key to it in the world of nature (for figuratively and poetically at least, his domain of morality included the world of nature), was to be found in his ever ready sense of pity. Mollusks, for instance, were "moral" in their effort because their task unfailingly performed seemed to him a touchingly humble one. It is said that the sense of the unity of life could make Emerson "feel a whole zoölogical series within himself."[16] Michelet

---

[16] R. Michaud, *Un intermédiaire français entre Swedenborg et Emerson: Egger et le vrai messie, Revue de littérature comparée*, 1921, juillet-septembre, pp. 389–397.

When he and the wife of his second marriage began their series of eager observations of natural life, Michelet used them to support his conviction that the universe was one great vital impulse, one vast *élan* of love. His scientific baggage, although not to be despised, was necessarily unsystematized and uncritical, and the use that he made of all that he learned, subordinated it to the task that he set for it. Flying birds, creeping things, mountain and sea, all

would probably have had difficulty in isolating, even in
this way, a single series from the inexhaustible multiplicity
of life. Mollusks offered for him at any rate an edi-
fying example through the faithful performance of whatever they were capable of doing, the performance which
he characterized as the "opening and closing" of their
"windows." Michelet was not averse to the use of the
methods employed by the authors of the old *Physiologus*
and *Bestiaries*, who found their lessons everywhere. But
with his lessons he found also poetry:

> These rocks seem to you to be covered by a layer of grey
> asperities, but they are living things. It is a world complete
> in itself established there, and at ebb-tide, left high and dry, it
> retires and shuts itself up within itself. It opens its windows
> again when its kindly nurse, the sea, brings back to it its food. . . .
> There these little stone-workers labor on, an inestimable popu-
> lation, an interesting folk and modest. These are the hard-
> working mollusks whose busy lives give to the sea its serious
> charm and its morality. . . . These little beings have nothing
> to say for the world, but they work for it. . . . Between the
> silent earth and the mute tribes of the ocean a dialogue goes on,
> deep, strong in sympathy. It is the harmonious concord of the
> GREAT ME with itself, and the great debate is love.[17]

In the "world obscure and humble, which the Germans
say the devil made," the "world of insects"—he found,
as he studied it curiously, the most vivid glimpses of

brought him the testimony that he needed, for naturally he found
what he went out to seek. But the spontaneous wonder and childlike joy that he felt at finding it made of his books, *L'oiseau, L'insecte,
La mer*, and *La montagne*, lyric expressions of hope and faith.

For the nature of Michelet's scientific information, cf. R. V. d.
Elst, *op. cit.;* and review of same by H. Hauser, *op. cit.*

[17] *La mer* (1861), p. 28. In *L'oiseau*, on the contrary, mollusks
appear among the eternal protestants who feel the impulse to "mount
higher." Ed. 1856, p. 24. (The passage cited is a portion of a dialogue between the author and "a woman's heart." The portion
spoken by the "heart," has been omitted here.)

"immortality and love." [18] They furnished added proof of the continuity of life secured by sacrifice and love. This continuity thus maintained, was the scheme of all existence; and from the beauty which he found in it, Michelet elaborated a faith which helped him to utilize all his beliefs and all his unbelief. After having sought satisfaction for his need of a personal and individual faith in his own instinctive demand for individual freedom, he came now to seek this satisfaction in the power and beauty which he found in community of effort and aspiration.

His intimate biographer said of him, "Michelet believed too thoroughly in himself not to believe in the soul." [19] There were, however, deeper sources for his belief than could be found either in the historian's self-confidence or in his desire for self-satisfaction, although these were both important considerations in the compounding of his articles of faith. Doubtless he believed in God because he felt the need of belief, "Je ne puis me passer de Dieu" [20] was a part of the confession of his faith. But this basic need came in time to be enriched by every imaginable impulse and argument drawn from his eager and passionate investigation of the problems of history, from his ardent study of life and by his deep concern for the general social welfare. All these considerations so deepened his sense of the interdependence of life that he came to say quite naturally such things as this,—that he felt himself lifted and carried on by the great flood of life, and that he could feel its palpitating force even to the farthest stars. He attained at last to an absolute faith in the unity of life. [21]

[18] *L'insecte*, ed. '59, Introduction, pp. x–xii.

[19] G. Monod, *J. M.*, p. 248: ". . . lui, résolumment hostile au catholicisme . . . mais homme de foi inébranlable, croyant trop en lui-même, pour ne pas croire à l'âme . . ." etc.

[20] It is characteristic of Michelet that this need is expressed in connection with his statement of his reverence for human love. *La femme*, pp. 352–356.

[21] *La femme*, p. 358: ". . . Est-ce que nous ne sentons pas le haut

In the course of his very long life, the impetuous "moi" which he had posited in 1830 as unwilling to accept the yoke either of man or of nature, lost bit by bit its defining restrictions and limitations, lost gradually the clarity of outline that critical reason or a different sort of egotism might have imposed upon it. With his ever-growing conception of the solidarity of life, his Me became for him immense, vast enough to englobe and hold within itself the great life impulses of the Great Me (*le Grand Moi*),[22] the love creative all embracing which was the universe itself. But since he believed this to be the privilege of the humblest creatures of the earth, he preserved always a sense of measure and of modesty, amazing when one considers that he never for one moment lost the conviction that his being was his own, his energy his own, and that every act that he performed was an act of his own free will,—"libre et voulu."[22]

From these convictions Michelet framed a "natural religion" from which, so he believed, a social faith might be derived. Every conception that it contained was determined by whatever ministered to that twofold sense of his own personality which we have just noted. These conceptions display a curious composite of rebelliousness,

Amour impartial qui règne par ses grandes lois? . . . Pour moi, j'en ai le flot puissant qui par-dessous me soulève. Des profondeurs de la vie je ne sais quelle chaleur monte, une féconde aspiration. Un souffle m'en passe à la face et je me sens mille cœurs.

L'amour, 1859, p. 454: "One word mounts in the whole living scale, one word: I desire beyond myself. I desire all, always." Another passage which shows how much mysticism was mingled with all conceptions of Michelet, is found in *La mer*, ed. '85, p. 347. *Ibid.*, p. 452: "It desires nothing less than the absolute, it desires itself as eternal love."

[22] G. Monod, *J. M.*, p. 100: "Si tout cela n'est pas moi, je me sens une compassion assez vraie, assez immense pour endosser toutes ces douleurs "

La femme, ed. 1885, p. 115, "L'effort est dans la nature, libre et voulu."

of individualism, merged into an ideal of social life as a manifestation of universal love set to the tasks which make up those activities by which life is maintained and developed. The interest that it presents lies in the fact that it was a sincere and personal aspiration toward a belief that human energy in so far as it springs from the common aspirations of humanity is divine and that it is a part of the creative activity of the universe. Michelet's faith in the divine in nature and man is what he called "Naturalism and Heroism."

The thwarted nobility of the divine energy when its force seemed unavailing, he celebrated in the tenderness with which he studied the tragedy of frustrate life and effort; he exalted its glory in the enthusiasm with which he depicted its moments of magnificent strength. Under this double aspect of life,—on the one hand pain and travail, and on the other the joy and exaltation of achievement,—he studied the art of God and of man; or if you will, just the art of God, since there could be for him none other.

Life was the universal artist unfolding gradually the revelation of her mysteries. Both in the world of man and of nature, Michelet believed that art spoke distinctly of its origins and that it carried a definite message. This message, as has been noted above, was the artist's inspiration. His personal achievement revealed, often without his knowing it, this profound inspiration and revealed as well an interpretation of life which was not necessarily limited to the conception that the artist himself might consciously hold of it,—

> "He builded better than he knew;
> The conscious stone to beauty grew."

The artist transcended his own ideal and was thus the medium of forces and of impulses which he freely guided because he freely participated in their source. Indeed his

artistry attained to artistry only in so far as it found itself
answering freely to this profound impulse.

The true greatness of the artist is to transcend his purpose,
to do more than he willed and to do something quite different;
to go beyond the aim he has set for himself, even the possible
itself,—and still see what lies beyond.[23]

The prodigality of nature was thus justified in Michelet's
eyes since it proved the unlimited power of the universal
artist and hinted at the mystery of aims and purposes
which had their source in the source of all power,—in
universal love. We have seen how startling he found the
"religious spark" in the "moral beauty" of the humblest
forms of life, especially in the world of insects where its
force was manifest to him in the fact that life was created
only by the sacrifice of life. On the other hand, wherever
he found the coincident triumph of life and love easily
and materially visible, as in the delicate transparency of
certain sea creatures, this revelation was for him something like an illuminating flame which played joyously
over the whole scheme of existence.

"Their charming varieties,—he says in speaking of them,—
mark the inner progress of life; and each degree of development,
the smile and grace of new born liberty (reveals) the admirable
artist who has created an infinite number of pretty variants,—
a deluge of tiny marvels." [24]

In the world of man the impulse of the artist toward
full and free development if balked might make of his
expression of it an eloquent protest against restraining
limitations, lending it as has been seen, a profoundly
prophetic significance. Art spoke of the infinite both by
what was unrestrained and free in it and by the trace it
bore of whatever had impeded and confined it,—causing

[23] *L'oiseau*, 1856, p. 252.   [24] *La mer*, 2e partie, chap. vi.

it at moments to "grimace." In the world of man and of nature, all life bore a double aspect,—effort and resistance on one hand, sacrifice and submission on the other. The glory of "heroism" seemed then to lie in living to the fullest capacity given, its morality in the joyous acceptance of the limitations imposed by the solidarity of life.

This is of course rudimentary. But in the simplicity of it Michelet found all the themes of the joy and sadness of existence. In his preaching of the glory of life there is sensuousness, there is often sensuality; but to read into it this alone would be to neglect the dignity which his respect for life lends to his admiration for its power. His tender pity for it when the sacrifice by which it is maintained appeared to him to be futile, was perhaps exaggerated, but there was a delicate sincerity in this tenderness which was inseparable, as has been pointed out, from the importance which he attached to each individual life, save perhaps when he found himself swayed by unreasonable prejudice. In each life "to love that which will never be seen again," would lend to life as a whole an inestimable value, and lend it pathos. This conception of the beauty of the transitory beauty of the individual life,[25] and of its sacrifice, and the celebration of the dignity and power of universal life made up the matter with which Michelet's "more popular science" was concerned. He found it to offer excellent polemic texts and appropriate themes for lyrical elaboration.

In such a conception of the scheme of existence, where nature is considered as infinitely good, there is no logical niche for the problem of evil. Therefore Michelet did not consider evil as a problem, but as a mystery. That death

[25] E. Estève, *Vico, Michelet et Vigny, Rev. universitaire*, mars–avril, 1919. M. Estève finds in certain lines of *La maison du berger* ("aimer ce que jamais on ne verra deux fois"), trace of the influence of Vico, as his influence was felt through Michelet.

should ever be overcome seemed to him improbable, but suffering might be suppressed. And when the world should have reached a fuller understanding of life, when love should be universally recognized as the source of life, another order of things might be revealed. "Ah, our globe is a barbarous world," cried Michelet at the thought of fear, hunger, suffering and death. But he used this impenetrability of evil as an argument that the world was "still young." Any other belief was impossible to him.

Death is not impenetrable, our souls have faith and hope enough to accept it as something which leads us on, as a step in our initiation, a door opening into better worlds. But suffering! Alas! was there a purpose in making it so wide spread? [26]

The struggle in the individual life, the presence of evil, of "pride and desire," hatred, all "the conflicts of the moral man," were formulated by Michelet as "the struggle of man against nature," or against "fatality." But it remained unexplained by this believer in the beneficence of life and its innocence. It was accepted as a part of the long combat by means of which, through collective effort, humanity is forged into shape by the generations of men. Man merits his salvation and wins it solely, so Michelet taught, through his effort for the salvation of all. This effort was to some degree a purely practical

[26] *L'oiseau*, ed. 1856, p. 24. A comparison might be made between the buoyant optimism with which Michelet consoles himself for his momentary doubts and the note of hopefulness of which M. Bergson has shown himself capable. M. Bergson has hinted at the possibility of conquering death itself.

Although Michelet could by imagination rise above the pity which paralyzes, the effort necessary left him with the sense of being an exile in the City of life which he had adopted as his own. "I had come as a son, and I went away as an orphan, feeling the notion of Providence lifeless within me!" In the meantime, he believed that the world "passed little by little into the power of the Being who alone has the sense of the needful balance between life and death."

matter, for it was in the useful and necessary arts that he believed religions to have been born, and "from every religion springs the divine fruit, the awakening of the conscience." The source of the ignorant conflicts in the individual and in the social life he explained through the divorce between science and the education to which the human conscience was subjected. Only when illumined by science could the power of human impulse make a winning struggle against all that taught it disbelief in itself.[27]

Civilization had in modern days failed in its aim because of trust in sanctions established upon ignorance and distrust of life,—of "nature." Michelet had very frankly substituted "the fall of society, for the fall of man," and he seemed to consider that the disaster was allowed to be repeated with futile and servile submission. For him every child came into the world "trailing clouds of glory," then because of ignorant traditions in education the prison house was allowed to "close about the growing boy." The task of future "heroic" society would be to knock down these prison walls through an understanding of the secrets of life and of its laws.[28]

The alternation of life defeated in its aspirations, and of life triumphant, was then the double theme which made up Michelet's story of the discovery of the value of life

[27] "The long and painful initiation" of mankind deprived of its birthright of self respect was the history of the humanity of modern times as he saw it. So long as he allowed himself to be swayed by his sense of pity he allowed himself to dwell much upon its sorrows. "The tree of life," he wrote, "is the Persian idea of the soul fecund and beneficent. The tree of sorrows (an Egyptian idea), has a soul imprisoned and suffering under the bark. The two beliefs sprang from a common source,—a great respect for the tree." Michelet's respect for the imprisoned soul made him look askance at the bark (although he realized that it was a normal part of the tree's growth), because he saw that it had imposed painful restraint and limitations.

[28] *La bible de l'humanité*, ed. 1864, pp. 120, 134–5, 197; *Nos fils*, passim.

and of effort. We have seen that in his earlier work, with other writers of the period, notably Ballanche, he had shown a certain inclination to present the nobility of failure as not unavailing. He even glorified and idealized it. The life which showed incompleteness, morally or intellectually maimed, might, he seemed to think, by its very imperfections serve as a type of expiation. The contemplation of its inefficiency or of its tragedy might bring, until the time that men should learn to trust in themselves, a sense of solidarity in suffering. Michelet seemed especially pleased at one moment to use it as a sort of humanized type of the Redemption, making of it an application of the dogma against which he showed himself so recalcitrant. He dechristianized it and brought it down from the cross; or if you will, he was pleased to take humanity and lift it up, even in very abject forms, in order to show that through any life the consciousness might come to man that he must hope in humanity alone, even in its weakness. The world had found its way toward salvation by means that it had chosen itself. The only danger that the historian foresaw was that humanity should be withheld from discarding ideals that it had definitely outgrown.[29]

As he grew older, he showed a growing tendency to rate less highly the efficacy and the dignity of suffering, in order to celebrate the joy to be derived from the consciousness of efficacious effort. Thus a book of his old age, his *Bible de l'humanité*, of 1864, which he thought was "a mountain peak" whence he could look down upon all the ages, marks a distinct reaction against all "Messianic Tradition" involving the tradition of unquestioning

[29] The mad king Charles with his "sick soul" was a symbol in which the people saw their wretchedness and were consoled. In England the imbecile Henry VI was such a type; such too were the fainéant Merovingian kings, cf. *Armagnacs et Bourguignons*, pp. 151–155. For Louis le débonair, as an example, cf. Part III, chapter 2.

submission to suffering, however humanized it might be. Michelet, at this moment, seemed to seek to discount and discountenance it in order to proclaim that man should frame his ideal of the divine from the sense of heroic and joyous energy which he could find and cultivate within himself. The historian pictured in this volume with especial predilection the two great heroes whom Greece had created, the heroes of daring, presumption and serviceableness,—Prometheus and Hercules, the last to do all the tasks of humanity and to scatter the terror of hell; the first, to scale Olympus and bring to man the knowledge of his own power:

Prometheus is the true prophet of the Stoic and of the jurisconsult. He is anti-Pagan and anti-Christian. His support is in the law and he invokes only his own deeds. He attests only justice, no privilege of race, of predestination, or of the prior rights of the Titans over the gods. The help he awaits will come sooner or later. The hero of justice, Hercules, will deliver him, will kill the vulture that is devouring him and Jupiter will yield to the right and will bow before the return of Prometheus.

Michelet's hero-worship was inspired by a distinct spirit of utilitarianism. His great men were not on the whole supermen. They were those who had done the tasks of humanity. The hero was for our historian distinctly a "son of Martha," whose labors were inspired by "an active passion," and whose example would furnish inspiration for effort:

The incarnations of India have shown their passion by traversing life in such a way as to learn its miseries. Those of Egypt, of Syria, of Phrygia, mutilated gods, have suffered and endured. But their *passive passion*, far from giving us force, has made our discouragement, and their fatal legend has created sterile inertia. It is in the *active passion* and Herculean that man will find his harmony and equilibrium.[30]

[30] *La montagne*, ed. 1887, p. 198.

Michelet stated that in writing his *Bible* he had thought to finish the book without a word of criticism and reproach. He failed of course to fulfil such a hope. This book presents with sympathetic appreciation all those heroes whose legend he believed to be such as could not dwarf man's pride in his own power to achieve. In this connection he chose to present the Christian tradition as a dead weight on humanity. In 1835, when Quinet in his criticism of Strauss's *Life of Jesus* had denied that the Christ was a mere figment of tradition, affirming him to be a man of extraordinary personality and power, Michelet had written to his friend a letter of unqualified approval.[31] Almost twenty years later, stricken by the death of his child, he confided to his *Journal* his feeling of reverence for this personality and power. But even here, although he pictured the Christ as a figure of great beauty, he noted sharply the alterations which it had suffered in that it had become the representative of principles which he believed had sprung neither from the life nor from the teachings of Jesus:

"Suffer little children to come unto me,"—gentle and beautiful words of the Gospel. The Christ had not foreseen what a Christianity men would make in his name. Christianity has failed as dogma. What remains ? The best, which is divine and human at the same time. To Him was reserved the great merit of having formulated and taught what men had felt and said, but vaguely: " Love each other, love each other in God." [32]

Thirteen years after this date, in his *Bible de l'humanité*, Michelet did not hesitate to make our Lord appear as the incarnation of confused hopes cherished by a people of slaves, and troubled by the superstitions of the Jewish imagination and by the fears of nervous women.[33] A

[31] Mme. Quinet, *E. Quinet avant l'exile*, ed. '88, pp. 266 ff.
[32] G. Monod, *J. M.*, pp. 266–286.
[33] *La bible de l'humanité*, pp. 439–468.

note in this book accuses Renan of having given "to that which is dying," (that is, to the Christian faith), a regrettable respite. Certain lines of the preface of Renan's *Vie de Jésus* might have been written in reply to such an accusation:

Whoever does not speak gently of Christianity and of the edifice of which it is a part, shows himself guilty of ingratitude. In answer to the aspirations of the heart, religions fall away, one by one, because so far no force has stifled reason.[34]

Michelet's contention was quite that found in the last sentence of Renan, and he believed with him that "our planet is accomplishing some profound task." But since he also believed that in this task the work of Christianity was done and that the sooner this was recognized the better, his attacks upon the "Jewish Bible" grew continually more bitter, while he depicted the holy books of Persia and the legends of Greece as full of gentleness, love, justice, and strength. He commented thus upon the contrast: "Pallas the austere virgin could no longer reign when Madeleine performed her act of worship, as if before the altar; bathing it with her tears. What does she say to this dying world ? . . . 'Let us die together.' . . . A tender sister's prayer, only too sure to be heard! But what if one remained thus in suspense—not able yet to die, not able yet to live?" [35]

The heroes then who had worked through the power of justice as well as through that of "love"; those who had revealed the pagan winged soul of Greece were chosen by Michelet as models. He sought to show that the great men of the ancient world had had active inventive minds

[34] E. Renan, *La vie de Jésus*, ed. 1867, preface, p. xxx.
[35] *Bible de l'humanité*, p. 457, An extract from the chapter, "Triomphe de la femme," where Christianity is represented as a religion of "grace" instead of a religion of "justice."

and busy hands. They were the hewers of wood, or they guarded the sacred fire and the furrow whence sprang the sacred grain. Human tasks were always waiting to be done and the hero was merely the man who had seen most clearly what these tasks were and who had not hesitated before them. He had, however, at moments, through the world's scorn of nature, been forced into being a protesting soul and all his activity had been organized into a program of resistance.[36]

The hero being great by his capacity for service, the problem of the future would naturally present itself in this way to Michelet's eyes: how might society be so organized as to use to the best advantage the rebelliousness, the innate 'heroic' strength of man. It seemed to him that this could only be accomplished by such a re-organization of society as would utilize the force which had hitherto been devoted to resistance to certain popularly accepted beliefs and traditions, in order to put it to the service of what he believed to be the actively "progressive" endeavor which modern life demanded. Michelet's ideal program for "the active passion" of the life of the future ended then by leaving him very cold to those types of human experience which he found to have

[36] The Gallic tradition represented for Michelet one great source of the inconquerable impulse toward the 'heroism' of resistance. Gaul had postulated human liberty. She had spoken through Pelagius whose name, the historian affirmed, "the Occident should cherish," for Pelagius had "uttered occidental aspirations." Heroic strength of will and unshaken self confidence were important items in his eyes of what made up the equipment necessary to the modern hero. The heroes of the past likewise for whom the historian felt an especial sympathy, were men who, believing themselves to be superior to traditions to which they were still subject, had resisted. They might be gentle and silent as was the dreamy mystic, Joachim of Floris, gentle and boisterous as were Rabelais and Luther, or keen and bitter as was Voltaire,—they had in every case placed their word of protest, and while and by protesting, they had carried on the work of the world.

been closely associated with the authority of the tradition of the Church.

On the other hand he had never shown any great sympathy for the romantic type of hero, for those beings whose "deep mysterious souls" made of them beings remote from the lives of ordinary men. Michelet permitted no aristocratic solitude to his heroes. Some of them were distinctly lacking in intellectual, and one may even say perhaps at times, in moral fastidiousness. The great men whom he ended by adopting as fitting social models might be described as being what someone has called "functionaries of society," those who had shared the common lot, or those who had sought to better it. The sum of them might be compared to a composite incarnation of the willingness to do hard work. He saw them collectively as a sort of giant Saint Christopher constantly bent under the growing weight of the human Christ-Child, standing, waiting to be borne across the floods by which the ages are divided. Each age had struggled on toward the revelation that the salvation of humanity had been confided to humanity itself. The great men had but helped it on its way. The great revelation of the instinctive nobility of man was, in the historian's eyes, the Revolution. Jeanne d'Arc had been for Michelet the great single incarnation of the spirit of the People, the Revolution was a multiple revelation of it. The People and the Hero were at last recognizable as one, and consciously one.

The historian's revolutionary sympathies, from 1842, had grown in strength and had found one channel of self-expression in an over-emphatic insistence upon what he found admirable in non-Christian civilizations. This somewhat self-conscious "Paganism" he offered, it has been seen, in later life as a corrective for "dangerous" Christian tendencies. The suggested promise of such a method is found in his earlier work. The over-use he made of it is more especially a manifestation of a comparatively late period. *Les Jésuites* shows in some respects more measure than his last volumes of history, his *Sorcière* or *La bible de l'humanité*.

In 1831, Michelet's preface to his *Histoire de la république romaine* had set forth his belief in the divinity of mankind, and added his conviction that it was essential to proclaim and popularize this faith:

Humanity is divine, but there is no man who is divine. The mythical heroes, Hercules, whose arm hewed out the mountains, Lycurgus, and Romulus, swift legislators who in one lifetime accomplished the long work of ages, are the creation of the imagination of peoples. And these peoples prostrate themselves before these gigantic shadows. The philosopher raises them up, and says to them: What you adore is you yourself, your own conceptions. These bizarre and inexplicable figures spring from poetry, but they become the matter of science. The miracles of individual genius are classed under a common law. The level of criticism reduces them to a common measure. This historical radicalism does not go so far as to suppress great men. There are without doubt those who dominate the mass . . . but their heads are not lost in the clouds. . . . They are not of another race. . . . Humanity can recognize itself in its own history, one and identical with itself.

Since the historian taught that the full revelation of this identity had come through the Revolution, he studied its origins and its manifestations with a peculiar enthusiasm. It was toward the radiant light that the Revolution had cast on all human affairs that the whole course of human history had led, and, as Michelet depicted the long line of those heroes who had prepared it, he seems to have felt more and more their accomplishment to have been a work of liberation which could but bring them joy. Their gayety, as he depicted it, was not precisely a rationally tempered one. Their occasional boisterousness, which at moments he gladly shared with them, especially in his

later years, has offended his critics. In his long preface of
1869 he wrote:

> I wrote the *Renaissance* with forces a hundred times multi-
> plied. When I turned around to look back on my *Moyen-Age*,
> that absurd sea of absurdities, a violent hilarity seized me, and I
> made a terrible fête of the sixteenth and seventeenth centuries.
> Rabelais and Voltaire laughed in their tombs! [37]

In his *Reformation* and *Renaissance* he had pictured
Galileo and Luther as given to hearty laughter, and he
emphasized strongly the joyousness of Gustavus Adolphus.

The manifestations of good temper and good cheer on
the part of these great men, as depicted by Michelet, is
far from suggesting a sense of measure. His own pleasure
in these manifestations has been qualified as both irrational
and ironical. His insistence upon the efficacy of joy may
best be interpreted as characteristic of the emphasis that
he came to place upon the nobility of emotion and upon
the dignity of instinct. He considered the response to
instinct, joyous and spontaneous, as an essential con-
comitant to progress. Rebelliousness, when it was the
expression of individual conviction, was a force of civilization which he deeply respected. However, as has
been noted, he himself was too reasonable and too
conservative to be a light hearted and uncompromising
rebel. This indicates what opposing currents of French
tradition had contributed to impart to Michelet's personality its odd complexity. His adoption of Rabelaisian exaggeration, partly intentionally defiant,—at any
rate fairly frequent in his later years,—was not perhaps
merely a mark of this complexity, it was probably
as well an indication of a decline in intellectual vigor and
in good taste. He seems to have believed increasingly that

[37] Preface of 1869, p. xxxviii. For comment, cf. Pierre Lasserre,
Le Romantisme.

it testified to a titillating sense of the innocence of instinct and of the beneficence of the forces of life.[38]

As time went on, coming more and more to look upon the past at certain moments, not as an integral part of human existence, not as that life of humanity, continuous throughout all ages, which he had been, at the outset of his career, so ardent to resuscitate; he defined it as an old, outworn and cast-off "form," an absurdly mechanical device, which still continued to perform its antics but which had lost all power to create the illusion of life. He treated this "form" with growing lack of respect, and seemed to

[38] Lamennais, who found the source of evil in an exaggerated individualism, considered laughter a mark of it and found it offensive. He quoted Lucifer's loud outburst. For quite another reason, Michelet's master, Vico, shrank from a loud laugh. He found it irrational and unbecoming. Whatever there may have been of the 'Satanic' in Michelet's laughter savors of the essence of that spirit to which he was pleased to give the name of 'Satan.' This spirit, it is clear, was not essentially either arrogant or malicious; it had, however, the irrepressible vigor and irrational strength of natural forces unrestrained in their operation. Michelet seems to have wished to represent his sense of joy as the expression of the natural jubilation of a soul happy in the consciousness of contributing to the triumph of human energy. Michelet's own jubilation, faintly indecorous at moments, seems often to have been instinctive and irrational, but it would be difficult to interpret it as the mere outlet of malice. May it not have been the laughter of which M. Bergson thinks he may have found the secret? His explanation of it has been often quoted. Bergson finds one source of laughter in the instinctive reaction attendant on the sight of the artificial, executing motions which are a mere imitation of those actions natural to the living being, or the reaction produced by the sight of the living being performing motions mechanical. May not Michelet's mockery at what he considered the artificial engaged in controlling and travestying the natural, be looked upon as Bergsonian rather than Luciferian? But there is little need to distinguish, since both are supposed to celebrate triumphant instinct. Michelet, at any rate, apparently felt that his occasional boisterousness had a legitimate source in his conviction that human energy was being increasingly released and that all that hampered it was becoming increasingly discredited.

see it crumbling before every Rabelaisian utterance, each example of which roused new life and vigor. Michelet described such utterances and proffered them himself as so many anathemas pronounced against all that past,— which he qualified as "Anti-Nature." [39]

The spirit which animated these utterances he believed to be an irrepressible and sometimes boisterous spirit of the "new life" which he hailed as a liberator. It was "young liberty," nature, instinct,—all that the Church had been prone, so he insisted, to condemn under the name of Satan. It is easy to understand that for the historian the name should stand for the spirit of the scientist, of the artist, for all that seemed to him to inspire human effort and social progress. He used it in this sense partly because it connoted defiance of the Church, but especially perhaps because it was the name bestowed by his contemporaries upon the spirit of the Revolution,[40] which he regarded as *the* final and supreme revelation.

What Joseph de Maistre had seen as 'Satanic,' according to his acceptation of the word, in the French

---

[39] *La Réforme*, pp. 359 ff.; *La Renaissance*, pp. 283 ff.; *Nos fils*, p. 407.

[40] R. Van der Elst, *op. cit.*, p. 127, comments thus on the fact that there was nothing blasphematory in Michelet's 'Satan': "Mais l'ennemi de l'Eglise, c'est précisément la Nature; ou plutôt, la Nature à force d'être désignée comme ennemi de l'Eglise, a fini par prendre nom et figure dans l'imagination des masses, et Satan, pour Michelet, n'est rien autre. Le livre, *la Sorcière*, qui est un commentaire de cette théorie, n'est peut-être pas un blasphème comme il en a l'air: mais si quelque chose l'en exempte, c'est l'absence totale de foi dans une personnalité diabolique." It is indeed apparent that the historian was trying to escape from all the traditional connotations of the word. As a species of "boutade" his insistence upon it is characteristic of his desire to show himself willing to accept the name which was sometimes applied to such opinions as were his. It was not an unusual weapon in the wars of opinion of this epoch. L. Liard (*L'enseignement supérieur en France*, 1894, vol. 2, p. 235), gives an example.

Revolution, would naturally be 'Satanic' for Michelet as well, according to his own quite different acceptation of the word. It was the great liberating force which moved peoples as though they were one man, and moved them to utter the same word of hope after years of suffering and silence. When all spoke together, then, so Michelet felt, justice herself was voiced. The inalienable right of peoples to act was a right which he taught with ardor. When all act together, the historian maintained, the legitimacy of the motive of action is not to be questioned. Such action to him was the great life of nations exerting instinctively its force and seeking new self-expression in law and government.

Michelet worshiped then with mystical devotion the manifestations that the French Revolution had afforded, as manifestations of 'pure reason' and of miraculous enlightenment. Men had cast aside for the moment their "foolish Messianic faith," and had sought, each with the consciousness of heroic power, the accomplishment of the will of all. He had greeted the same spirit in 1820, in 1830, and he believed it to be present in the hopes of 1848. Michelet's 'Satan' would perforce continue to be a spirit of rebellion until the whole world should move forward as one, until there should be no more laggards, until each man could feel and find himself accepted as a "chosen one" and thus refuse to relinquish his personal responsibility, whatever submission might be due to law and order. The Revolution had been betrayed and lost because freedom had been revealed to men as a possibility before they had learned to know what it was to be free, before they had had time to learn how to trust in themselves. Their premature faith in themselves had been both their glory and the source of their temporary defeat.

It is an ocean which mounts from infinite profound causes, stirring in unknown depths. Oppose to it, I beg of you, all the

armies of the world,—or the finger of a little child,—it will make
no difference. . . . God impels it forward, and tardy justice,
expiation for the past and future salvation. The glory of the
Revolution was its greatest menace. What might render it
less certain of its course was the fact that it sought to dispense
with men; it went forward alone through the pure impulse of
ideas . . . without idols and without false gods.[41]

But, although frustrated, the Revolution remained to
Michelet and to Quinet as the revelation of the soul of a
people. Quinet always insisted that there had never
been found in all its showing, a single trace of the meanness and misery of the "Plèbe." The people had risen
and stood as men. The Revolution had performed the
miracle of "creating an infinite number of proud souls."
Michelet's contention was the same, and to all who tried
to point out to him what complications might result
from such a universal sense of personal dignity and pride,
he did not consent to argue,—

Take care, said someone; you are teaching man his rights
when he is only too sure of them. You lead him up to a high
mountain-top and show him unlimited space. What will happen
when, having come down, he finds himself forced to halt before
the law, facing barriers at every step? [41]

To such warnings he only replied by the assertion that
the world could never have too wide a vision, and that
laws would not be regarded as stumbling blocks when
they should be framed in accordance with the 'natural'
development of the human sense of justice. Such a development would make of instinctive love and sacrifice
the motive forces of society.

Laws emanating from such sources were to govern his
"City of Providence," and France was to be this City.

[41] *Hist. de la Rév.*, vol. i, p. 317; vol. ii, p. 152: "Etrange *vita
nuova* . . . qui fait de toute sa Révolution . . . une sorte de
rêve. . . . Elle a ignoré l'espace et le temps."

For France was the outward manifestation of a "principle" which was to bring the reign of "Naturalism and Heroism." And in his "City," as Plato in his, Michelet would have no evil imputed to its gods. With what conviction, albeit with what vast difference of content, he could have echoed these words of Plato:

> That God being good is the author of evil to anyone, is to be strenuously denied; it is not to be said, or sung, or heard, in verse or prose, by anyone, whether young or old, in any well ordered commonwealth. Such a fiction is suicidal, ruinous, impious.[42]

This, Michelet naturally would maintain, the Church had done. She had made of what to him was "God," an author of evil. She had condemned the God of Life, the God of 'Nature'! And 'Satan'? But Satan as the Church saw him was the creation of the Church herself!

Plato asks in a sentence beyond the one just quoted: "And what do you think of a second principle? Shall I ask you whether God is of a nature to appear insidiously, now in one shape, now in another; sometimes changing himself and passing into many forms?" What Plato's God because of his nature could not do, it was in the very nature of Michelet's God to perform. This God could not be God unless he could so change and take upon himself the shape that human need demanded. Michelet's mythology of religions admitted that all possible forms might be God-like if they would but change with the changing life around them,—and disappear when their time was come. He could be "tender" with all gods if they would but consent to die when their day should be over.

Why is there strife in the world of men? Why had humanity been forced, now into open rebelliousness, now into sly subterfuge? Christianity had replied that it was

[42] Plato's *Republic*, translation by Jowett, 1892, vol. 2, pp. 390 ff.

through man's misuse of liberty.   Michelet found it to
rise from the undue constraint of human liberty.   He
interpreted the dogma of the "fall" as an attack upon the
dignity of the human will.   This attack was explicable
only through ignorance of life and distrust of nature.
The future hope which Michelet proclaimed was the hope
that men might discover in the universe such evidence
of an all-informing beneficent love that they would learn
to feel themselves the participators in the impulse of divine
life, and realize that they were co-creators of it.

It was this impulse that the Church had called 'Satan.'
It was 'Satan' who worked, 'Satan' who sought knowledge, 'Satan' was life in the never-ending process of becoming, always eager to cast out the "old Satan" of ignorance, unbelief and distrust.   The light-bearer had
been hitherto the outcast.   When man should feel himself
a co-worker with God, then all conflict would cease; not
by compact or compromise, but through the sense of
unity in common effort.

Michelet had written in 1825:

If one wrote the memoirs of Satan, one would have to show
him furious at first, believing himself equal in right . . . and
telling history in his own manner . . . then growing smaller
every day, finding himself absorbed in God, of whom he is only
one form.[43]

In 1859, the evolution of Michelet's thought had brought
him to the point where he could more clearly follow this
conception of the life history of Satan.   The historian had
begun the task of writing history as one long struggle of
the spirit against 'nature,' and so in a certain sense he
still saw it.   But he now placed this spirit of freedom in
nature, not over and against her,—"Effort is in nature,

[43] *Mon journal*, p. 311.   The young writer gave it here as an
adaptation from a passage of Kant.   At the end of his *Sorcière* he
attributes to George Sand's *Consuelo* the notion of Satan's submission and reconciliation.

free effort and free will." [44]   It was this effort of nature,
the artist seeking to transcend herself, to do the works
of freedom, that the ages had known as 'Satan.'

It is this gigantic work that the Church has cursed, this
prodigious edifice of science that she has excommunicated.
Name to me one science that has not been a rebel. Every new
one has been Satan. No progress but it has been his crime. [45]

The old feelings of schism, of divided interests and of
partial aims, had been lost, according to Michelet,
in one supreme moment. This was when the Revolutionary spirit had laid hold upon men, when their souls
had risen to one hope, when their faith had been fixed,
not upon things of the past, but rather upon the promise
of the future, brilliant with all the transcendent light of
"justice" and "right." He saw man at that moment
rising to a vision of his Promethean task, reaching out to
fuller and freer life:

> passa benefico
> di loco in loco
> su l' infrenabile
> carro di foco.
>
> Salute, o Satana,
> o ribellione,
> o forze vindici
> della ragione.

All compact or compromise with the past which cast
doubt upon the revelation of the Revolution was henceforth impossible. [46]

Therefore if it was impatience of restraint, belief in
absolute right, scorn of priestly sanction, supremacy of

[44] *La femme*, p. 115.

[45] *La sorcière*, ed. 1878, p. 411.

[46] *Ibid.*, p. 410, "Ceux qui sérieusement proposent à Satan de
s'arranger . . . ont-ils bien réfléchi?"

reason, which Satan proclaimed, could Satan be called a spirit of evil? If science, which could deck 'Satan's chariot' with smoke and flame, was a rebel, if the daring of discovery was to be deprecated and hampered; then, asked Michelet, whose the fault? And he continued to proclaim that man should learn that his impulses toward freedom were one with all the energy of the universe, and that this energy was irresistible. Michelet's definition of evil would have perforce included all that cannot minister to the glory and efficacy of life. The "carro di foco" celebrated by Carducci (the comparatively inoffensive steam-engine), must have been for the historian as it seems to have been for the Italian poet, a practical and every-day symbol of the future and certain victory of this particular 'Satan,'—the power of human initiative, increased by scientific knowledge, the revelations of which had brought the revelation of what human effort may accomplish.

Such was the paradoxical and rebellious note with which Michelet's *Sorcière* ended. This book and his *Bible de l'humanité* show certain characteristic forms which his expressions of belief in the dynamic force of life came to assume. As a gentle, earnest and comparatively solitary scholar, seeking to bring himself into harmony with all that seemed to him noblest in life and its manifestations, sharing the widespread convictions of his day that the destinies of mankind were just at that moment being revealed as august in a sense quite unforeseen, and that even fuller revelations were at hand; he had at first trusted to social institutions as he had found them to take on such significance and to undergo such transformation as would prove them to be the means of self-expression for a humanity which had new convictions and fresh hopes to express.

The Church had seemed to him to hold a better title to authority than the various social sects and social philosophies which had claimed a right to take precedence of her. But when the historian had kissed the cross in the Coliseum, his reverence for it was probably but an expression of his reverence for man. His belief in humanity as the arbiter of its own destinies, inspired him with confidence in hopes for future change and transformation in human ideals, as great as had been his reverence for the past. After 1850, this reverence was expressed almost exclusively in terms compatible with those convictions which had to do with belief in the necessity of some immediate social and political transformation and regeneration.

His sympathy for the progressive and democratic ideals to which he had believed humanity had attained, found itself homeless and an alien in the France of the second Empire. There was no immediate promise of any realization of the dream of national life finding its expression in the fraternal association constituting the "social church" of the future which he had predicted in the fervor of the excitement born of the promise of the Revolution of 1848. Since he could not preach faith in the present, he sought instruction in examples of a past as far removed as possible from the present, and matter for admonition in all manifestations of natural life. This gave to much of Michelet's "Heroism and Naturalism" its paganism, which is not without a touch of self-conscious rebellious Titanism.

The reverence for life which in his earlier work (showing perhaps some trace of the old Celtic tradition of reverence for the dead?) had been translated by such sympathy for all effort and endeavor of the past, such compassion for defeat, such respect for the struggles incident to the individual and the general life, was replaced in this his later work by a more militant interpretation of human dignity. The "unity of life" was to be demonstrated not so much by the recognition of the dignity of the continuity of traditions as by the projection into the future of new hopes and ideals which had been born in his own epoch.

Thus Michelet's humanitarianism having ceased to show an all embracing sympathy and understanding and having taken on a shade of impatience and of defiance, he exalted the revolutionary spirit as a new revelation of the dignity of human instinct and of human endeavor, as a supreme expression of the divine impulse by which the universe was guided. In such championship his compassion for failure still found satisfaction; his lack of a sure faith in a personal immortality found there its compensation, and he believed that the national tradition of respect for the dignity of the human person was supported by it.

His mystical faith in life as the immediate manifestation of universal love gave a peculiar significance to his desire to dignify and ennoble all conceptions of human relationships and of human association. In this mystical faith his ardent desire for some basis for a religious faith found its profoundest satisfaction. At no time does he seem to have fully shared Mickiewicz's faith in an extraordinary "Messianic" revelation in a single life or in 'exceptional lives,' but his faith in all life as a continuous and maintained divine revelation imposed upon him an imperative desire to interpret the individual life as the supreme opportunity, given but once and for a brief moment to each individual, ennabling him to participate in divine impulse. Such a conception of existence especially inspired his pronouncements on the family and on woman's rôle in it. It increased too his tender reverence for childhood.

The chapters of Part III constitute a study of these pronouncements and of the character of this reverence.

PART III

WOMAN AND SOCIETY

Tes pleurs lavent l'injure et les ingratitudes,
Tu pousses par le bras l'homme . . . il se lève armé.
Alfred de Vigny, *La maison du berger*.

CHAPTER I

INFLUENCES PRIOR TO 1843 WHICH MAY HAVE CONTRIBUTED
TO FORM MICHELET'S IDEAS ABOUT WOMEN

Je me sens profondément fils de la femme.
Michelet, *Les Jésuites*, Preface.

In the society of the future which Michelet desired to
see "energized" by faith in man's power to reveal himself
master of the destinies of the world, the problem which
gave him most serious pause was that of determining in
what way the tremendous influence exercised by women
might be recruited to the cause of the "Naturalism and
Heroism," which meant to him, as has been seen, trust in
the nobility of instinct and faith in the efficacy of human
effort. His approach to this problem was determined
naturally not only by his conception of life in general but
by his personal and intimate experience and more than
all else perhaps by the tenderness, hauteur and pride
with which his instinctive and cultivated sense of pity
was tinged. His pity for woman revealed a sincere and
gentle regard for her, but it was founded too upon the
conviction that woman could only think and act to some
purpose in so far as her thought and action might be inspired by man. He found therefore some difficulty in
defining and championing her right and capacity to look
upon herself as a "person" save through whatever sanction man's reverence might secure to her. Furthermore,
this reverence, being found on analysis to be composed
largely of man's willingness to pity and protect, Michelet's
study of woman's rôle resolved itself into the justification

of the moral authority which would give full sway, sup-
posedly, to man's pitying and protective impulses. He
lent, we shall find, a somewhat especial significance to
these impulses. Even had he attempted to do so, he
would have found it difficult to study impersonally the
question of woman's place in society, or to look on her
as an individual capable of estimating and determining
her own conduct and action. He was making no such
attempt in his books on woman, love and marriage. He
was rather trying to create a poetic myth where respect
for woman should appear as the supreme opportunity
offered to man for the manifestation of his moral dignity.

Now since this dignity lay in man's power and preroga-
tive to pity and protect, the ideal woman would of necessity be she who should most completely yield to the power
which ennobles man. In the consideration of the problem
of woman's place in society, viewed from the angle offered
by the loftiest height of manly superiority, one does not
necessarily ask where woman's dignity as an individual
may lie. It is natural, however, that Michelet should
have considered the question from this angle of manly
superiority. It is the one which most easily gives the
desired perspective to those who are dominated by a desire to idealize woman, especially when they feel that
this power of idealization is a proof of moral fineness.

One might further add that the question as to what
constitutes the highest personal dignity is not one to be
easily and immediately settled to the satisfaction of all.
As for woman, there are still those who would maintain,
as we shall find that Michelet maintained, that her dignity
is largely incidental to "the exclusive and delicate"
affection of a husband.

Michelet had felt at recurring intervals during his life
that "something should be done for women." What he
finally did by attempting to define her rôle in society in
the two books *L'amour* and *La femme* and by whatever

comment he made upon it in his historical works and in his attacks directed against the Jesuits, became the occasion for some of the bitterest criticism which he was destined to encounter. On reading the books directly concerned with his views on woman, one is at first rather inclined to think that he might better have formulated his interest in the subject by the statement that something should be done for society, since society presented the problem which the presence of women there had actually created. It is, however, quite evident that he fully recognized the importance of the problem to women themselves. His books about them were written primarily for men, and seem to have been intended to encourage marriage and to institute outside the Church a sort of family religion, in which women should play a rôle the character of which may best be explained by an attempt to coordinate Michelet's various pronouncements on the subject.

They constitute an important part of his polemic undertaken for the vindication of the dignity of life. Like many of the so-called solutions of the problem of how this dignity might best be assured (solutions with which his epoch was much occupied), they aroused a resounding storm of protest.[1] Fired by the convictions which he had under-

[1] Some account of Michelet's second marriage and of his life just prior to it is given in Chapter V and its notes. The whole discussion concerning Michelet's books about women has been colored by whatever preconceptions are likely to be determined by religious and social traditions. What made his course very hard to steer was the fact that he tried to trim his sails to very contrary winds. The criticism listed in the accompanying bibliography under the names of E. Schérer, O. d'Haussonville, R. Van der Elst, and A. de Pontmartin, will give the inquiring reader some idea of the way in which Michelet's books have been judged. E. Seillière disposes of the question by pronouncing Michelet's conceptions about women to be "Christian ideas spoiled in spots by bursts of senile eroticism and interrupted from time to time by attacks on religion." There is much truth here, but it is not quite the entire truth and it neglects

taken to formulate, Michelet dragged woman, metaphorically speaking, into a very indiscriminate fray. He could hardly hope that she would come out of it untouched. She did not. No one would be rash enough to follow him into it without uttering the prayer of one of his bewildered commentators, who begged heaven that he might find himself fighting on "the right side." [2] It was indeed the "side" that Michelet took which accounts in part for the sensational interest that his opinions concerning woman and woman's place in the world aroused in his day as a part of his attack on the Jesuits. The interest in these opinions today lies rather in the revelation that they afford of Michelet himself, and in the relation they bear to his consideration of other social problems. His polemic led him to consider from a particular point of view woman's place in history, in society and in the family. Michelet's position had been determined to a certain extent by his own personal experience. But, without some knowledge of what other people had been saying about the same matter, one would have difficulty in explaining to oneself just why Michelet said what he said, in the way in which he said it.

The whole question of woman's rights, duties and destiny had been made the pivot on which some of the most debated questions of the nineteenth century had turned. In fighting some of his sharpest social battles in woman's name, Michelet was but following the bent and custom of his time. From the beginning of the century woman had been sent out in the front ranks of the combats that had been waged over matters of social well-being and happiness.

some of the significant aspects of Michelet's views on woman's place in society.

[2] H. H. Milman, *Erasmus and Other Essays*, 1870, pp. 357 ff. "If we were disposed to throw ourselves into this conflict, we would be disposed to adopt the prayer of the honest Irishman who rushed into the thick of an irresistible fray shouting: God grant I take the right side!"

Michelet and many others of his day had sympathized with the earnestness and zeal with which the disciples of Saint-Simon had sought to throw fresh light on the way in which men might attain happiness; and he found much wisdom in certain theories of Fourier, as well as much foolishness in the way in which Fourier would have applied them.[3]

Now "the rehabilitation of the flesh" had been an

[3] Traces of the hopes and disappointments that these thinkers had brought him are to be found in various portions of Michelet's work. In *Nos fils* he gives evidence of having taken more or less account of Comte, of Fourier, and of Littré. Leroux is often referred to in *Le peuple*. Michelet judges Proudhon to have expressed in *De la justice* (1858) many of the ideas that he had made his own, but refuses to subscribe to his paradoxes. (*Hist. de la Rév.*, t. 4.) Saint-Simon in the Introduction to Michelet's *History of the Nineteenth Century* is characterized as the author of a sublime idea in that he would have constituted a world council of "geniuses" and learned men. For a discussion of all these men, cf. *Un hiver en Italie* (Marpon-Flammarion, without date), pp. 171–179, and notes, *ibid.*, p. 297. In regard to Fourier the following note (p. 242 of *Le peuple*) suggests the possible nature and extent of his influence on Michelet:

"Je suis l'homme de l'histoire et de la tradition; donc je n'ai rien à dire à celui qui se vante de procéder par voie *d'écart* absolu. Ce livre du Peuple particulièrement fondé sur l'idée de la patrie, c'est à dire du dévouement, du sacrifice, n'a rien à voir avec la doctrine de *l'attraction passionnelle*. Je saisis néanmoins cette occasion pour exprimer mon admiration pour tant de vues de détail ingénieuses, profondes, parfois très applicables, ma tendre admiration pour un génie méconnu, pour une vie occupée toute entière du bonheur du genre humain. J'en parlerai un jour selon mon cœur. Singulier contraste, d'une telle ostentation de matérialisme, et d'une vie spiritualiste, abstinente, désintéressée!"

Michelet's contact with Fourier's ideas was perhaps facilitated by the fact that Toussenel, a Fourierist, was his first secretary. Moreover, sympathy with all the socialistic agitation of Lyons and its history is very apparent in *Le banquet*. Michelet spent many months at Lyons in the course of his life. For some further discussion of the parallels that one might establish between the "reformers" of his epoch and Michelet, cf. note 12 of this chapter.

essential part of the contention of Fourierism, and of Saint-Simonism as well, at a certain stage of the development of these philosophies. It was considered to be inherent in the claims for natural rights and human dignity. Rousseau, one of the great common ancestors of these rebuilders of the social machine, had set the example of recognizing and studying from a new angle the fact that there had been entrusted to woman an important rôle in the influence that she exercised through the forces of sentiment and that these are the forces which keep the social mechanism running. In his discussion of woman and marriage he had found the means of preaching the supreme right of passion, and of moralizing at the same time on its devastating effects. It was this latter theme that Madame de Staël had chosen to develop. The odd mingling of passion, frankness, prudence and hypocrisy in the *Nouvelle Héloïse*,[4] formed an imaginative background in which one could pick out patterns according to temperament and taste. George Sand found there the justification for the release of passion and sentiment. The novel could be taken either as an example or as a warning. It had been offered as both. George Sand used it as an example [5] and Michelet, we shall see, used her in his turn both as an example and as a warning.

The temperaments and tastes of the social reformers

---

[4] For example, *La nouvelle Héloïse*, Lettre xxvi.

"Ah, what a gift from heaven is a soul sensitive to feeling! He who is the recipient of such an one must expect nothing but pain and suffering on earth. He will seek supreme felicity without remembering that he is a man. His heart and reason will eternally be at war, and unlimited desires will prepare for him eternal privations."

In a long second preface to his novel, Rousseau argues the *pros* and *cons* for the moral value of his novel, showing equal conviction on both sides. Cf. note 12.

[5] Cf. Chapter IV, note 4.

just mentioned had been greatly influenced by the tradition formed by the philosophies of Condillac and of Destutt de Tracy;[6] as well as by the doctrines of the right of all men to happiness, so ardently preached by the philosophers of the end of the eighteenth century. Rousseau's ideal had been permeated by such doctrines. "Emile's" perfect right to a woman formed and fashioned for him in such a way as least to complicate his intellectual and moral existence[7] was a natural corollary to the doctrines that were to be developed by the "Utopian" philosophers, and incorporated into their social systems. Fourier had topped all these claims to the right to happiness by positing the right of men and women to the fullest liberty in the relation of the sexes. This was a part of his theory that all the discords of social life were to be silenced, not by the suppression, but by the fullest and freest expression, of all natural impulse. There would be no more need of remaking man to fit society; society on the contrary would be remade to fit man.[8]

These new social systems had invited Michelet's curiosity. In a certain sense his social ideals and theirs held

[6] M. Ferraz, *op. cit.*, Introduction, passim.

[7] *Emile*, ed. 1792, tome iii, pp. 330–376.

[8] Cf. Fourier, *Oeuvres*, ed. 1841, vol. i, p. 319:

"The French, because of their mania for exhibiting their *bel esprit*, and because of their numerous prejudices, are not adapted to the study of *Attraction*."

Fourier found the Germans more fitted to it. R. Gillouin on the other hand cites "a good judge, George Sorel" as saying that "out of ten Frenchmen, there will be nine, of whom one may say that they are incomplete and illogical Fourierists." (*La grande Revue*, mars, 1921, no. 3, p. 58.) Such of course was Michelet in a certain sense, and such are others today outside of France, if the general trend of educational movements may be taken as an index. Louis Franck (*Essai sur la condition politique de la femme*, 1892, p. 9) states that Fourier originated the expression "feminine emancipation."

common hopes and looked toward common ends. He agreed with them in their contention that the problem of woman's rôle in society was a fundamental one. "It has been seen since the beginning of the century that the question of love was an essential one which underlies the very foundations of society." But in examining the solution that "the illustrious Utopians" had given to this essential question, the historian discovered that they had made for it far too easy a solution. They had bowed to realities as they found them. "Frankly admitting that society was polygamous, they had created their Utopias accordingly." [9] They had failed to find for their solution of the problem the solid basis without which all social life is insecure. "Where it is firm, all is strong, solid and fecund," was Michelet's assertion. It was indeed the lack of this "force and solidity" which had brought about the spectacular downfall of Saint-Simonism.[10]

These systems, however, despite the bizarre way in which they had met an important social issue, had put it squarely before the public, and the conflict about it had been so noisy and far-reaching that books on love and marriage both by the orthodox and the heretical took on fresh actual interest. Saint-Simon himself had not touched directly on the points debated, but he posited so definitely liberty and equality that the whole question of woman's place in society had to be met very early by his followers. Some of them met it in such a way as to bring themselves quickly into the civil courts and into general disrepute.[10] Fourier's harmonization of society might have had a similar fate but for the fact that his theories never received the same practical application as had those of Saint-Simon. His followers, moreover, had set themselves almost immediately to modifying what was not in accordance with accepted social morality in his system, a system—as

9 *L'amour*, ed. of 1859, pp. 3–5.
10 M. Ferraz, *op. cit.*, p. 77; H. Louvancour, *op. cit.*, pp. 164–169.

Fourier had stated with fond regret—that "might have carried the French immediately and safely out of civilization" had they only been willing to go!

The economic problems created by woman's activities in the industrial world became very pressing during the last years of Louis-Philippe's reign and were seriously considered by Pierre Leroux, an ardent champion of all causes that presumably could further woman's welfare. He worked earnestly for these causes, aided and inspired by George Sand's sympathy and collaboration. Their demand for greater liberality in matrimonial conventions was based on the conviction that marriage as it existed was for women an injustice and an oppression. Leroux formulated his conclusions thus: "When man says selfishness, woman says liberty." [11] Quite another way of facing the problem was offered by the interestingly paradoxical Proudhon, who was often quoted by Michelet, and who in his turn insisted that Michelet had at times used his doctrines much to the undoing of the same. Proudhon considered that the dignity and nobility of marriage was best safeguarded by basing its ideals on a lofty conception of justice; and he measured man's dignity by his superiority to all personal and sentimental considerations.[12] The

[11] P. Leroux, *Oeuvres*, vol. i (ed. 1841), p. 41.

[12] P.-J. Proudhon in his posthumous work, *La pornocratie, Oeuvres* (Marpon-Flammarion, without date), vol. 2, gives ample evidence of the embitterment inspired by the polemic that the author had sustained in defence of the position that he had taken in *La justice*. The preface to this work (signed C. E.) states: "il concluait au couple androgyne comme unité sociale sans toutefois attribuer une valeur équivalente aux deux parties qui la constituaient . . . des réfutations ne se firent-elles pas attendre. Des articles de journaux, des brochures, des livres entiers . . . ne tardèrent pas à se produire sur une grande échelle." The attack apparently was sharp indeed, and Proudhon irritated by it and all that it revealed to him seems to have ended his days as an irreconcilable adversary to all efforts that would in any way over-exalt woman. One of his last notes (edited under the above title), runs thus: "Suppress all that

idealized picture that he draws of woman's rôle in the family and society lends her the same importance as does that which Michelet drew. It is not less gracious and elevated indeed than that of Auguste Comte, whose final adoption of a patron saint, his "suave Clotilde" may have been one of the many inspirations for Michelet's statement, made in 1859, of his belief that "la femme est une religion." [13]

In many of these considerations of marriage and of love there was a bizarre mingling of sensual mysticism, and of lofty idealism. With them, as with many others, the use of the word "love" (Janet has pointed this out) [14] was often an equivocal one; it led them into an

I have said of the beauty of woman!" There is a certain tonic note in most of what Proudhon says of women. After a prolonged examination of Michelet's fragile ideal carefully guarded against all experience of the hard tasks of housework, one reads with a sense of relief the injunctions of Proudhon. They recall what Victor Hugo has somewhere said of the woman that is over-careful of her hands. Proudhon insists that all women should be willing to tuck up their skirts and plunge into the heroic tasks of scrubbing and washing. He austerely warns against any outspoken expression of tenderness. Proudhon's *Justice* appeared in 1858, and the stir that it occasioned may have inspired in part the assumption of the conciliatory tone of *L'amour* and *La femme* (1858, 1859).

In *l'Amour et le mariage* (Oeuvres, ed. cit.), dated 1876, vol. i, p. 213, P. writes: "La justice, mère de la paix, ne serait pour l'humanité qu'une cause de désunion sans ce tempérament qu'elle reçoit surtout de la femme." Proudhon judges (*ibid.*, p. 178) that *La nouvelle Héloïse* "revealed love and marriage, but prepared the dissolution of the latter." Of Michelet he said (*La pornocratie*, ed. cit., vol. 2, p. 185): "En résumé, Michelet donne de petites recettes pour cultiver le mariage et la femme, imitées des auteurs comme Rousseau, Beaumarchais, etc. Il reste esclave de *l'amour* qui n'est dompté que par la *conscience;* il reconnaît à chaque pas l'infériorité de la femme, et cependant il la déclare égale . . . de l'homme. Il me prend beaucoup de choses qu'il s'efforce de raccommoder."

[13] A. Comte, *Système de politique*, 1852, vol. ii, préface; *La femme*, ed. 1885, chap. vi.

[14] P. Janet, *Le socialisme moderne*, ed. 1876, p. 608.

inextricable confusion between what is most noble and what may be least so in human emotion. It was to a public more or less accustomed to such confusion of terms that Michelet was to address his exhortations. He himself, we shall find, was not always guarded in observing distinctions in the meaning of the word.

One thinker to whom both Michelet and Comte undoubtedly owed much was Condorcet. This revolutionary sage had had a prudent, reasonable, but very real respect for womankind. He considered carefully and discussed rather fully the status of woman in society. He would have granted her a great deal of personal and political independence. He showed himself disinclined to treat her as a superhuman or indeed in any regard as an extraordinary being, and would have given her power to participate in national and political activities. He considered that although she might not show the highest genius, she might well be able to outstrip the average man. "She would never have been an Euler or a Voltaire, but she might easily be a Rousseau or a Pascal." [15] This may show a hint of some inclination to underrate Pascal and Rousseau, rather than suggest an attempt to overrate women.

In the compiling of his books on women, Michelet noted gravely and disapprovingly Senancour's treatise on love; condemned that of Stendhal; and qualified Balzac's treatment of marriage as a "cadavre." He had apparently studied carefully Madame de Gasparin's book on marriage, of which his own seems in some portions a dechris-

[15] Condorcet, *Oeuvres complètes* (1804), XII, pp. 19–27; 1847, v. 6, p. 632. In his *Esquisse d'un tableau historique des progrès humains* (ed. 1822), pp. 293–294, Condorcet wrote: "Parmi les progrès de l'esprit humain les plus importants pour le bonheur général, nous devons compter l'entière destruction des préjugés qui ont établi entre les deux sexes une inégalité de droits funeste à celui même qu'elle favorise; cette inégalité n'a eu d'autre origine que l'abus de la force." Louis Franck, *op. cit.*, pp. 19–30.

tianized version. To paint the duties of marriage in an
amiable light without having recourse to Christianity,
and yet to maintain all of the dignity that Christianity
has endeavored to lend to the institution of marriage,
was a very considerable part of Michelet's self-imposed
task. Among the many pronouncements by the champions
of traditionalism on such a possibility, Joseph de Maistre
had made the following characteristic protest: "Before
doing away with the Bible we should have to lock women
up, or put them under laws as terribly repressive as those
of India." [16] Here was just the point at issue. To meet
it will be the object avowed and unavowed of much of
Michelet's writing from 1843 until the end of his life.
But on the other hand he had, as well, to combat the ideals
that some of the Utopians had set up as to what might
be done with the enfranchisement of society from the
Christian tradition, without undermining too completely
the grounds on which these philosophers had set up their
ideals: the unquestioning trust in human nature and the
absolute respect for human impulse.

To liberate human impulse and at the same time to
discipline it was the problem. It was to understanding
and to the sense of pity in man that Michelet appealed
as the disciplinary powers. Man with the sense of pity
for life that understanding of it would supply should
undertake the direction of all the force that love, wisely
interpreted, could lend to life. The education of women
for a life in which knowledge and understanding would
be the guides for service and sacrifice was the ideal which
he undertook to set forth to men.

The difficulty of this task had given the more cautious
Bernardin de Saint-Pierre serious pause. He, too, had
looked upon the education of woman as a means of reforming man, and thus of regenerating the whole world—

[16] Quoted by P. Leroux, *op. cit.*, p. 35. Leroux says for himself:
"La femme est le mal quand le mal existe autour d'elle."

but from a different standpoint. He had treated marriage
as a supreme refuge, the quiet rest for the soul which has
essayed in vain many other experiments; and he had
asked hesitatingly if one might not have reason to be
afraid of caricaturing both sexes "by seeking their im-
provement by means of an examination of the defects of
both,"—whether there might not be some danger "of
alienating the sympathies of all those whom one is seeking
to reform?" [17]

There was indeed such danger! Michelet had the instant revelation of this when he offered himself as the
counselor, champion and mediator in what he looked upon
as the one definitive clash among the many conflicts which
constituted all the social and political disquiet preceding
and following the years 1848 and 1852. In 1836 he had
felt an impulse to take the task upon him. He had, he
said, "hazarded a few words on the education of women"
and then had stopped. He read a *Mémoire* on woman's
education before the Institute in 1838. In 1842–'43 he
may have touched the subject in his lectures on the
Philosophy of History. In 1843 he launched, with the
sympathy and aid of Quinet, an open attack upon the
Jesuits, who were threatening to invade the official sanctity of the University.[18]   His pamphlet *Les Jésuites*
was the occasion of a noisy polemic, and the echoes of it
were loud in every succeeding volume of Michelet's *History of France.*

He undertook to study the moral and social evils
which he believed the Jesuit order had contributed to

[17] Extract from an interesting collection of sayings about women
and their education compiled by a woman who was in her day a
poet of some note, Madame Dufrénoy, in collaboration with Amable
Tastu, *Le livre des femmes*, 1823, vol. 2, pp. 15–16.

[18] In the beginning Michelet received the sympathy even of those
near the source of authority, but this situation was not long in changing. Cf. G. Monod, *Revue historique*, 1903, vol. 83, pp. 77–79,
Cuvillier-Fleury et J. Michelet.

produce in France by their influence in the family. This
situation, he proclaimed, was the result of the ignorance
in which men and women were kept in regard to life. This
state of ignorance in the whole French social system was
more especially the fault of men. They did not regard
properly the responsibilities of life; they were indifferent
and selfish. Every woman's folly was due to man's stupidity. The cure for all this might be found in a clear knowledge of the facts of life acquired by scientific and medical
investigation. What above all else was necessary was
good will and more knowledge. These would put an end
to the debated question of superiority and equality between men and women. There was really, he declared,
no fundamental quarrel whatsoever. The assumption of
the superiority of man had been a stupid one, it had
passed into a tradition which science had shattered. If
the quarrel continued to rage, it was not because there
could be ground for misunderstanding, but because the
ground on which understanding is easy had not been clearly
enough revealed. He took upon himself the task of
revelation, and made of it an appeal to men that they
should make of their love for woman a part of their reverence for life.

He thought that his inexperience of life in general made
of him a sure mediator. "Living outside of my epoch,
having slight knowledge of men (and very little of books),
my battles were those of ideas against ideas." He told
of how broken hearts came to him for help, and found it.
Men sensitive and distrustful, in the fear of general
mockery, opened their souls to him. He said simply, "I
never laughed," and touched to the very quick his fitness
and unfitness for the task which he assumed—that of
lay priest and public confessor. It was indeed given him
to consider gravely and delicately matters grave and
delicate. It was not given to him, alas, to see that when
he made them a matter of exhortation in the market

place, he could not always count upon all his listeners, however delicate, to be grave.[19]

However, to these men of 1849, and women too, who had come to him from everywhere, he gave what he had. He searched about in his own experience and "invented" old things, in ignorance of what was the common knowledge possessed by the popular mind. Someone has said of Voltaire that "plus que tout le monde, il avait l'esprit de tout le monde." It was just this lack of the "esprit de tout le monde," Michelet felt, that put him in living contact with the emotional experience of every man. His freedom from those currents of opinion on which one takes sides, and which serve as lines of demarcation between group and group, made of him, he seemed to feel, a sort of democratic superman—one more like everyone than anyone else.

But when, in 1858, he tendered to the general public admonition and reproach, the public either turned and rent him, or, what was worse, it mocked at him. He had the usual fate of the mediator. He was equally ill-treated, he complained, by friends and foes. He had laid himself open to every variety of attack. The violence with which he was assailed he found to be but a manifest symptom of the need of his ministrations. Therefore, undaunted by the public judgment and by any misgivings as to his possible indiscretions, he persisted in trying to solve the contradictions offered by the question of marriage. To see this question clearly and see it whole, it must, he stated, be looked at from both sides and reviewed in detail. He continued, therefore, to present woman both as the world's supreme salvation, and as the greatest menace of the universe. Around the problems of her destiny he grouped the great problems of religion and of humanity with all

[19] Cf. works, cited in Bibliography, by A. de Pontmartin, E. Schérer, and E. Faguet, for some knowledge of the nature of the criticism which Michelet's expansiveness and frankness inspired.

its needs. He made of the study of them an occasion for discussing the imperfections and all the unbounded possibilities of human destiny.

He believed that many things in his life had given him a very especial preparation for his task. It was natural that when asked for help he should seek it there. He had early shown an impulse to see himself as a counselor and friend of women. Almost from the beginning, both in imagination and in practice he took upon himself some of the burdens of their lives. Even before birth, so he thought, he had shared those of his mother; and in his childhood he had lived her life. It was a very shadowed one. He reproached himself later for the quick passion with which he took up her defense when, lonely, discouraged and hopelessly ill, she had irritated her too optimistic husband with reproaches. In his 'Robinsonades,' of which he had at first confided the complete organization to her, he very early made a place for women. Thereupon his confidences ceased. A part of his early reading had been *Les reines et les régentes de France*. He had devoured, too, Boileau's satire upon women! [20]

After his mother's death, he had followed his father to a combined boarding house and insane asylum, in which the latter was employed. He thought that he saw there the neglect and sacrifice of women: he learned, too, how elsewhere they were exploited—ruined. If what he represented in *Ma jeunesse* as having existed in this place,— if what he thought to be the lives of women living in it really did make up their lives, there must have been much which might have troubled an imagination far less sensitive than his. The autobiographical notes compiled after his death show him haunted with a disturbing knowledge of indifference to misfortune, and suspicions as to much that he could not know. All this turned his

[20] *Ma jeunesse*, pp. 20, 27, 34.

thoughts quite naturally towards the necessity of jealously safeguarding a woman's existence.

In these same notes (edited, compiled—and undoubtedly composed in part—by Madame Michelet) there is a curious tale of the plan of adoption that Michelet is supposed to have meditated while yet a mere stripling. His ward would have been a little girl whose loneliness had seemed to him very pitiful, and with whom he had fallen in love. The memory of this "Thérèse," and of a little Sophie Plateau, who had touched his heart at the age of nine, and whom he later rather daringly compares to Beatrice, seem to have always remained vivid memories.[21]

He had been cared for and counseled by one of the employees of the place, whom he had adopted as his "marraine," the "Mme. Hortense" of his *Journal*. She had told him the story of her own daughter's life and he understood then what he must have known before,—that there are problems in the lives of men and women not to be solved by confidence in oneself and faith in one's mission. It was a story of suffering and suicide. It is represented as the occasion which had made him feel once for all that there was need of finding help for women and that he himself might be one of those who might bring it to them. It awakened at the same time in him very natural and justifiable doubts as to his fitness for the task. All his life long, this sense of his need of being better than he really was, enhanced his pity for women, and his distrust of them served to feed his pity for himself. This double sense of compassion helped to hold the problem straight before him.

He and a young friend had pondered deeply over Madame de Staël's thesis on woman's unhappiness, and

[21] *Ma jeunesse*, pp. 43, 137, 159–174. Michelet cited in one instance the age of Beatrice incorrectly. Cf. *La femme*, p. 250, where he states that she was twelve years old when she first met Dante.

they had mourned together over *Paul et Virginie*. As a young tutor, exhortation in regard to women had risen easily to Michelet's lips.

Some of his earliest associations then had to do with the illness, tragedies, and mental and moral suffering of womankind. Comparative poverty in his own home had made them more poignant, the glimpses of that refuge for the feeble-minded, "l'Etablissement Duchemin" (not more unpleasant perhaps than other contemporary establishments of the same order, but still distinctly unpleasant), had deepened his sense of neglect and wrong as an undeserved portion of a woman's lot. He had been the confidant of a woman who had not been able to protect her own daughter. We have seen that he married eventually one of the caretakers of the *Etablissement*. She was some years older than himself, had grown up outside the security of sheltered, conventional society, and she had in many respects a difficult temperament. Although this marriage was less unfortunate than it might well have proved to be, still it lacked some of the essential elements of happiness, and when Michelet's wife died he felt that he had often wronged her. Reflections on what had been unworthy in his own marriage and in himself, must have added to his conviction that marriage could and should be ennobled.

Quite other associations supplied him with knowledge of women of a different type. In his staid, intelligent aunts of the Ardennes, Michelet had interesting models of a certain category of French women to whom, in spite of his zeal as a reformer, he paid sincere tribute from time to time, acknowledging their courage, their good sense, and their good judgment.[22] His affection and rev-

---

[22] Michelet's maternal aunts were women whom Michelet always deeply respected and whom he seemed to find it wise either to convince or to conciliate when matters of importance were to be decided.

erence for the German wife of his beloved friend, Edgar
Quinet, must have increased the idealization he so often
showed of the Teutonic woman. She was his confidante
and counsellor in some of the difficult moments of his
life. She seems on more than one occasion to have saved
him from disasters that might have followed adventures
into the realm of sentiment. One may perhaps consider
that some of his tributes to the woman of Germany were
personal tributes to her.[23]

Cf. Mme. Michelet's preface to *Rome*, p. 21 and *Mon journal*, 42–45,
Ma jeunesse, pp. 267–276.

It has been seen that Michelet found that what had influenced
him "in all his passions" had been a sense of pity, and that he had
the conviction that arriving "as a consoler" he had a "better chance
of being loved." The three women whom he mentions as having
been the recipient of this feeling of pity are Madame Fourcy, his
"marraine," tormented by remorse because of her daughter; his
second wife, because she was frail and had had to make her
own way in the world, and his first wife, because of her neglected
youth. Pauline Rousseau was the daughter of a musician of some
note and of a mother with some pretensions to nobility. For
Michelet's regret at having allowed his married life to become
so poor a thing, cf. G. Monod, *J. M.*, pp. 77–79. Whatever may
have been his own shortcomings (and M. Monod admits that
he was perhaps guilty of some), his first wife seems to have been
eminently fitted to make, for herself and all those about her,
an unhappy life. Michelet's ideal of the dignity of married
life had in the course of his career to withstand much that
seemed to threaten it. For all that his own temperament contributed
that might have compromised his faith and loyalty to this ideal,
one must consult his intimate biographer G. Monod, *J. M.*, pp. 72,
220, 222. It was his second marriage which brought him some realization of it. In spite of the devotion and the affection which Michelet felt for the daughter born of his first marriage, and for the man
whom she married, this second marriage presented eventually some
occasion for estrangement. This daughter, Adèle, described by J.
Levallois as a woman of great charm, died in 1855 of consumption;
her brother Charles, who lived separated from his father, died in
Strasbourg in 1864.

[23] Mme. Quinet, in *Edgar Quinet avant l'exil*, gives an extended
account of Mina Moré.

When his quick rise to an assured official position and authoritative dignity came, it brought him varied and interesting social contacts and responsibilities.   It has been seen that he was selected on Guizot's recommendation to teach history to the granddaughter of Charles X. Later under Louis-Philippe he was the master of history to the young Orleans princesses.[24]   This rôle gave him opportunities for developing very differently the delicate and chivalrous idealism which was always to triumph over his disillusions about himself, as well as over all of his disenchantments in regard to women.   This idealism and the contrast that it offered with his own life deepened the sense of tragedy which touched his sorrow at the death of his first wife.   This death seemed doubly a tragedy, because it left him memories of a marriage which, as has been noted, had little in it which could foster idealism.   There had been much in his married life which left him with a sense of pity for his wife, and pity for himself.   There seems to have been that, too, which left him saddened with remorse.   His self-accusation and regret run like a thread through the volume he was busy composing during the year of her death.   His portrait of Louis

---

[24] Mme. Michelet in the preface of *Rome* (p. 56) gives an enthusiastic description of her husband in court costume: "Ses cheveux d'un blanc de neige . . . paraient sa jeunesse austère d'une sorte d'auréole."   Of the little granddaughter of Charles X Michelet said, "Elle a ému mes entrailles de père."   In a letter to Mario Proth (30 janvier, 1859) Michelet called himself "a courtier of Queens and not of Kings," with how little basis the following chapter may show.   In speaking of the Princesses, daughters of Louis-Philippe, he wrote: "J'avais cru . . . qu'on me croirait et plus que le père même.   Trompé en cela, j'ai quitté.   Elles étaient charmantes.   Je crois que je les aime encore, Dieu et la République me pardonnent.   (Etienne Charavay, *Lettres inédites de Michelet*, Rev. Bl., 28 mai, 1898, p. 702.   He said of Mlle. de Berry: "Ah, l'aurais-je tant aimée, si elle n'eut été, à ce point, la fille de mon esprit?" (Preface to *Rome*, p. 57).

d'Orléans seems softened and touched by his own need
of forgiveness and his desire for self-justification.

Every life has its autumn, its season of falling leaves,
when everything withers and pales. At that age of action
when circumstances prevent one from acting, one looks back
with violent longings towards departing youth, towards the
caprices of an earlier age. But his fancy has changed, anything appeals to it, nothing satisfies it: pleasure first of all,
but that does not endure, for into pleasure there creeps the
bitter savor of secret sin.

He made thus of his *Histoire de France* a confessional,
and added a cry for help.[25] His course on the Renaissance

[25] The fifth volume of Michelet's *Histoire* seems especially full of
frank or half-veiled autobiographical intimations. Many of the
notes (dated 1839) correspond almost textually with his *journal
intime* of this year, which was the year of his first wife's death. On
p. 213 one finds the passage containing "Admirable vertu de la
mort! Seule elle révèle la vie," . . . accompanied by the note,
"Je faisais l'autre jour cette observation dans la forêt de Saint
Germain (12 septembre, 1839)." This reflection is indeed to be
found *en germe* in his private notes of that date (cf. G. Monod, *J. M.*,
p. 80). Under the same date, in these same notes, one finds: "J'ai
vu le plus fin spiritualiste, quand on avait touché à sa peau, comme
dit Satan, mené invinciblement par les puissantes attractions de
la tombe . . . s'attacher, poursuivre avec une avidité douloureuse
la terrible laideur du sépulchre." Such avidity Michelet himself
displays by introducing on p. 217 the extraneous episode of the ex-
humation of Inez de Castro: "En vain, s'obstinant à douter, s'irri-
tant . . . il ose soulever le linceul, et, montrant à la lumière ce
qu'elle ne voudrait pas voir, il dispute aux vers le je ne sais quoi
informe et terrible qui fut Inez de Castro." (The body of Michelet's
wife was exhumed September 4, to be reinterred in a tomb prepared
in Père Lachaise). This same episode begins with, "C'est que
les mots de l'union: *Vous êtes même chair*, ils ne sont pas un vain
son. . . ." Michelet's private notes read (Monod, p. 80): "C'est
qu'il faut convenir que ce ne sont pas de vaines paroles: Vous êtes
même chair." Michelet's exoneration of his wife's faults and his
own self-accusation are perhaps translated in many portions of this
volume; in his treatment of the episode of the murder of the Duc

in this year "acted," he says, "violently on many persons." Madame Dumesnil, the mother of one of his students, was among them. She wrote him letters in which he felt the delicacy and sympathy that he craved. This led to her joining her fortunes and her son's as well with those of Michelet's household, and it resulted ultimately in the marriage of Alfred Dumesnil and Michelet's daughter, Adèle Michelet. The charm of this daughter and her great musical gift must have helped her father both to idealize women and to appreciate music. Madame Dumesnil's health had been shattered before their acquaintance began and her death was to be foreseen from the beginning. The bitterness of it was prolonged, and to Michelet, more than the bitterness of death, for at last in her illness she turned from him to her confessor. His diary records the change. "All association has entirely ceased—not a tender word except a word for Alfred. She showed me the Virgin and the crucifix of her alcove: 'there are our saviours,' " and he despairingly cries: "Alone! deserted!" It seems clear that one more document had been added to the growing evidence that complete union and understanding could never be assured with one who found her consolation in a religion which might demand the sacrifice of human affections, even though such sacrifice might seem inseparable from the renunciations imposed by death. The mystical ideal that Michelet had framed of affection

d'Orléans, for example. M. Monod hints that some self-accusation was justified, however great the excuse offered by the poor thing that Michelet's married life had perforce become (Monod, *J. M.*, p. 70): "Peut-être même l'histoire ne fut-elle pas la seule rivale de Pauline". Michelet's notes contain: "Et avec tout cela, elle a été fidèle. Combien sous plusieurs rapports elle valait mieux que moi," *ibid.*, p. 73. Another note, vol. 5, p. 295 (dated 1841) runs as follows: "Douceurs infinies du travail, celui seul les sent bien, dont le foyer s'est brisé. Cette larme sera pardonnée (à l'homme? non) à l'historien au moment où la famille elle-même est compromise dans plus d'un pays, lorsque la machine à lin va supprimer nos fileuses, celles de Flandre," etc.

between man and woman demanded an exclusive communion of spirit that precluded all that could jeopardize it.[26]

Such in its large outlines is the chapter which woman had filled in Michelet's life up until 1843, when he openly began his attack upon the Jesuits. Into this attack he puts bitterness, some of which springs from his personal prejudices, some from his patriotic resentment toward the stranger in the land; but most especially it had its origin in a keen jealousy of the intruder in the household. "The family is at stake," wrote Michelet in his preface to *Du prêtre, de la femme, et de la famille.* His *Jésuites* ends as follows: "Your name is the outsider. . . . You have a hundred thousand confessionals from which you direct the family. . . ." [27]

This was Michelet's war cry as he formulated it clearly in 1843 in *Les Jésuites.* First it was a battle upon an issue of university education in which he found himself engaged. But as time went on, the struggle came to mean to him a struggle for every phase of the life which composed his vision of the future—a future for which the entire history of France might have been a preparation. All this work of preparation had been, he proclaimed, a slow resistance to impeding forces, chief among which had been woman's.

[26] G. Monod, *J. M.*, pp. 116–119. The account of this friendship, of which every shade of sentiment is noted in Michelet's *Journal intime,* is contained on pp. 105–120 of Monod's *J. M.* Monod says: "Il n'y a pas une ligne . . . qui n'eût pu être lue par sa fille ou par son gendre."

[27] *Les Jésuites* (1843), pp. 109–110.

CHAPTER II

WOMEN IN MICHELET'S *HISTOIRE DE FRANCE*

"Enfant, tu as en toi une grande et redoutable puissance."
Letter to Mlle. Miarlet, January, 1849.

Until 1842 Michelet, in his historical writings, had not seemed disposed to emphasize unduly woman's influence as one of the gravest problems of history, although he had indicated plainly its importance. In this year, in his Introduction to his *Renaissance*,[1] on passing in review and interpreting anew the period studied in the first six volumes of his *History*, he apparently formed some fresh conception of what had been and what might come to be the power and menace of her influence. This backward glance showed him woman degraded by the superstitions of sorcery and shamed by the mockery of popular satire. He concluded, therefore, that the guardians of woman's conscience and destiny had been unable either to guide or to safeguard her. He found them especially guilty in that they had not been able to control an influence which needed control. The need of this control became increasingly apparent to Michelet. He had always accepted naturally and easily certain limitations to which he found it subjected. Far from regretting with Fourier that woman had been excluded from royal succession in France and thus robbed of 'rightful authority,' he noted

---

[1] Later in *La Renaissance*, p. 180, he affirmed: "la femme à ce moment prend possession de l'homme"; and in *La Ligue et Henri IV*, p. 49, "Il [the sixteenth century] sent que tout tient de la femme, *non pars, sed totum.*"

with approval that the government of "mobile France" had been stabilized by the exclusion of woman's mobility.

In 1837 in his *Origines du droit* the symbolic significance and the civilizing influences which he had found associated with woman's power of sacrifice and her will to serve, were set forth with comments which revealed his capacity for idealizing her as a symbol of all the forces of life and of love. But in this idealization of woman he kept her well within the limits imposed by the conception of her as a human being, whose humanity constituted a particularly knotty problem. In 1838, he read a *Mémoire* before the Institute on the education of women in the Middle Ages which showed some understanding but no deep sympathy for what he called the "metaphysical poetry" in which "chivalric adoration" of woman had been expressed. He found in Dante the logical outcome of the development of woman-worship of this type. He showed the great poet following Beatrice from star to star, and the reflection which this vision inspired in the historian is eloquent of his sense of its inadequacy. The poetical beauty to which he was sensitive had a content which was more simply human. In his closing passage he suggests that in the dazzling glory of the vision of Paradise, when his eyes had grown strong enough to endure it, Dante must have sought in vain the woman:

Such is the strange height to which women were borne in the Middle Ages, carried on the wings of mystical chivalric verse. But she disappears here. Dante seeks for her with anxious eyes. Paradise itself does not at once console him. Perhaps without quite daring to say so, he regrets having lifted her so high that at this sublime point her radiant face, having lost all humanity, is swallowed up in light. As for myself, however glorious this apotheosis may have been, I wonder if woman was not divine when she was still woman; when doubtless less lofty but more touching, uniting in herself more perfectly the harmony of poetry and nature, she held in her arms that which constitutes her real beauty, her charm and her grace,—a child.[2]

The quest of the divine outside of the domain of what is purely human early seemed to him idle and vain. In the second volume of his *History* Michelet had noted the great flood of worship which was poured out to the Virgin in the thirteenth century, but he mentions it merely as a curious fact.[3] "In this century woman is enthroned in heaven and on earth," is one of his comments on a cult which left him cold. On the other hand, the beauty of the human devotion which Héloïse had felt and which she had awakened held his undivided interest and sympathy. Here was the woman who had not escaped the common lot of joy and sorrow which was very human. It was not her learning or her wide influence which gave her a title to glory, it was her "constant and unselfish love."

This ideal of pure and disinterested love, Abélard, before the mystics, before Fénelon, had posited it in his writings as the aim of the religious soul; woman attained to it for the first time in the writings of Héloïse, who bestowed this love upon her husband, who to her was a visible God.

Thus she stands already as the proof of woman's inability to rise above what passion and sentiment make of her, an inability which to Michelet was regrettable only when

[2] *Fragment d'un mémoire sur l'éducation au moyen âge lu dans la séance publique de l'Institut de France*, published with *L'introduction*, etc., 1843, p. 282.—In vol. 5 of his *Histoire*, p. 162, Michelet wrote: "Nous connaissons assez mal les femmes de ce temps-là." This fragment may be a portion of that study of woman's education which Michelet states that he "began in 1836" and "fortunately" did not complete.

[3] *Moyen-Age*, vol. 2, p. 253: "Dieu changea de sexe, pour ainsi dire." The respect and restraint which characterizes Michelet's consideration of woman in his earlier volumes aroused J. S. Mill's admiration. He quotes at length from them in his essay on Michelet. Cf. bibliography.

not frankly recognized. "The fall of the man proves the grandeur of the woman," [4] was the historian's summing up of the great medieval romance of Abélard and Héloïse. Such in his eyes were statics of the forces of love between man and woman, and they seem to have commanded for the moment his unreserved approbation. But at the same time he indulged an innate distrust of this power of woman to make man love her, and his resentment was quite as great as was his admiration of the power of woman to love. His volume, *Armagnacs et Bourguignons*, of 1840, contains many traces of an overweening sense of woman's "fatality." He visited his resentment in one instance with seeming capriciousness on the most unexpected object—upon the exemplary and admirable duchesse d'Orléans. Is it because she as a foreigner had gained such an ascendency over the sick mind of the king that he questions so gravely her influence? Or was the historian, through such suggested doubts, translating his own private questionings as to the helplessness of man when facing the influence of woman? For this volume of Michelet is eloquent with self-confession. In his description of Valentine's influence upon the king, he dilates with seeming irrelevance upon the fascination by which women bring both peace and trouble to disordered minds. "It is love and yet not love," and he vaguely confuses it with the fascination of certain places,—with a lake from which Charlemagne could not take his eyes, on which he gazed for hours.

If nature,—he asks,—still forests and cool waters can hold men captive, what may not women do? What power may they not hold over a soul which suffers and which seeks near them the charm of solitary communion and voluptuous compassion?

[4] *Ibid.*, pp. 246–250. Later, in the Introduction to his *Renaissance*, Michelet apologizes for having treated Abélard with too slight consideration.

"Sweet medicine," he cries, "which calms and troubles!"
Then he proffers one of his bizarre comments, clearly de-
noting his instinctive desire to interpret popular sentiment
—so full of suspicion for the foreign—and with this intepre-
tation he mingled his own sympathy for the exotic, and his
sense of the power of nature and of instinct. "The people"
—he says—"have crude judgments but they are never mistaken, and it was whispered among them that this Visconti
had brought her charm from the land of poisons and of
wicked enchantments." Does the historian mean to hint
seriously that he shares the popular judgment,—that he
does indeed suspect that there may have been some wick-
edly subtle spell in the address of this Italian woman, some
secret poison in her? [5] Surely not. Then he is, perhaps,
speaking here in the same mood as that of the man he was
when, in this same volume, he dwelt on the "aigre goût
du péché secret"? In such moods he was a fine sceptic
with regard to the beneficent power of love which he elsewhere so idealized.

He had moments as well of speaking of women in a
tone of easy superficial gallantry which led him into such
offhand statements as the following: "Peter the cruel was
a furious madman yet he was a lover too." [6] With all
the world, and more perhaps than most, Michelet loved
a lover, and he painted France as amiably setting the
example. Louis d'Orléans was "her favorite son." "A
woman gave him this grace and a woman cultivated it in
him." And Michelet paused in the midst of his recital
of French national tragedy and disaster to exclaim, very
much in the tone of a man who pledges the toast after
which all glasses are broken:

What would we do without women! They give us life, which
is little, but they give us too the life of our souls! What

[5] *Armagnacs et Bourguignons*, pp. 134 ff.
[6] *Ibid.*, p. 16. "Cet homme sanguinaire aimait pourtant."

does not one learn from them as son, lover, friend? It is
through them that the French intelligence has become the most
reasonable of Europe. This nation, by finding pleasure in
the conversation of women, by chatting with these amiable
doctors who know nothing, find that they have learned everything.[7]

As he treated the women of this old-time France, so he
treated this France herself, "la vieille France!" He spoke
of her tenderly but not always with an entirely serious
respect. It is the tone of Montesquieu, of Voltaire, of all
those who had seen or imagined the France of Louis XV
and of the Regent:

Such was in general our primitive and natural France,
somewhat light perhaps for present day seriousness. As she
showed herself in verse, so she was in her wines and her women.
The French beauty is not immediately visible. What constitutes it? Movement, grace, all that is indescribable, all the
pretty nothings![7]

Thus he saw the France of the past and thus she spoke to
him through the verse of Charles d'Orléans, slight, capricious and infinitely graceful, and thus for the moment he
was content to consider in general the influence of women
in the history of France, save in moments when both
France and her women revealed unsuspected heroism.

He early saw women, to be sure, as one of the possible
determining influences of social and political life, but they
had not come to be for him the means of positing certain
ideas and ideals through the revelation of what an all-
embracing problem they could make of life and history.
He had not yet come to study the full force of their "fatality." They were good or bad as women may be with the
goodness or badness of the life about them. How bad
they might become is indeed fantastically set forth in
certain pages of his volume on the France of Charles the

[7] *Armagnacs et Bourguignons*, p. 162; *Jeanne d'Arc*, p. 43.

Sixth.   The recital of the bloody deeds of Frédégonde and Brunhilde fills pages of his first volume. These might, however, be those of any chronicler.[8] The grip that his wicked Italian wife had on Louis le Débonnaire was used to show how the "fall" of a man may make of him a figure of tragic dignity (as saintly as the figure of the other Louis whose saintliness was unimpaired) rather than to emphasize the power of women.

His story was the story of the man of the Bible,—his Eve was his ruin. On the other hand, in this marvelous example of suffering and patience, those who insulted and outraged him saw in this man, ready to bless those who offered him outrage, the patience of Job, or rather the image of the Saviour. Nothing was lacking to it. [9]

As far as historical events are concerned, women are not usually represented as playing a rôle of exaggerated importance.   Or if our historian does sometimes dwell unduly upon a woman's influence in connection with historical events, her significance, as has been seen, seems to lie for him elsewhere.   As for the practical or actual achievement of women (when there was such) he granted them briefly the honor they deserved.   There is a passing word for Blanche de Castille, for the countess Mathilde, for the brave women soldiers of the Ardennes, as well as for other good and great figures of old.   As for the wicked ones, unless they were English or had played into the hands of the English he did not dwell upon them over-long.   The strength of woman both for good and evil he conceded in his earlier work with comparative reasonableness,[10] nor was he, on the whole, inclined to overrate it.   But it is plainly to be seen that in history it

[8] *Moyen Age*, vol. I, pp. 189 ff.

[9] *Ibid.*, pp. 311 ff.

[10] *Jeanne d'Arc*, p. 162; *Moyen-Age*, vol. 2, pp. 150 ff. *Le Tableau de France*, passim.

was woman, rather than women, whose interest and influence arrested his attention. The Visconti, we have seen, was pictured less as an historical person than as a type of influence and a force; and the picture which Michelet drew of her was drawn rather by the man than by the historian,—although in Michelet's case it is usually difficult to establish any real distinction between the two.

Everywhere the human note in the symbolically poetic legends about women found in him a ready echo. The woman in the old Germanic legends who was the fighting comrade of her husband, or the "spirit of combat, the Walkyrie, terrible and charming, who caught up the warrior's soul as if it were a flower," [11] the Indian woman who told her love and obedience in the household rites which law and tradition had formed for her, and which she humbly performed as an inarticulate expression of sentiments for which she had no words,[12]—such symbolic figures had their place of importance in his epic of history; in its *Iliad* and in its *Odyssey*. Woman he noted as one of the sources and satisfactions of the vaguely nostalgic capriciousness which he presented as a cause of the great folk migrations. "First Helen; then, as morality progressed, Penelope the chaste, and the heroic Brunhilde" had led men far. But if woman had figured for him as the vague lure, the call to unknown adventure, the quest outside reality,—she figured too in a particular way as the symbol of the highest duty which stable reality could offer to him, she came to symbolize the human city in which alone, in Michelet's eyes, a man could learn to know himself a man—*la Patrie*.[13] For *la Patrie* was also "a person."

The historian had begun very early to try to disengage

[11] Vol. i, p. 149. "L'or et la femme voilà l'objet des guerres, le but des courses héroïques. Elevée par un homme . . . la vierge manie les armes."

[12] *Les origines du droit*, Introduction.

[13] *Moyen-Age*, vol. 2, p. 188.

from the divergent elements which somewhat obscured it, the "soul" and "personality" of his own country. He had in 1833, in his famous *Tableau de France*, attempted to model the body of this "loved one," and he sought at the same time to detect her soul and spirit. But until he came to the story of the long despair of the Hundred Years War, he had caught but fitful glimpses of them.[14] Then, just when all life seemed dead in France, when all material and political order had disappeared, he had the full revelation of what he sought, and it was through a woman that it came. This France which, as he put it, had "longed to be," *was* at last! She existed because French loyalty and faith existed in one woman's heart. The harm and wrong which had been done by men and women were to be repaired by woman. The historian had seen France in woman's love and devotion, seen her as "a person." "La France est une personne" and she is Jeanne d'Arc![15]

He was never able to see her clearly again and see her whole, until the Revolution. From now on the history of his France became for him a prolonged betrayal, of which Jeanne's own was a significant and poetic symbol. This saviour of France was a woman such as he believed that French women might be, such as they were when in this dark moment the women of Orleans, being full of pity, had thus become unchangingly French. At this moment, when the national faith was alive in women's hearts, when the priests themselves were French, and all the down-trodden people were lifting up their souls in prayer, they found their inspiration and their salvation

[14] *Ibid.*, vol. ii, *Tableau de France*, Michelet was very proud of the insistence that he placed upon the importance of the study of geography and of provincial characteristics.

[15] *Jeanne d'Arc*, pp. 288, 290. "Car il y eut un peuple, il y eut une France. Cette dernière figure du passé fut aussi la première du temps qui commençait. En elle apparurent à la fois la Vierge . . . et déjà la Patrie," p. 288.

in the spirit of the *Imitatio Christi*. This book was theirs "through their supreme need of it," and they alone could detect in it the spirit which it taught, and it came to them, Michelet explains, under the title which indicated the need of the moment, "*Internelle Consolation*," without "the dangerous last book" of the *Imitation*. For the Churchmen, the historian insisted, the book spelled only patience and submission. But out among the people the true message was caught. The people understood how much more it taught than resignation, how full it was of inspiration for the effort which saves and of the impulse towards heroic action. What more natural than that it should be translated in the spirit of the woman who was herself the spirit of France?

The impulse of a simple heart! France herself was a woman. She had a woman's mobility, but with it the loving gentleness of ready pity. Purity, kindliness, heroic goodness,— that these supreme powers of love should have been found in a daughter of France may surprise foreigners; they should learn that under her seeming lightness this old-time France was none the less the people, to whom had been given love and grace.

This marvelous spirit of the *Imitation* translated into the essence of the French spirit was full of a sense of measure, full of the good common sense which enables the soul to pass quickly and unheedingly by any temptation towards "mysticism,"—which for Michelet meant merely inaction. "She passes as if she did not note the peril, she passes in all simplicity." [16] This was, the historian stated, the spirit of Christ himself, and it was passing now forever from out "the Cathedral," into the hearts of men. The Church had grown so narrow as to be unable to hold it; the "temple" now was to grow and spread its walls until it could embrace all humanity. It was outside the Church

[16] *Ibid.*, p. 139.

that Christ was to find his refuge. Michelet claimed that "the People," obedient as they were to priests, had early seen that "the saint," the Christ of God, was a spirit of another sort,—something quite apart from the spirit which filled the hierarchy of the Church, and that this spirit was now revealed by a simple peasant girl, "Jeanne la pucelle,"—"The woman in whom the people dies for the people shall be the last symbol of Christ in the Middle Ages." Jeanne was not only France, she was the revelation of the divine,[17] she was for Michelet that greatest of wonders, the simple wonder, "a human miracle."

But this revelation of France, of humanity and of God was a prophecy as well. The last figure of a time which was passing, it was as well the symbol of the time to come. In Jeanne stood revealed the hope and the tragedy of France. *La Patrie*, as soon as she came to know herself and to be known, found herself face to face with a force which robbed her of faith in herself and confused her; an inquisitorial force, unloving, distrustful and pitiless; in league with foreign force,—the Church. This could but have been for Michelet the supreme "pitié qu'il y a au royaume de France."

In the year in which *Jeanne d'Arc* was published, Michelet, in writing to Quinet in regard, seemingly, to some proposed concerted action, added: "It is the last farewell to the Cathedral." At this moment he felt that the "walls" which he believed threatened to shut "the spirit of Christ" away from the people, the "walls" from which he had believed that France had forever freed herself, were swiftly closing about her again.[18] His "last farewell to the Cathedral" was indeed to be pronounced the following year, when he undertook to shatter these "walls" of priestly authority which he maintained had sheltered tricks for the deadening of national life, for

---

[17] *Eclaircissements* (dated 1833), end of vol. 3, p. 313.

[18] Mme. Quinet, *op. cit.*, p. 113.

sacrificing individuality, for "putting souls to sleep." This last accusation of Michelet's was for him a crowning one; he insisted that the "mystic's dream" was a purely human one in which reality was only deformed and disguised. It was naturally to be expected that he himself should prefer the waking reality.

His *Histoire* was, after 1842, to become a tribunal before which the guilty were summoned; by which they were tried, and condemned.[19] Their bad faith, their "shameful secrets" were all laid bare. By them life had been betrayed. Whatever life of the soul, of the body, of society and of the nation survived had lived on in spite of them. His works on History were written to show that all the crimes of society had their origins in the disregard of respect for life. It had been crimes of ignorance into which humanity had been betrayed, and priests, prelates and princes had all been parties to them. They had used women and allowed women to use them. Thus all the powers of life and love, both social and individual, had been diverted and perverted.

Henceforth, as an historian, Michelet yielded resistingly and regretfully, or else refused to yield at all to whatever poetry and romance might be found in the charm which woman had exercised, in so far as history had revealed it. A fitting symbol for it, so he seemed to suggest, could be found in the art of the

---

[19] *La Ligue et Henri IV*, pp. 352 ff. "Je le déclare, cette histoire n'est pas impartiale. Elle ne garde pas un sage et prudent équilibre entre le bien et le mal. Au contraire elle est partiale, franchement et vigoureusement, pour le droit et la vérité. . . . Plaisant juge, celui qui ôterait son chapeau à tous ceux qu'on amène à son tribunal! . . . L'historien, comme juge, a démenti les deux partis, et au lieu de les écouter, il s'est chargé de leur dire qui elles étaient. Au Catholicisme de la Ligue qui dit: "Je suis la liberté" il a dit sans hésiter: Non. Et il a dit Non encore au Protestantisme, qui se disait le passé et l'autorité. Il l'a relevé, défendu, comme parti de l'examen et de la liberté, intérieurement identique à la Renaissance et à la Révolution.

late sixteenth century,—"a sorry art, sad and ugly. . . . From the day in which the good Saint Ignatius brought forth his bastard order, art and letters grimaced." [20] Even Michael-Angelo surrendered to the spirit that now held sway, this new "God-in-Death" which reigned in life. Another artist, Germain Pilon, had left the tortured image of it, "la mort galante," which he had carved with a cruel chisel. Michelet followed every stroke of it with an intense participation in the purpose which he lends to the artist:

A learned work full of ardor, but shocking and painful! Enough, cruel artist; enough, spare her! show pity for woman and for beauty! No, he is implacable. Woman the fatal queen of the sixteenth century, who brought such understanding and such ruin, shall endure this expiation. Let death reign, and let it be perceived by all the senses! Woman or corpse, he presents her and gives her over to the supreme humiliation of being the object of nausea. He puts into the odious stone a sickening foretaste of the period which is to follow. [2]

There is no need to follow Michelet step by step down the long descent, into the subterranean channels of intrigue and crime, full of "the sickening odor of corruption," where he felt that his country's soul had been held captive. Of all the women whom he found there, he dealt tenderly with very few, but there were very few that he did not pity. His compassion might be his crowning condemnation, as it was in his description of the duchesse de Berry, or it might condone. When it was put to the latter service, it could make of his Henriette d'Angleterre a Francesca da Rimini in this his Inferno of French past history. Even in his tender treatment of her, however, his pity held the cool severity of the physician whose paramount duty it is to be intent on his diagnosis. It had

[20] *La Ligue et Henri IV*, p. 52. "Un pauvre art triste et laid, etc."
[21] *Ibid.*, pp. 53–55.

the indiscretions of one whose right it is to hazard the theory which may explain, when the symptoms are obscure, and to pronounce upon the case accordingly. It had, above all, the keen curiosity of one who, suspecting what the cause of disease may be, is keen to put his hand upon it in order to add one more item to all the sum of his professional evidence. He moved along the great historical gallery of women as a busy surgeon might in some huge clinic where a devastating epidemic reigns, sure of detecting the universal marks of the scourge even when most subtly disguised. This is far from being a figurative presentation of the historian's attitude, for as he began after 1855 carefully to ponder on the physiological and psychological puzzles which the history of his country offered him, his assumption of a physician's attitude became more and more apparent. We will not follow him into the difficult complications where he rendered his physical diagnosis. We will content ourselves with some examination of his study of woman's influence as a source and proof of the moral conditions of his country.

He interpreted Roman Catholic discipline as a wanton sacrifice of personality, and he protested against it even more keenly than against the wanton sacrifice of human life. Witness the tenderness with which he painted the killing of the personal and spiritual aspirations of the Waldensian heresy, comparing it to the trampling down of Alpine flowers.[22] What he considered the murder of a soul was a subject over which he lingered long and he found such murder everywhere, in courts as well as in the haunts of "mystics" and of saints. Everywhere women had been used, misused and sacrificed. Marguerite de Navarre was a psychological and sentimental puzzle over which he toiled long and tirelessly with all the cruel keenness of Germain Pilon's chisel, insinuating his final guess as delicately as a firm faith in his own

[22] *La Réforme*, pp. 297 ff.

sagacity permitted. Marguerite's mysticism was the refuge into which she had been driven after all her human native tenderness had been betrayed by her brother.[23] Her life had been one long harrowing effort of self-sacrifice and self-abasement.

With an equal ardor of pitying curiosity he traced later the tragedy of Henriette d'Angleterre. "Corrupted from her childhood almost innocently, she had in her the moral miseries of two great monarchies." It was this her moral tragedy which he studied, rather than those political misfortunes which he believed to be due in part to her clouded judgment. He analyzed in detail all that had filled her desires and her decisions with contradictions, making her out to have been a complete sacrifice to the pious cabals of the court and to the court's corruption, showing how she had willingly acquiesced to her own undoing,[24]—"And with all this, three men plead for her and try to disarm history!" Michelet, however, refused to allow himself to be completely disarmed, albeit he recognized a charm which he felt everywhere,—in Racine's work, where the women were a reflection of her soft radiance, and in the inspiration which had lent to Molière the strength to hazard "in a sublime moment" his Tartuffe. Her tragedy he painted as implicated with that of Molière, two great souls debased together and not strong enough to scorn what so debased them. The story of this tragedy did not, however, totally obscure his picture of the social and political issues among which it played its rôle, although it did for a moment trouble his judgment of Bossuet,[25] whose truest inspiration he found in the great man's admiration for "Madame."

But there was another woman's sacrifice which dwarfed

[23] *Ibid.*, pp. 153–161.

[24] *Louis XIV et la révocation de l'édit de Nantes*, pp. 28–141.

[25] *Ibid.*, p. 383, "Bossuet qui reçut son anneau et l'inspiration la plus vraie qu'il ait eue."

temporarily all the great national and international interests of the moment. It was the case of Madame de Maisonfort. Let us take this as one of the most convincing examples of the way in which Michelet allowed a purely personal problem (especially if this problem involved a woman with whom he sympathized), to disturb the logic and the perspective of his historical treatment of events. The choice is perhaps the more permissible here because in this instance he himself almost admits that he may be considered to have gone too far.[26]

It is a question as to whether, at a certain moment in Madame de Maintenon's St. Cyr Madame de la Maisonfort can be brought to proper submission. To break her soul and her resistance, the "tyrannical force" of Madame de Maintenon and the director which the latter has given to her protégée, do not suffice. The gentleness of Fénelon is called in and the girl's destiny hangs on him. But Fénelon himself is not free, and he does not dare to give the support which might have come from his pity and sympathy. "Let us explain the situation," says Michelet.[27] Whereupon he outlines the story of a threatened descent of the French upon England and brings the story to a close with the announcement of Madame de la Maisonfort's moral discomfiture, as if the breaking down of her resistance were indeed the logical sequence of military and naval exploits. The recital of some slight success on sea and of some misadventure on land, followed

[26] *Ibid.*, pp. 37–60; also (note to *Louis XIV et la révocation*, etc., p. 361). "Si j'y suis un peu long, if faut m'excuser." He proffers his own excuse as follows (*ibid.*, introduction, p. 12). "Qui tient trop, ne tient rien. Les grands objets échappent. On a trop à faire des petits. . . . Le testament de Charles II ne tient plus de place dans les pensées du roi de France que la réforme de Saint-Cyr et ses dames cloîtrées malgré elles, que le mortel combat de Bossuet et de Fénelon pour Madame de la Maisonfort."—Such at least one may be sure was Michelet's own perspective.

[27] *Louis XIV et le duc de Bourgogne*, p. 47.

by the account of a plot against King William of England
ends with the following reflection:

> Into the cruel necessities into which one was forced through
> the defence of the faith, if the great aim of such defence did
> not suffice to sanctify the means employed, it was something
> to be able to offer up the virginal martyrdom of a young soul
> to God.[26]

It is true that this episode was used to support the historian's thesis that France lay for a moment helpless in
the hands of Madame de Maintenon. Thus her protégée's
sacrifice was but a symbol of the hopelessness of resistance
to the influence of this great lady. It leaves one, nevertheless, somewhat confused as to the scale of importance
of events. This confusion grows when in the same volume
one tries to follow the historian in his championship of
that "gentle soul," Queen Anne, in her struggle against
"the spirit of damnation," Sarah Marlborough. Happy
on the whole was any woman whom Michelet found to
be without a history—in his account of the many decades
in which women had held in their hands the destinies of
kingdoms, playing with these destinies as with the delicate
webs of lace in which they had woven threads according
to their caprice or according to the caprices which they
had awakened.[28] Mary of Scotland was the supreme
figure of them all,—and for her, in spite of the charm
which Michelet admits that he is near to feeling, he will
show no yielding pity, only regret that he may not yield.[29]

These queens of old were slayers of national life and
their irresponsibility was the source of all the harm that
they had wrought. They came bearing as their wedding
gifts numberless human destinies, "a realm, as a wedding
gift," and from court to court the threads were woven
which complicated the destinies of the world. In their

[28] *La Renaissance*, p. 303.
[29] *La Ligue et Henri IV*, pp. 133–140.

arms they held the national hopes and in their hearts were
the shameful secrets of the way in which they had misused
them. The glamor that their royalty had cast about
them, Michelet shattered with slight compunction. It
was as women that he judged them, and he found them
guilty one and all, guilty with respect to that which was
to him the supreme trust of the world—womanhood.
Victims or victimizers, their course had been almost unfailingly fatal.

There was, however, one exceptional figure that stood
quite apart from the others, that of Elizabeth, "the pal-
ladium of nations." [30] He had no lurking suspicions of her.
He permitted her to appear as the queen whose conception
of her responsibilities outweighed her mere personal
weaknesses. He gave her the honor of having fulfilled a
national and political rôle in which his sympathies fully
justified her. He even tried to prepare the sympathies of
others, for he made of Anne Boleyn's life a romance in
which he wove the history of English and French national
relations, imagining in detail a chapter of it, apparently
without any historical ground, and supposing it to have
taken place during the visit of Henry VIII to the Field
of the Cloth of Gold.

This prince went to see her (Queen Claude) and found
her surrounded by that beautiful garland of ladies. Was he

[30] In his *Précis*, pub. 1829, Michelet had termed certain policies of
Elizabeth "hypocritical," p. 210 (ed. Flammarion). In a note, R.
Van der Elst (*op. cit.*, p. 59) sees in Michelet's reference to Elizabeth
as a "belle vestale assise sur le trône d'Occident," only a reference to
the *Origines du droit*, p. xliv. Is it not quite possible that Michelet,
who knew his Shakespeare fairly well, may have been quoting
Puck's reference to the Queen, *Midsummer Night's Dream*, Act II,
Scene I. There is added reason for this belief since in *La Ligue et
Henri IV*, one finds (p. 301): "Shakespeare fut historien, . . .
quand il salua en elle 'la belle vestale assise sur le trône d'Occident.' "
Of Coligny's wife, and of certain other women Michelet speaks with
deep respect and reserve, but of such he has little to say.

so blind that he did not see the youngest and most charming? I affirm without hesitation that the kindly Queen would surely have paid the King a compliment by saying as she introduced them: "Here is the loveliest of all, my pearl, my English maiden." [31]

Elizabeth and Protestant France, the possibility of co-operation and common interest between them exonerated her from all littleness and made of her a symbol of one of the lost hopes of France, the hope of an alliance with non-Catholic Europe.[30]

The mistresses of kings, in whom general curiosity and popular sympathy in all centuries have found objects of interest, received from him on the whole such gentleness as one might expect of him. He found, seemingly, their irresponsibility more in harmony with their rôle than that of the royal ladies in theirs. But here, too, his severity was not over-yielding. Agnes Sorel he characterized by citing the old quatrain, proof of popular affection, and by an admission that historical evidence supported and justified it:

> Gentille Agnès, plus d'honneur tu mérites
> (La cause étant de France recouvrer),
> Que ce que peut dedans un cloître ouvrer
> Close nonnain ou bien dévot hermite.[32]

He admitted, however, that she was found to be a "public scandal." The historian had but little of the romantic tendency to make a paradox of virtue save on occasion where it would help him point his moral! One could rarely accuse him of having used it to adorn his tale.

---

[31] *La Réforme*, p. 134.
[32] *Charles VII*, p. 6.

> Gentille Agnes, plus de los en merites
> (La cause estant de France recouvrer)
> Que ce que peut dedans un cloistre ouvrer
> Close nonnain ou bien devot hermites.

Where royal manners and customs were such that a
contrast with the manners and morals of those scorned
by royalty seemed to him salutary, he may be said to have
used it on occasion by way of contrast.   It may be because of this as well as because of the human interest that
Michelet found in Henry IV, that Gabrielle d'Estrées [33]
is accorded generous consideration, with apologies for her
having had too little space accorded to her, albeit she fills
chapters.[33]   And in the horrors with which the historian
chose to surround Louis XV, Madame de Pompadour
takes on an official and personal dignity which she seems
indeed to have assumed, but perhaps with less effort and
suffering than Michelet would lead one to suppose.   As
for Madame Dubarry, he makes of her an inoffensive,
somewhat debonair apparition which he pictures with a certain forgiving tolerance.[34]   On the other hand, his picture of
Louis XV's consort robs her of all moral dignity.   In spite
of Michelet's sympathy for her, she is shown, as someone has said, not as "an ill-treated queen, but as a sick
wife."

At the end of the long gallery of portraits of all these
women who helped to bring about the ruin of France,
was the one who would logically close the series.   Marie
Antoinette was the incarnation of all the powers that a
queen may exercise to wreck and harm.   She was the
incarnation of woman's total irresponsibility.   As an un-

[33] *La Ligue et Henri IV*, pp. 322 ff.; also *Henri IV*, pp. 2–40.
Michelet's sympathy for the king is clouded by his regret for the
lack of dignity displayed by the "vert galant" in some of his adventures.

[34] Michelet found means for supporting his arraignment of royalty
by his account of certain episodes in which he showed that the great
of the earth had sacrificed comparatively unimportant persons as
scape-goats, cf. *Louis XV et Louis XVI*, pp. 235, 285, where the
Valois is thus pictured; and in *Louis XIV et la révocation*, etc., pp.
205 ff., Madame de Brinvilliers plays a like rôle in the trial of "Quié-
tisme et poison."

loving wife she had humiliated the King (and for a moment Michelet's sympathy lends to Louis XVI a real
royalty), she had set French royal dignity under her way-
ward foot, she was the exploiter of the affection and of
the trust of a nation. But this was not her supreme crime.
She had committed a great and crowning wrong,—that
of bringing unmerited disrepute upon the Revolutionary
movement by the necessity in which its leaders had found
themselves of putting her to death. She represented in his
mind (and so he had pictured Mary of Scotland), woman's
disastrous power of escaping all cool-headed judgment by
the pity which her punishment awakens. Women should
be morally responsible, but alas they are unpunishable!
This woman represented for him the fact of how helpless
the world is when it faces a woman. All the wrong of
which they have been the cause will become as nothing
when set beside their own suffering, and Michelet seems
on the point of adding: "Et c'est presque tant pis!" [35]

Mystics, saints, and sinners, all the crowned queens of
the many volumes published by Michelet after 1843, form

[35] *Louis XV et Louis XVI*, p. 113. Michelet's impressions of the
Queen were derived in part from his father's own memories, cf.
L'Hist. de la Rév., vol. 6, p. 152: "L'attitude de la reine, il faut le dire
(je parle ici d'après le témoignage de mon père, qui monta la garde
au temple) était souverainement irritante et provocante." The
Hist. de la Rév. shows Marie Antoinette sacrificing her husband and
her friends (the Princesse de Lamballe among them) without compunction. His baffled feeling when he faces woman before the bar
of justice is well expressed in *Hist. de la Rév.*, vol. 7, "Il n'y a contre
les femmes nul moyen sérieux de répression. Elles sont souvent
coupables; elles sont moralement responsables; et cependant, chose
bizarre, elles sont impunissables. Malheur au gouvernement qui les
montre à l'échafaud, on ne l'excuse jamais. Celui qui les frappe se
frappe, qui les punit, se punit. Elles sont le monde de la Grâce;
la loi ne peut rien sur elles." It is interesting to compare with this
Proudhon (*La pornocratie*, p. 269): "O, j'ai dit trop de bien de la
femme! Je le regrette, je ne le retracte pas; j'ai peint la femme
idéale; elle est toujours idéale quand elle n'est pas mauvaise, la
femme! Cf. also *La Ligue et Henri IV*, p. 151.

a long procession of examples of the tragedy, to herself
and to the world, that the simple fact of being a woman
may bring. Such was the background against which
he set his study of latter-day France, and out of the convictions which such a study afforded he framed his exhortations. He used a very schematic treatment. In his
volume, *Charles VII*, he indicated its outline: "What one
woman has obscured, another woman shall set right." [36]
All questions which women, misled by bad counsellors,
had obscured, it would be the rôle of enlightened woman
to make plain.

[36] *Jeanne d'Arc*, p. 164.

CHAPTER III

MICHELET'S IDEAS ON FEMINISM

Michelet, it is said, was asked in 1848, to take a very definite stand in regard to the question of the political enfranchisement of women. There is little need to state that the stand that he is reported to have taken was against it.[1] This question had already precipitated quite a chapter of history in the social agitation that had marked the period of years between 1800 and 1850. Before that time feminism had hardly been recognized as a social issue. It had not been one of the first considerations of the Revolutionary government. The National Assembly, on its adjournment in 1791, had merely entrusted the guardianship of its work "to the vigilance of fathers of families, to wives and mothers." No suggestion of according the vote to women had been considered. Babœuf, who would have suppressed all "political inequality," considered that the inequality based on sex could not be suppressed. It has been seen that Condorcet was a sturdy champion for women's claim to political freedom. But on the other hand, the most influential woman of his political group, Madame Roland, was keenly opposed to it, on the following grounds: "I do not believe that our civilization would permit as yet that women should appear (in the public

---

[1] J. Tixerant, *Le féminisme à l'époque de 1848*, 1909, p. 91. "Michelet pressé de donner son avis sur la question des droits politiques de la femme, etc." Michelet's reply, suggesting the right and justice of giving women political rights and denying the capacity of women to exercise them, is the answer that his ideas on women would dictate to him.

arena). They should inspire all that is good, nourish, inflame the sentiments that are useful to the country, but should not appear to enter into political activities." [2] As the ardent disciple of Rousseau that she was, she could have taken no other stand.

Michelet could have found other precedents, furnished by the proceedings of the Revolution; for the Convention considered the question in formal debate during a long period of weeks, and ended finally by refusing to women all political independence.[3] In 1848, when the matter was debated anew, an attack upon all projects for granting liberty to women was couched in the following terms: "The historical scenes of the presence of women in political assemblies are enough to exclude them from such assemblies." However, the right of women to sit in assemblies was a question that had already been the subject of keen discussion in 1830, and continued to be discussed during the next twelve years; not only in the many women's clubs that were formed during those years and in the press, but as well in the National Assemblies themselves. *Le Globe* in 1830 asked that the wives of deputies sit with their husbands.[4]

The great English thinker John Stuart Mill was in advance of certain great French reformers. He broke lances with Comte on the subject of woman's suffrage, and when Leroux in 1851 brought before the Assembly a project for woman's enfranchisement, Mill wrote him a letter of hearty congratulation. The establishment of the national workshops in the last years of the reign of Louis-Philippe

[2] Jeanne Chauvin, *Les auteurs de la tradition, étude historique sur les professions accessibles à la femme*, 1892, p. 170, quotes a letter from Madame Roland, dated July 29, 1784, as follows: "We desire influence through virtue solely, and no other thrones than those of your hearts."

[3] J.-J. Aulard, *Le féminisme pendant la Révolution française*, Rev. Bl., le 19 mars, 1898.

[4] J. Tixerant, *op. cit.*, pp. 28 ff.

had brought up the question of the means of protecting women against over-work, bad treatment, and under pay; but the problem had found no solution. Cabet had written in his *Icarie* alluring descriptions of perfected industrial society in which women charmingly dressed stood weaving beautiful fabrics in vast sunlit rooms filled with a beautiful spirit of peace and contentment.[5] Women in the industrial ateliers of 1847 offered a bitter contrast to such pictures. All efforts made to pass laws which should correct abuses where they were concerned and which would prevent their assignment to night work, were defeated. All projects for adequate pay completely failed.

The revolution of 1848 was the occasion for fresh agitation and this agitation was very ardent. Proudhon declared that it was largely responsible for bringing the Republic into the disrepute through which it met its defeat. "La République tomba en quenouille."[6] George Sand ardently shared in all the eager agitation for lighter work and shorter hours for women, but manifested no great sympathy with the demands for equal suffrage.[7]

[5] L. Cabet, *Voyage en Icarie*, 1848, p. 136: "What a view! Two thousand five hundred young women, working in one atelier." Cf. also J. Tixerant, *op cit*.

[6] P.-J. Proudhon, *La pornocratie*, p. 166: "L'influence féminine a été en 1848 une des pertes de la République. G. Sand, femme et artiste, composant avec J. Favre, autre artiste, les bulletins fameux, c'était la République tombée en quenouille. Où était l'homme dans le gouvernement provisoire?"

[7] J. Tixerant, *op. cit.*, p. 12. Michelet was naturally far from feeling any immediate necessity for schools for women. He found, however, as will be seen, that teaching was the only suitable resource for women who had no experience of maternity; and seems to think it desirable that every girl should have some experience in training little children. He even admitted that little girls might perhaps be best trained in kindergartens. His enthusiasm for teaching as the fitting training for motherhood was probably due largely to the fact that his second wife had been a teacher. One of his first letters to Mlle. Miarlet advises: "Soyez mère par le cœur," *Lettres inédites*, p. 18.

The law which in 1833 had fixed a minimum wage for men teachers, had made no provision for women, and they were poorly paid. When the former Saint-Simonist, Carnot, became minister, he was keenly interested in all these social problems which concerned women. He established a university lectureship where they should be treated, naming Legouvé as lecturer. With Reynaud's aid he tried in 1848 to provide for free elementary instruction for girls up to the age of fourteen, and to establish equal pay for the services of men and women teachers. The only result of this effort was the fall of his ministry.[8]

Michelet in 1848–9 was lecturing on the education of women. He is said to have been asked if he would accord them suffrage and he is quoted as having answered: "Women have the same rights as men but the exercise of these rights is not possible under actual circumstances. We appeal to women themselves. To grant to women the right of voting would be to cast immediately 8000 votes for the priests." Such a reply must have formulated not only his predominating habit of mind, but also that of a great group of the French thinkers of the moment; a ready tendency to test the solution of any question, by asking what influence such a solution would have on the influence of the Church. Such a reply, moreover, was characteristic, showing the combined reverence for woman and distrust of women which always spoke clearly in Michelet's ideas on any subject where woman was concerned. The clearness of his reasoning was sure to be disturbed, not only by fear of woman's submission to church influence, but by the fact that he either idealized her in theory as a creature instinct with love and tenderness, or accepted her as a part of an imperfect present which an enlightened and progressive future was destined to transform. He found himself unable to grant her any

[8] J. Tixerant, *op. cit.*

political freedom. That apparently could not be accorded
until some drastic change had been effected in society—
Republican France had demonstrated to him how disastrous her influence was when she held power, just as
fully as monarchical France had proved it.

We have seen by his pronouncements on Marie Antoinette and Mary, Queen of Scotland, how he would have
answered the plea professed by Olympe de Gouges:
"Women ought to have the right of mounting to the
tribune, because they have the right of mounting to
the executioner's block." [9] He denied her both rights;
"Woman is responsible but she is unpunishable." Yet
while he refused her the right of a practical share in
political action, he granted her an all-dominating influence. The women of the Revolution were for him its
most touching figures, but wherever they really came
into contact with it, they had ruined it. He drew
with apparent sympathy a picture of Condorcet and
Fauchet pleading for woman's suffrage in 1790, Fauchet
violent and romantic, poet, preacher, prophet,—"This
Saint Paul is speaking between two Theclas. One will
never leave him, so great is her fervor. The other woman,
of Dutch birth, of noble mind and heart, is Madame
Paulin Aedler, the orator of women, who preaches their
emancipation." He called Condorcet a "precursor of
socialists" because on the third of July, 1790, he had asked
formally for the enfranchisement of women—"l'admission
des femmes au droit de cité." [10]

His sympathy was however aroused only because of the
abstract justice of the principle, and because the scenes

[9] M. Ostrogoiski, *La femme au point de vue du droit public*, 1892,
p. 29.

[10] *Les femmes de la Révolution*, 1854, in chapters under title of
women named. This is a compilation drawn largely from the *Hist.
de la Rév.*, with a preface laudatory of the services of women in
time of war. (There was at the moment the unrest attendant on
the threat of war with Russia.)

in the assemblies where the principle was discussed were dramatic and imposing. Moreover, whatever his belief in the principle may have been, he stated plainly enough what the practical influence of woman was. If one wanted to see her making it felt, it was to the Jacobins one must go, where the women thronged in crowds, surrounding and strengthening Robespierre by their unquestioning devotion. The real origin of women's clubs he found in the gathering of anxious mothers, some seeking news of their sons, and in the groups that they formed for discussing ways and means. "Earliest and touching origin of women's clubs," he said, but he hastened to show that the development of these clubs had brought about such violent scenes among angry women that the convention had been forced in the end to forbid their meetings. They were the tools under the Republic, as they had been under the monarchy, of men who exploited them. The Vendean women launched civil war, women worked the political ruin of Danton, they brought discord into republican councils—even the most admirable of them: witness Madame Roland, so shocked at Madame Robert's feathers and paint that she held herself coldly aloof from her advances, quite heedless as to whether she awaken her rancour! Madame Roland's rôle was typical of the way in which women conduct themselves in public life. Admirable in self-control so long as she found, as was fitting, her liberty in obedience and duty, she had been carried out of herself by sharing political responsibilities,—with the result that from having been the glory of her party, she became its ruin. She also overshadowed her husband. Madame de Staël, bourgeoise, German-Swiss, had been too easily carried away by the advances and admiration of men of rank, and by her own personal vanity. In Michelet's eyes she had had but one really great moment in her life: it was the moment when, by her absolute faith in her father, she lent him power to be greater than he really was.

After all is said and done, the really admirable woman was she who could give hope and courage to men.[9]

Of "emancipated" women, one only, Théroigne de Méricourt, drew from him spontaneous and unqualified expressions of admiration. He felt that the breath of the Revolution was the very breath of her being. He described her thus: "Her round head has not lost its aureole of flame, the trace of the violent love on which this woman lived and of which she died—the love of a man? No, but the love of an idea, the love of liberty, and of the Revolution." She was sacred to him because she had inspired all the Republican fathers. She was endeared to him in the first place by the memories of the heroic resistances of Liége in the fourteenth century, by the fact that Liége was again, during the Revolutionary wars, a "France of Flanders." He showed her mounting the tribune of the Assembly, her intrepid figure brilliant in its redingote of red silk, girt with the sword which she had worn as one of the bravest and most daring of the Revolutionary troops:

Already she has traversed the whole Assembly with the light step of a panther, she has mounted to the tribune, and her charming head, seemingly radiating lightening gleams of the inspiration which fills it, appears among the somber apocalyptic figures of Danton and of Marat. [9]

This vivid incarnation of adventure dazzled him, not only because she had so inflamed the minds and hearts of these apocalyptic personages of 1793 and had become a part of the revolutionary tradition, but because she had asked for precisely the great public act which for Michelet would have been the manifestation of the essence of the Revolutionary spirit and the final consecration of the Republic. She had asked for the founding of a great Temple of Liberty, that this temple should be built on the Place de la Bastille, which would thenceforth be the heart of the "City"—the true temple of the true City to which Michelet had finally committed his soul when he had made up his mind to smash all other temples. The great edifice should show forth the sovereignty of the people:

" The people ought to be able to know when it seeks among edifices, where the true sovereign lives. What is a sovereign without a palace, a god without an altar? How would one be able to know what religion is? Let us build this altar. Let all contribute to it, let all bring their gold, their jewels. These are mine! Let us build the only true temple. None other is worthy of God, save that one in which was made the Declaration of the Rights of Man."

Théroigne de Méricourt was the manifestation of the popular spirit, and also of the power which Michelet thought was a peculiar gift of women, that of voicing great aspirations, of organizing and beautifying the great public festivals which he believed would be the natural and supreme expression of universal brotherhood. The dream of a whole nation, gathered around the altar of the "Cité" was a hope which never failed him. To see the great Revolutionary *fêtes*, repeated in the peace assured by the Republic, was the chief item, almost the only one, of the program which his fancy clearly outlined for the future cult of France. He hoped, in time to come, to see the State organizing imposing processions on all great occasions. Among these the christening of children should have a place of prime importance, so that the people might follow the mother to the civic altar and thank her publicly for being a mother. When France should have deserted the cathedrals for this great civic temple, then women might enter freely and work there in complete equality with men.

In the meantime what might they do? Here we meet the inevitable contradiction in Michelet's sayings and admonitions concerning woman. He was as recalcitrant to change as he was desirous of progress. His desire in his less idealistic moments to keep in their places women of different social rank was as pronounced as was his inclination in his mystical moments to set woman high upon a throne. Women who tried foolishly to push their sons into the learned professions were disturbing the equilibrium of life.[11] He insisted that peasant girls must be recruited to do household tasks for the fragile ideal of womanhood that he worshiped, and he pointed out that a peasant girl brought up in charity was lost if she but left off her peasant's cap.[12] Women, he recognizes very sensibly in his more reasonable moments, should do what they must, may, and can. He admitted that they make admirable post-mistresses, that they had written books which had stirred nations, that they had fought like good soldiers.[13] He saw and admired the beauty and valiant strength of the wives of the Breton fishermen. He insisted that women ruled wisely the majority of households. "The women of the people, particularly obliged to be the providence of the family, of their husband, forced even to use an infinite amount of ruse and address, attain an astonishing amount of wisdom." [14] He asserted that the French marriage law giving women a certain economic independence was a commendable measure of which French women were worthy, and that women were shrewd and full of good counsel in commercial matters. They made excellent teachers too (and schools there must be), they were past masters of skill at a microscope; to handle that instrument well, one must be more or less a woman.

---

[11] *Le peuple*, pp. 56–57.

[12] *La femme*, pp. 450–451: Qu'elle eût mis un chapeau, un seul jour, tout serait perdu. Qu'on la laisse en bonnet, ou mieux, dans ses jolis cheveux.

[13] *Jeanne d'Arc*, p. 165.

[14] *L'étudiant*, ed. Flammarion, without date, pp. 151–152.

All of this was very rational and sensible. Michelet really saw the busy sturdy life of France about him, respected it, and extolled it, and granted quite simply that women did their duty in it according to their capacity, their powers, and their station. He admitted that women have intelligence, he "dedicated" this intelligence poetically at one moment to reason, and in various notes he showed an admiration for them as artists, as scientists, and—as just simply women.

That he could not throw himself with any intense feeling into the great discussions as to the status of women in the world of economic industry will become apparent when one examines his ideal of woman. This ideal stood in the way of any belief that women would as individuals be called upon there to play an important rôle. Questions of wage, accordingly, he naturally refused to discuss. But he gave much consideration to the unfortunate influence which industrialism had exercised on the personal well-being and on the physical health of women. He insisted without exaggeration that overwork for women and children spells disaster. His protests were not unreasonable, and his imagination, fed on all the traditions of pre-industrial France, was full of a natural regret for the sustained, easy, rhythmical movement that the spinning wheels and looms of other times had supplied as a matter of wholesome routine to women-workers. For the loss of this he is only partially consoled by the bright colors and gay designs which cheaper cloth, mill-woven, has put in the reach of almost every French woman.

The importance of the protection of working-women, and the rôle that women can play in assuring it, he affirmed repeatedly, but offered no definite program. The reform of prisons and of hospitals assuring personal care, attention, and sympathy for women by the direction and oversight of women—which are among those social measures that are actually being developed—was a possibility which

he foresaw. The coöperation of women in social reform
he posited as indispensable. But to be completely useful
in any capacity a woman must, he maintained, have been
married. To the unmarried woman he conceded that
she might teach if need be. Such contact with children
would be for her the one possibility of a certain kind of
maternity. A woman who had not learned to understand
motherhood to some degree was without the only insight
which could help women to use those gifts which were
essentially theirs.[15]

Chief among these gifts was the "medical" one. It
made the usefulness of women very great. Their natural
gift for divining all the curative powers of plants was,
however, not so much a matter of intelligence as of instinct: they were made by nature to heal, comfort, cure,
and to find the means for doing so.

But it was only in the science of "life" that their intelligence was sufficient. When they were brought to that
step of scientific investigation where some study of death
would have to be made, they were entirely without apti-
tude. They could work to advantage only when they were
inspired by the love of life. Their inspiration to men was,
however, what made them really useful—but it was rare
that their practical usefulness was great in matters of scientific investigation; and in any case this usefulness was in
direct proportion with their power to love. Their lack of
the power of creative intelligence gave them a certain
sureness in their tasks. They were full of poetry but they
are not poets, therefore in their labors at the microscope,
their fancy did not interfere with their fingers. It was
most certainly through love and instinctive insight that
they did their work—"untiring love, lasting, unfailing,
that is what gives strength to weakness! They have more
respect, more condescension than man for the humblest

---

[15] *La femme*, pp. 408, 430.

forms of life." [16]   Women were quick to seize what to
Michelet was the true source of the enlightenment of
science; not knowledge, but the inspiration which is
"religious"—"l'étincelle religieuse de la science nouvelle."
A woman naturally had divined this inspiration: "la
théologie des insectes."

He could see small value in the individual activities of
women, except when they had been put to some man's
service.   Madame de Châtelet had a head, he admitted
that she used it, he called her "cet ange de Newton," but
he admired her really as the angel of Voltaire; and in the
same way, as has been seen, Madame de Staël's one great
moment was that of her father's greatness, which she, by
her faith in him, did so much to create.   A woman had
"breathed" upon Rousseau, and behold the world was
changed!

It was Rousseau's conviction that masculine and feminine intelligences produce the twofold understanding
needful for the "moral individual": a moral individual of which "the woman is the eye, and the man the arm."
Michelet's contention was the same.   Women, it was
plain, were not made for the struggle of existence, they
had not the strength to take them through it.   As writers,
actresses, they could have no success alone.   In any conditions it was through men and their influence, by their submission to such influence and only in this way, that they
might succeed.

There was no dignity, no consideration granted to the
unmarried woman, and without the protection and encouragement that this respect could give her, how could a
woman live? [17]   She did not.   Morally, she had no life
of her own.   "La femme ne vit pas seule, moralement." [18]

[16] *L'insecte*, Introduction.
[17] *La femme*, pp. 47–48: "Maudit qui brise une femme, qui lui
ôte ce qu'elle avait de fierté, de courage, d'âme."
[18] *Ibid.*, pp. 96–97.

A woman was totally isolated morally where she has no sense that her work, and that she herself, could awaken sympathy and understanding. The multiple tragedies in the lives of women who were forced to find their way in the world were saddening enough; but they were only symptoms of a general process of social decay and death.

It has been seen that he put aside all economic considerations which might be involved in the protection of the unmarried woman. "Agitation about a few cents more a day paid to the man than to the woman," such questions of wage as were being debated in France as well as in other countries, were not fundamental matters. He appealed to feeling, to man's chivalry and sense of manliness as the surest and most welcome protection for the woman who was forced to make her way alone. Other considerations were as negligible for the moment as the question of woman's vote. On the whole, the assurance of an economic independence to women was not the matter which should be considered, for women lived, in the true sense of the word, only when they were surrounded, protected by dignity and respect, and it was only by giving them these that France could hope to live a vigorous life.[17] This, he thought, was not so much a concern of material adjustment, as a matter of opinion. Therefore he made his appeal to humanity and to sympathy rather than to any sense of the necessity of assuring to women political equality. Such equality would ultimately have to be recognized, he admitted, because justice demanded it, but in the meantime women must have a better world in which to live, it was a part of their own duty to make it such. For the time being, it was man's formative control that should determine in all respects the nature of woman's influence upon the world. Women were a power with which the world had to reckon. Before turning this power loose upon the world, it would have to be carefully directed and disciplined.

To one inclined to admit Michelet's contention as to the danger of Roman Catholicism as a political force, his hesitation on the subject of the enfranchisement of woman could only seem perfectly logical. The program of what should constitute her preparation, as outlined in the next two chapters, will serve to show what apprenticeship Michelet considered would be necessary for the women of France. With his insistence on the necessity of change in the education of women, he still found means, it has been seen, of conciliating his admiration of the French woman as she was. His judgments of her power, her good sense, seem full of a quiet understanding and of sagacity. They served to fill many pages of his books with a pleasant sense of reality. They are ennobled by a real appreciation of the usefulness and dignity of the lives that he probably had seen around him. Much of his zeal as a reformer seems to have sprung from his pity for women whose lives could not show just the dignity which he so respected, and with which he would have desired to see all women adorned.

But when Michelet presents his abstract ideal of woman, that is another matter. For then he speaks as a prophet, taking small account—or no account—of stern reality except when it insists on playing the rôle of an unwelcome intruder; or, in case it lends itself to his purpose, utilizing it as so much added beauty and poetry with which to embellish his vision of loveliness.

CHAPTER IV

MICHELET'S IDEAS ON THE IDEAL EDUCATION OF THE IDEAL WOMAN

In his prophetic presentation of the ideal woman, Michelet sought, as he had always sought from his youth up whenever he had touched upon the subject of woman, to find some middle ground whence he might pronounce authoritatively upon the problems of the past and proffer admonitions in regard to the future. Naturally, in 1858, he brought fresh and abundant documentation to his task. His enthusiasm for science, his second marriage, had contributed much to the "message" with which he felt himself charged. Seemingly he had acquired, moreover, the power to imagine himself in something of the rôle of Balzac's Seraphitus-Seraphita, with a suggestion of the power of that mystical being to feel as a woman and to judge as a man. He looked eagerly to the future, which should reveal what the eternal feminine might some day prove to be; and in the meantime, contemplating with commiseration some of its actual manifestations in the society of his day, he found much ground for sorrow and for regret. We have seen that he had always considered the problem of woman's well-being and the question of her education very puzzling and of paramount importance. It would have to be met in the family, so reorganized as to make its solution possible. This would mean the transformation of woman herself, in so far as it could be accomplished by means of an education of which he was ready to indicate the essential features.

In prescribing what he believed to be essentially wise

and useful in the bringing up of children, Michelet considered and approved many things which have entered into the educational traditions of today. He had pondered over all that Comenius, Pestalozzi and Froebel (the application of whose methods he had learned to appreciate through an acquaintance of the Quinets')[1] had taught him in regard to it. He had always felt an unbounded pity and sympathy for the exaggerated sensibility of children. He had memories of his own childhood which helped him here. He had tried, moreover, to make a scientific study of this emotional capacity by dissecting tiny brains in order to look with his own eyes on the material evidence of it.[2] The necessity of training a child to simplify its complex mental life by free natural choice was recognized by him almost as fully as it is recognized today. He insisted, quite as modern educators do, upon the importance of a healthy and free enjoyment of wisely graduated tasks as the desirable discipline for a little girl's

[1] *La femme* (1860), pp. 456–457, note 2: Quelle est l'éducation propre à un âge créateur? Celle qui habitue à créer. Il ne suffit pas de faire appel à l'action spontanée. . . . C'est ce qu'a fait le génie de Froebel. Lorsque en janvier dernier, son aimable disciple, Madame de Marenholz m'expliqua sa doctrine, je vis au premier mot, que c'était l'éducation du temps et la vraie. Rousseau fait un Robinson, un *solitaire*. Fourier veut profiter de l'instinct de la singerie, et fait l'enfant imitateur. . . . Froebel fuit le bavardage. Son éducation n'est ni extérieure ni imposée, mais tirée de l'enfant même . . . l'enfant recommence l'histoire, l'activité créatrice du genre humain.

Madame de Marenholz was recommended to Michelet by Quinet. Mme. Quinet, *op. cit.*, p. 256. "Une femme admirable qui faisait la propagande des jardins d'enfants," says Mme. Q.

[2] *Ibid.*, pp. 103–104, "Voilà le nœud de la pitié qui doit faire trembler, cet être infiniment mobile, n'oubliez pas qu'en même temps il est infiniment sensible. Grâce, patience, je vous prie!" Cf. also Mme. Quinet, p. 298, "At other moments he made you shiver by his anatomical descriptions. Since he had begun to use the microscope he had discovered that the brain of a dead child looked exactly like a camellia."

excess of nervous energy. Fourier had exploited to the full the rôle that all forms of activity might play in helping develop physical and nervous control of those tendencies which he himself qualified as "papillon."[3] Rousseau had insisted that music and dancing should be permitted even in austere ideals of education.[3] For Michelet music, although "the crowning art," was the supreme outlet of emotion, and was therefore by no means to be accepted as an accomplishment without some possibility of danger for a growing girl. As for outdoor occupations, which Rousseau had accepted with a hint of remonstrance, as outside the traditions of a girl's bringing up, Michelet emphasized them as a necessity.[3] To a certain point also, he insisted upon the importance of giving serious instruction to women, but he restricted so definitely the field in which it might be safely undertaken, and formulated so vaguely such eminently sensible ideas as he had upon the subject, that one is left with a clear conviction as to what he thought a girl might do with her hands and heart; but one is less sure as to what he would have had her do with her head. All considerations as far as woman's education was concerned, were subordinate in his eyes to the problem which he accepted as broadly and preëminently important, and he imagined his ideal woman as the product of an environment in which this problem had been fully met.

The ideal of a world in which a girl might grow naturally and happily to womanhood, in which her womanhood should be as sheltered and respected as her girlhood had been, was the world in which Michelet placed the girl brought up to love and to be loved. Only such a girl could come to be his ideal woman. Her education would teach her respect for herself, and understanding of the sources of such respect.

[3] Rousseau *Oeuvres* (ed. 1790), *tome iv; Emile*, pp. 170–185; *L'amour*, Livre ii, chap. ii: "le besoin, la manie de la variété (mot très bon de Fourier)"; *La femme*, pp. 307–308, 140–144.

His thesis was that the air of society was vitiated for women unless they could feel themselves surrounded by a regard for their weaknesses, and by a reverence for their strength. The wife in her own protected home without such reverence was as lost a force as her stranded sister, so far as the social world was concerned. His ideal world would give her this reverence.

The actual world, which he studied and condemned, was the world in which he thought that this intelligent regard for women was lacking. It was the domain of the bourgeoisie which Augier, Dumas, and others were engaged in analyzing with the same reforming zeal as that which inspired the historian. Michelet maintained that the souls of women were being fed upon just such poor trivialities as this society offered. The theater, the novel, and their own idle imaginings were blinding them to what life really was.

Women were beginning to write novels and had revealed the futility of such imaginings. They had shown what a poor thing woman's ideal of man had grown to be. It was a sorry image, but men were willing to conform to it, and thus both women and men were coming to live an increasingly futile life. The squalid obscure tragedies of *Madame Bovary*, many of the *Contes* of Maupassant, come to one's mind in reading the little sketches which Michelet used, to show the furtive eagerness for adventure of these women whose ideals had been dwarfed, and to bring out their instinctive impatience of constraint. He analyzed briefly in these tales not only many of the themes of the social satire which the sad facts of social life in every time and place have justified, but also the bitterness and disillusion which reigned in the literature of the middle of the century.[4]

[4] *L'amour*, ed. '59, pp. 279, 297–348. Michelet, as will become apparent, showed hearty sympathy with George Sand's rebelliousness in so far as he could interpret it as a respect for the dignity of

It is indeed very evident that the sources of Michelet's aspirations and disenchantments are to be found not only in his own sense of an actual moral dislocation in the world he studied, but also in the literary agitation which was proclaiming it and disclaiming it. The supreme right of Passion (with a capital) that the romanticists posited had revealed indiscriminately, without questioning its legitimacy, the sublimities and atrocities of which passion was capable. Their heroes and heroines were its personifications.[4] Indiana, Manfred, Antony, Fièsque de Gène, Hernani, showed various characteristic phases of such power. In 1845, the fatalistic "hero" had begun to lose his halo. From Antony to Rastignac, even to the hero of Stendhal, there had been already a shifting of the point of view which promised some transformation in the conception of the hero of drama and fiction. In the contemplation of such types as the world of letters offered, the reaction of Michelet was twofold. It was against the literature which celebrated the fatality of the passions on the one hand, and on the other against the literature that consented to paint a man as a poor sort of thing unable to find in himself any capacity for passion, noble or ignoble. It was in this way that he struck the vein of inspiration which establishes a kinship between some of his pages and those pages where the lifeless indifference of the bourgeoisie is scored by Augier or Dumas. He was animated by a desire to

passion, but he deplored such undisciplined strength. The following extracts suggest what was Mme. Sand's thesis in her earlier work: G. Sand, *Indiana*, ed. 1832, preface: "Indiana . . . is woman, the feeble being, representing the passions, or if you will those passions which the law would suppress; she is the human will in conflict with necessity; she is love finding wherever she turns the obstacles of civilization pitted against her weak strength. Raymon . . . he is man according to the conventions of society."

Lélïa (1833), ed. 1855, vol. i, p. 190: "Was there a paternal eye open upon humanity the day upon which the idea came to it to create within itself division by putting one sex under the domination of the other?"

preach the right and value of disciplined passion. He preached this as a man might who had studied all the pathological data which a scrutiny of modern society might be supposed to afford.

In his study of a social world of selfishness and indifference he detailed then a series of scenes that might have been taken direct from the serious bourgeois drama, and which depicted woman as this drama was at that moment so often pleased to consider her, either as a hunted creature, or as a hunter herself of human prey. He made of her capacity to awaken respect in man and of her incapacity utterly to wreck his own respect for himself, the touchstone of man's character. He showed on one hand the infinite patience and understanding which the ideal respect for women demanded of man however undeserving women might be of it. On the other hand he presented the utter lack of such patience and intelligence in the ordinary man as he found him. His survey gave thus in quick succession the two sides of the medal, man as he was, then man as he ought to be; and furthermore—Michelet would have added—man as he was destined to become.

It was in order to show that nothing really stood between men and women and their marital happiness but the maladresse and ignorance of men, that Michelet sketched his little scenes. In his study of subjects—which he considered it the duty of the artist who writes for his country's good to study—he foreshadowed the zeal that Brieux was later to show in trying to put his finger upon all the abuses and misuses of the social order. In one of his little ébauches there is to be found a modernized and popularized version of the *Princesse de Clèves*, its austere delicacy trampled ruthlessly underfoot by his eager marshalling of all the arguments tending to prove that a perfect understanding between husband and wife might be very simply and easily assured. It was only necessary that men should know woman's weakness, respect her in spite of it, pity her, be patient with her and be able to forgive her with an unfailing generosity.[5]

He had taken over in its entirety Madame de Staël's thesis that a woman is unhappy in the possession of a mind of her own—a gift which merely brings with it suffering so long as it is hers and hers alone. Woman's intelligence as a personal possession would be worse than useless should she try to use it unguided, should she ever learn to pronounce the fatal word "deux." [6] It must be the object of society, so the historian seemed to think, so to train her that she would never desire this disastrous power.

Continually he came back to the assertion that a woman would never learn what she should learn, that she would never be what she should be, until she should have the poise and equilibrium that unfailing regard from without could give to her. Perfect respect must be hers, she must be assured of it, not only as her portion as an individual; it would have to be hers merely and simply because she was a woman and because it was a woman's right. To give her this sense of protection, she was not to be subjected as a child to close and searching questionings—questionings which Michelet believed would inevitably be inflicted on her in the confessional. With her mother and father as her only confessors and directors, the clearness of her vision would not be blurred by a consciousness of contradictions in herself or in life. Romance and revery

---

[5] *Ibid.*, pp. 296–7, 300–4. In his *notes et éclaircissements* (note 8) Michelet states that all his examples are taken from life and science, "N'ayant pas cette lumière, les littérateurs ont flotté un peu au hasard." But he himself quotes a play by Madame Collet, and *L'aventurière* of E. Sue, and questions at frequent intervals the legitimacy of the conclusions reached by men of letters.

[6] *Ibid.* (ed. 1920), p. 182. "Elle ne peut pas dire 'deux,' la femme est l'union elle-même."

must be quickly forestalled.[7] She should not even be allowed the privilege that Rousseau granted his Sophie, that of cherishing an ideal patterned after the admirable Télémaque. She should be taught the power to love by no other way than through the discipline of active service for the welfare of others, and by the love with which she might feel herself surrounded.

As for her education, she might study mathematics and nature; not history, which was too bitter a draught for girls. This study was to be reserved for men, whose portion it was to meet the problems and the conflicts of life. History was in fact the most fertile source of ideas and aspirations for men; but she who was to be the gentle mediator between the father and the child, should not be fed on the food of bitterness, the history of moral and political strife; she might at the most be taught the legends of her country, for her country was her second mother,—

The second mother, the great mother, *La Patrie*. God has given you this nobility, to have been born in this land of France, which the whole world enthusiastically admires. It is here and here only that one can suffer gaily. In France dwells the people that knows how to die. Paris means for France the wish, the will of all, to lose themselves in the great whole. It is through this effort of unity that France became a person, through the will to deliver the whole world. [8]

In addition to the lessons that the legends of her country might bring her, she must learn those of all other peoples,

[7] *Du prêtre, de la femme et de la famille* (ed. Flammarion, without date), p. 284, note to Chap. X: "What I have said, I repeat. The most loyal director in the world is dangerous, his language dictated by the purest of intentions is none the less apt to trouble the senses. Even when Bossuet blames, warns, forbids, he does it in just those terms which invite the thoughts which he forbids. I do not like to look at a great man in such moments; he has a right to our respect in all other regards." *La femme*, pp. 184–185.

[8] *La femme*, p. 161. For the study of mathematics, *ibid.*, pp. 176–178.

those at least which could teach her the lessons of 'heroism' inspired by love.

We have seen in what way Michelet believed that these legends should be presented, and how, in order to give to the world the book which could teach men and women the needful lessons, he wrote in his old age, *La bible de l'humanité*. The "Jewish Encyclopedia," he thought could only give to woman the shock of discovering the gloom of which Christianity was compact, and which was inherent in its teaching; that of the struggle between good and evil in the soul of man. Dante and Shakespeare were full of its devastating experiences too. The historian at times maintained that they offered no food for girls, who must see all life and history in the dancing light that is reflected from great and universal love, and who were to find their inspirations in books which showed life as varied manifestations of this power of love. There religion might be learned through the study of all religions.[9]

To this conception of woman as a being of infinite delicacy, of intrinsic superiority, Michelet added the picture of her as a creature bearing a tragic destiny, beautiful with the charm of those "fated perhaps to die early." It was this vision which he tried to set before man's imagination as one which could bring a new vision and a new conception of life to men. We have seen that Michelet's epoch was one which had been forced to reckon with the welfare and happiness of women. It had become apparent that the welfare and destiny of the race depended upon it. The agitation which would have given her a certain degree of independence continued to increase; laws which might insure her protection multiplied, while the plea for an increased consideration for her dignity had become

[9] Mme. Miarlet-Michelet's diary shows that after the death of her infant son, she read, by Michelet's advice, Quinet's *Génie des religions*. G. Monod, *J. M.*, p. 291. Cf. also *La femme*, pp. 167–172, and *Mon journal*, p. 47.

a commonplace in literature. Michelet's physician-like contentions were, as has been stated, those of other writers of his period. He preached the same necessity for respecting a woman's struggle to safeguard her self respect, and her incapacity to succeed in this; he emphasized her need of affection and the total irresponsibility that she showed as the guardian of affection—in a word, her need of the constant guardianship of man.[10]

A creature nervously unbalanced, morally irresponsible, of uncertain intelligence, of uncertain physical health,—she could, through love and respect, attain to as much moral dignity as those around her would be willing to grant to her. Her help could not come from women themselves until they should have learned how to give it. It would have to come from a change of heart and a change of attitude in men, who in trying to effect such change would, after all, be working quite in their own interests; they would need the hope and courage that women could give them, but they could not have it in its fulness until they had given to women a full sense of security, a sense even of superiority.

Michelet, it has been seen was not inclined, as were so many of his contemporaries, to exploit overmuch the paradox of the good bad woman, and the bad good woman. His sympathy and pity lent him the desire to look on all women very kindly, but he did not idealize the courtesan and the prostitute nor seek to embellish and idealize their tragedies. He could not bitterly enough reproach himself for the stupid tears that he had as a boy shed over Manon Lescaut. Such a creature was just what one would expect to find as the imaginative conception of the ecclesiastical

[10] Cf. references given for notes 2 and 4. Rousseau stated in *Emile* (ed. 1792, tome III, livre iv, p. 321): "We could more easily live without her than she without us. Women depend on men by reason of their desires and of their needs. Their honor lies not only in their conduct but in their reputation."

mind trained, according to the historian, to split hairs in all questions of sentiment. Only such an imagination could have lent any romance to the woman who traded on her own emotions and on those of men. Manon's losing struggle left him cold. She was, he said, woman as the confessional consented to see her. He contrasted with hers a tragedy in which he found greater dignity, that of the Mlle. Aissé in whom both he and the brothers Goncourt had seen an example of the most profound sacrifice of single-hearted devotion. She presented none of the strange contradictions of a woman who consents to sin against her own affection.[11]

The problem of the courtesan and of the prostitute then was to him only a very prosaically painful one, a menace to social life and one of its shameful symptoms. As such, the personal tragedy which it involved offered him merely the problem of how the personal redemption of such women might be accomplished. He found it in requiring of them strict self-discipline, or in the solution which the old-time France had tried, their exportation. Another kind of life might be begun in another land. He did not rob the 'Manons' and 'Camilles' of their tragedy, but he stripped them of all romance.

The right of woman was then for Michelet the simple, natural right to love and to be loved. Her instinctive desire for it must be reckoned with, and the way one went about it meant social salvation or social damnation.[12] The church, he contended, had tried to feed this desire upon "reveries and dreams." The historian saw nothing but cheap deception in the ecstacy of mystics, and in the contemplative life of cloistered women. Their confessors and their directors, he reiterated, had always been obliged

---

[11] *La Régence*, p. 301: "Les critiques ont été étonnement faibles . . . pour Manon. On sent ici les mœurs, les habitudes du prêtre. . . . On pleure, et on est furieux de pleurer."

[12] *La femme*, pp. 29, 50–51. *L'amour*, pp. 356–367.

to struggle for them and against them in order to maintain holy and sacred the illusions of their penitents. Mystical devotion was to him only a regrettable travesty of human love. He depicted Saint Francis of Sales as forced to feed the fire which burned in Madame de Chantal's heart with every kind of subterfuge, and as unwilling to take upon himself her direction until he had completely broken her spirit. "She ends by disregarding her son and her father; she arrives at Annecy—What would have happened if the Saint had not found an aliment for that powerful flame, which he had set burning more strongly than he had intended?" [13]

Sometimes these guides to the religious life were caught up and carried away by the mystical aspirations which they tried in vain to direct and control. In this way Fénelon had been swept away by Madame Guyon and her *Torrents*. Bossuet in the full combat against Fénelon's Quietism was forced in self-defence to give the very counsels which he had condemned in his opponent. It was a losing fight, Michelet maintained, this fight against the great human right however it might be carried on, and divine love gained but little in the sacrifices that were made to it. Sometimes the final submission was abject, a mere passive closing of the eyelids to shut the daylight out. Such he maintained was Quietism as it had been accepted in the sleepy stillness of the great Roman palaces, its stealthy insinuation hardly noted. But when an energetic French spirit faced the problem of complete surrender, it had to undergo a struggle which the very energy of the soul seeking submission revealed as being human in its essence. Madame Guyon's *Torrents* was a revelation of the true nature of this struggle and of its end. He followed thus her description of the soul's gradual self-surrender; which she had compared to the flowing of the waters losing themselves in the sea:

[13] *Du prêtre, de la femme* etc., chapter ii.

"One might hear in one's dream the murmur of waters—they fall, keep falling with charm and gentle beauty, their monotony varied by untold accidents of sound and light. Then there are the waters, in greater haste which run and dash themselves there—these streams pass through terrible rapids and they *become sometimes foul and troubled.* Ah, poor torrent! Where are you?—But it is not lost. It comes back to the surface, it is far from its goal. It must first be broken on the rocks, scattered; it must be almost lost! No one has ever so deeply dug down to the depths in which the soul is to be buried. Madame Guyon puts a sort of desperation into going deeper and deeper, further and further beyond all doubts, to a death still more complete, a death more full of death." [14]

It was this ideal of a mental, moral death which Michelet was pleased at moments to set forth as the ideal of the Church. He represented the confessional as having lent to it images and motives that disguised its true nature; but wherever the tradition of ecclesiastical direction survived, it bore the blight of an ideal which he found false. As Michelet's attacks on the Church grew more bitter, he sought the trace of it wherever a flicker of the faith was visible, however faint and intermittent. Rousseau's Julie was not immune. He found to be moments lost to life the moments that she stole from her busy life in order to consecrate them to devotion and to communion with God in the prayers that she offered up in behalf of her husband ("un réprouvé" according to her own religion).[15]

Michelet would have safeguarded a woman against self-abandonment to feeling which isolated her in any way within the family. He considered that a woman should pass from her father's tutelage directly into the tutelage of her husband.[15] In her training, with the father and

[14] *Ibid.*, p. 162 (ed. Flammarion).

[15] *La femme*, p. 182. This was also a contention of Julie's husband, *La nouvelle Héloïse*, Part VI, lettre vi: "He thinks that worship is an opiate for the soul."

mother as confessor and director, every sign of a desire
to substitute the dream for the reality was to be noted; all
tendency toward "revery" must be forestalled by the
revelation of human life, and by the teaching it brought
with it of the force of human love. Both father and
husband must be tender, but with all their tenderness
they must teach the use of whatever strength a woman
might possess.[16] Knowledge of the facts of life were necessary in order to develop it, and such knowledge would
only add to her understanding of the potency of love.
The first revelation must come from the father:

A devouring force is in you, but I shall give it food. Drink
(it is your father who fills the cup) bitterness and grief. Save
for a glance for the child who weeps but is so easily consoled,
you have not suspected what an infinity of sorrow there might
be here. You were tender and delicate—but today we would
be guilty if we did not tell you all. Then I take her by the
hand and I lead her through this ocean of tears which flows
beside us, and which we had not seen. I tear the curtain with
no regard for physical disgust, for false delicacy. Look, look,
my child, here is the truth. In the presence of such things,
you would have to be endowed with a marvellous power of
egoism to be able to go on with your dreams along the flowering
banks of the Stream of Sentiment. She blushes for having
been so ignorant of all this. Then the flame sent by God
mounts in her. All the forces of love, turned toward charity,

[16] This was Napoleon's theory and the French code has perpetuated
it in certain of its provisions; cf. Louis Bridel, *Trois études sociales et
juridiques*, Tokio, 1905, pp. 34–35; *La femme*, p. 309. For a vigorous
characterization of the dependence of women in the middle of the
century, cf. E. Legouvé, *Conférences parisiennes* (ed. 1872), pp. 52,
53, 60–62. On the other hand, statements quite as emphatic as
those of Michelet on the subject of the importance and decisiveness
of the French woman's influence are to be found in *Le mariage aux
Etats-Unis*, A. Carlier, 1860, pp. 26–29. *The American* of Henry
James seems written in support of Michelet's statement: "French
mothers are terrible."

give her an activity, a force—a regret for being able to do so little.[17]

These lessons of "heroic" charity, the symbol of which Michelet found in Andrea del Sarto's *Caritas*, were the only ones that might fill an ardent heart without endangering its ardor. Art, letters, history might all have their dangers, and music too! If a girl had but so much as sung a duet with a man other than the one destined to be her husband, she had wasted precious emotional strength! After marriage she could without danger see and know everything, because she could see with her husband's eyes. All art would then be open to her, and as for the novels that are written about her, she would then know them to be false!

This morbid literature does not have a very strong hold on healthy souls. The young woman who has not from her youth up been stung by the poison of mysticism is not drawn toward romance. A healthy, sane, loyal love, and mother love, two powerful purifying forces have kept her from contagion. She would not have been able to understand Balzac. [17]

She must be taught from the beginning that her life was the supreme flower of the life of the world: "The flower and charm of life are in me." No secrets of the history of her own life must be hidden from her. She must know its dignity, but she must learn humility too by seeing how humble are the sources by which her life is renewed. She would have to learn what it meant to "die a little every day before dying entirely; and every day at this smiling table, have my rebirth through the death of innocent creatures." [18] Through such homely lessons she would

---

[17] *La femme*, pp. 184, 185.

[18] *Ibid.*, pp. 145–146. This passage is characteristic of the regret that Michelet felt in finding himself forced (because of what he thought was requisite to the cultivation of physical vigor), to aban-

attain to gentleness, measure and humility. Her teaching would need just that gentle surveillance which would make of all her life a glad and useful outlet for her emotional impulses. That most of this teaching should be in the hands of the father was for Michelet, of course, a foregone conclusion. He did, however, consent at last to believe that she should receive some of it from schools, which he seems to have imagined as being much the same as those which have actually been organized by Madame Montessori,—schools designed to vivify and direct impulse. And he insisted too that every girl should have tried and tested her imagination and her heart by teaching little children.

This exquisite being, woman, that Michelet by his theories of life and love had created, would be the supreme and delicate blossom to the flowering of which all the strength and all the forces of social life must be consecrated. Women were by instinct aristocratic and would form the bond by which the classes of France should be drawn together. Woman could, in the last analysis, be made a supreme symbol of the ideal and should be made the object of solicitous and watchful but universal worship. In his religious mystical reverence for life, he exalted

don insistence on one point which had established in his eyes the superiority of the French over the English: the fact that they were not as a nation such meat-eaters as were the English. Compare with J. Delille's statement of his vegetarian faith:

Cruels, que vous a fait l'innocent brebis,
Dont la molle toison a tissu vos habits:
Ah! cruels, rejetez un aliment barbare,
Digne festin des loups, des tigres et des ours!
La nature en frêmit! Inutile discours,
Dès longtemps l'habitude a vaincu le murmure.
Soyez donc leurs tombeaux, vivez de leur trépas!
Mais d'un tourment sans fruit ne les accablez pas.
Malheur et pitié, ed. 1824, pp. 20, 21.

Cf. also *La bible de l'humanité*, p. 64.

her and set her upon a throne, where she would rule and be ruled by an understanding of love.

Her greatest power would lie in the reverence of her family, united about her. Fashioned by what her family demanded of her, she would become a "progressive being," made and remade by loving service which she rendered and which she received. Strengthened and formed by this service, she was to be the fashioner and arbiter of life and of its ideals. Thus he pictured her: "the woman according to the heart of God," the woman who was a living symbol of the worship of God, and the interpreter of life. She would learn from those she taught and she would be taught in turn by those about her; and thus he pictured her as growing in wisdom from decade to decade, learning the lessons of each and putting the essence of them into her own life, so that those about her might in their turn receive it again from her. Led gently on from age to age, she might come to learn at last the lesson of death, and by the grace with which she learned it, she would show this gravest lesson of all to be the supreme lesson of life, rich in all the secrets of life. Such a gracious being woman might become by being loved and worshipped in the family. Thus, and in no other way! This was the ideal that man her rescuer must have, and this he must teach to her!

For rescued she must be. This poor Andromeda must await her Perseus! Should she escape alone, said Michelet, she would be badly thought of, "la pauvre si elle venait à s'échapper toute seule on l'appellerait une coureuse." The responsibility of the modern world was in her hands, but it was a husband who must hold her hands up for her. La femme libre, the woman who dared to set herself free, was merely freed from all that a woman should and might have: the privilege of teaching by her own service the lessons of sacrifice. It was from these and these alone, that the child might learn the true meaning of

life, and the child was in itself continuity of life! Therefore, the agitations of 1848; and the theories that the
Saint-Simonists and Fourierists had taught would condemn society to moral death; for outside the family the
child could not live: "l'enfant meurt moralement."
Women might try to solve the problems of their own lives
(and on them depended the problems of all life) but it
was in vain; alone it could not be done. In all these agitations, however, Michelet saw a sign of promise, a rainbow
sign. They betokened the desire of love and the demand
for respect. Women were demanding it for themselves!

"Woman has spoken at last," [19] cried Michelet, "and
if what she had to say shows at first only her power to
hate, this is of small importance; if she can hate, then she
can love. But she must be taught what to love and how.
She sorely needs such teaching." In proof of which he
cited the most notable figure among the daring An-
dromedas who had boldly broken their own chains, and
were seeking their salvation for themselves: George Sand.
He used her as an example and as a warning. She was
an example of the woman impatient of conditions created
by a system of marriage which might have been the best
in the world, but which, in practice, had been the worst.
She served as a warning because her revolt only widened
the gulf by which France was divided. France was composed of two peoples: women on the one side and on the

---

[19] In the first pages of *L'amour*, Michelet greeted all feminine
impatience with existing social conditions as woman's declaration
that she had a soul, "j'ai une âme." He cited Valmore, Harriet
Beecher Stowe and George Sand as notable examples of women
conscious of this possession. But it is evident that he considered
that any strength displayed in revolt must be quickly mastered
and controlled by man. Cf. chap. V. For full account of the acquaintance and correspondence of George Sand and Michelet, cf.
G. Monod, *J. M.*, pp. 339–383. The author of *Uncle Tom's Cabin*
was particularly interesting to him because she combined happily
the dignity of authoress and housekeeper.

other men, who were willing to live the "new life," the life of thought and action; women still lost in unintelligent "sterile mysticism," still conning over passages from the "Roman du Confessionnal."

Michelet's admiration for George Sand's courage, and for her talent in painting the family, however little she had respected it at times in her own life, was but an added proof to him that an unprotected woman, however admirable, was a wasted power. He saw woman quick and ready for sacrifice, a sacrifice of small avail if not well guided and directed, bringing no help for others and uncounted loss to herself. He painted her alternately as the angel to whom love brings her own ruin, such a soul as A. de Vigny had symbolized in *Eloa;* or else as the being whose destiny it was to jeopardize the glory of the destiny which should touch her own,—the being depicted with poetic splendor by Lamartine in his *Chute d'un ange.*

But since at last woman had revealed herself as a person, demanding consideration and respect, there was promise of another order of society, and Michelet hailed it with enthusiasm. Woman has spoken! The "femme libre" could have no place in Michelet's conception of feminism, but the woman who demanded freedom for the rest of the world, held in it a place of prime importance.

> Voici enfin qu'elle a parlé, oh bonheur! C'est une personne. Du fond obscur et fatal, sa liberté s'est détachée. Elle peut haïr—tant mieux, car elle peut aimer aussi! [20]

The words of hatred and rebellion in the novels of George Sand were a revelation of the desperate condition of the moment. Such an outburst of rebellious passion, such vehement accusations were proof of its lack of character. Words of hatred from a woman capable of strength of sentiment and with the birthright of greatness, were enough to create alarm. Her outcry, Michelet insisted,

[20] *L'amour,* Introduction.

proclaimed what every one had long known, that man as a husband and a lover had fallen very low. Men had but to rouse themselves and they would have nothing to fear; a man who risked his life every day, whose life was a heroic effort, might allow his wife to read every day and all day long such novels as those which so traduced man—she would never find him among the husbands painted there.[19]

Michelet welcomed then for the moment women who were clamorous in their protests; women who could hate; but let there be found the wherewithal to quiet them! Woman has spoken! Silence her quickly, said the historian and moralist. Teach her how to love! Life is not woman's affair, it is man's! The solution was marriage, and marriage was for man the supreme and intimate revelation of his power to refashion the individual, the social and the national life. Marriage must be "heroic"; that is to say, a moral effort and an aspiration by which, and by which only, the enigma of the social world might be solved once and for all.

CHAPTER V

MARRIAGE

Marriage then, according to Michelet, was man's affair, not woman's. Marriage he treated as the means by which man may save himself by saving woman, and thereby bring about the world's salvation. There is much that is true in this, and all of it, truth and error, had been said before. Michelet admitted as much, but he claimed, and very justly, that he said it differently. He did, very differently! He said it with great splendor and magnificence and with strange contradictions. There could be, indeed, no simplicity at all in his presentation of marriage, woman being, of course, essential to the institution and yet its most grave and constant menace. This, too, had been said, and all along the ages, but Michelet's statement of the old contention was absolutely without cynicism, and he put into its exposition all that he had to say upon his hopes and aspirations for the world, and upon the boundless promise of the future!—all of which implied, of course, his unbounded condemnation of the past; for the little books *L'amour* and *La femme* which he sent out in the guise of doves of peace, were really camouflaged carrier-pigeons bearing full instructions for the routing of the enemy.

Woman, he stated, was no longer inarticulate, but still inscrutable. She had ceased to be an idle mouth-piece for the long tradition that for many centuries has defied her, scorned her and perverted her. "Woman has spoken!" said Michelet, "she has spoken too soon." She must be silenced until she shall learn just what woman may say.

Only a husband can teach her this, and she will not listen
to a husband unless he be the hero that the great modern
life creates. Marriage was, then, to be heroic, but the
hero husband should be warned to teach his heroic power
infinite wisdom and patience. This enlightened strength
of his that could move mountains and hew out the secrets
of the earth would have to be set to the humble but subtle
task of drawing out from the heart of woman her inmost
hidden thoughts. "I hold here the strife or the peace of
the world, what may trouble all hearts or bestow the lofty
harmony of God." [1] This was the lesson to be conned
over and over again by both mothers and husbands and
in order to penetrate its truth, husbands must penetrate
to the very heart of the thoughts of wives. "Marriage
is confession" and it was the husband whose office it was
to be the priest and the confessor. It would be his duty
to remember that one reason for being a husband was
the motive which Michelet imputed to priests for being
priests—"pour savoir le secret de la femme." [2] To this
constant care and direction of the woman's mind and
soul must be added the constant provision for her physical
needs, her health. The husband must have the vigilance
of a physician in charge, whose duty it is to follow every
fluctuation of the pulse, each change of color, to appor-
tion each morsel of food if need be, and to put down on
paper the whole life history of the life whose responsibility
is his.[3] That was one side of the matter; on the other hand,
marriage was the highest revelation of love, of life, of God,
the husband must make himself worthy of this revelation,
whereupon peace would reign and heaven would come to
dwell upon the earth. All of this was set forth with the

[1] *La femme*, p. 117.

[2] *La Réforme*, p. 117: "Il [Luther] abandonna la confession,—la
chose pour laquelle tout jeune homme se fera prêtre (savoir le secret
de la femme)."

[3] *L'amour*, livre II, chap. viii.

ardor and conviction of the prophet who had found his supreme message and gave utterance to it from his heart.

Michelet did utter it from his heart, for he gave it from his own experience, of which a most decisive chapter was constituted by his second marriage in 1849. These rather amazing precepts are those which he seems to have set for himself when, through the event which so profoundly changed his existence, he found himself guide, philosopher and friend to a girl of twenty-three. Some examination of the circumstances of this marriage may be useful here. Michelet married Mlle. Athenaïs Miarlet after an acquaintance established through about a year's correspondence. His books upon woman and the confessional, *Les Jésuites* and *Du prêtre, de la femme et de la famille*, had revealed a great desire to help any woman who might feel the need of a lay confessor. Mademoiselle Miarlet, it seems, had felt this need. She wrote to him from Vienna: "The world does not admit that a young woman may seek a guide save among priests. If you take the priest from her, what remains?" [4]

[4] *Lettres inédites de J. Michelet adressées à Mlle. Miarlet*, 1899, These letters were arranged for publication by Mme. Michelet, but did not appear until after her death. For comment of a personal nature, cf. J. Levallois, *Rev. Bl.* 1894, Dec. 8; 1899, Oct. 21. D. Halévy in *Rev. de Paris*, 1902, vol. 4, pp. 243–253, *Le mariage de Michelet*, treats very delicately and discriminatingly the content of the *Lettres*. He shares with other critics a certain tendency to deprecate the influence exercised on Michelet's life and work by the belated happiness which the historian was perhaps a little too prone to advertise. It is interesting to note that Michelet had characterized it many years before,—whether inspired by Hugo's *Don Ruy Gomez de Silva* or by a prophetic sense, it is impossible to say. (*Jeanne d'Arc*, p. 133.) The persistence with which Mme. Michelet safeguarded, according to what seemed to her best, this happiness, and her presentation of whatever personal claims she deemed just and fitting to press, as the one who had created it, have exposed her to some rather unkindly criticism. She had the misfortune, apparently, of not being quite the rare being that Michelet believed her to be, but she seems to have had great discretion and an abundance of

She must have felt that Michelet himself "remained." She felt perhaps, as well, a call in the books of this man for a woman whom he might help. She answered the call quite as Musset's "white blackbird" had answered the cry for sympathy and comradeship, and in the end this "rare mate for a rare being" proved to be indeed a real white blackbird—the one exceptional woman for the one exceptional man.[4] To her had been given, she said, the same "gift of tears" which she had divined in Michelet. Her hopes, too, were the same. She, too, had been fired by great hopes in the days of Revolution of 1848. "When the revolutions of Europe broke out, I felt that my faith was born." She was "la prédestinée." Michelet welcomed her as such in his letters. Her sympathy and understanding stood the test that had revealed the falseness of Musset's false "soul mate." The many blasts of emotion and sudden showers of tears to which this sympathy was exposed in the sharp temperamental storms that troubled the early days of her marriage, constituted for it a somewhat severe strain. It endured without suffering any change.[5]

common sense, in spite of her "don des larmes." Exquisite simplicity and a total lack of self-consciousness could hardly be expected in a wife adored by Michelet. Mme. Athenaïs Michelet (née Miarlet) before her marriage had lived in Vienna in the capacity of "companion" in the household of the Princess Catacuzène. When all the documents necessary to constitute the biography of the historian shall have become available in 1942, one of the most interesting chapters of his psychology will probably be found to be bound up with the story of his second marriage. For Mme. Michelet's autobiographical notes, cf. stray pages in Michelet's "nature books," her *Mémoires d'une enfant*, 1867, and the *Lettres inédites*. G. Monod has published extracts from her diary in his *J. M.* Mme. Michelet was born in 1828, and died in 1899. For the reverential cult she offered to her husband's memory, cf. her prefaces; A. de Brahms, *Les curiosités de Carnavalet*. For the liberty she took with his MSS., G. Monod, *J. M.*, pp. 3–7.

[5] Quotations from Mme. Michelet's diary are drawn from Monod's *J. M.*, pp. 243–251, 281.

She had alighted one day at Michelet's apartment like
a tired storm-driven bird, almost a total stranger in Paris.
His letters had hinted at a need of affection and of sympathy and she had come. They seem both to have hesitated for a moment at the end to undertake so strange
an adventure, but they were married, with Béranger and
Michelet's old friends Quinet and Poret as witnesses.
Michelet, in announcing his marriage to his staid aunts
in the Ardennes, had made a great show of prudence and
sage reflection. The young woman whom he was wedding
possessed, he seemed pleased to point out, various accom-
plishments. She could be generally useful. She was, to
be sure, extremely fragile and the birth of a child might
cost her her life. But, although she was very young, she
was very ready to be taught.

She was indeed fragile, she was also accomplished and
she could be useful. It was this very desire for usefulness
that created a problem which had early to be met, and
which ended eventually in her sharing, as has been noted,
in the work of preparation of Michelet's "nature books,"
the charm and delicacy of which seemed like a late flowering of his genius. But in these first days of marriage,
the young wife records:

" His writings, he says, are works of art; they can only be
the work of one [author]." She adds, however: " Our life
henceforth must be *one*. I shall enter as deeply as I can into
the life of his work and of his thoughts." [5]

She ended by penetrating them, but only after she had
been penetrated, herself, by the convictions that inspired
them. She was an excellent listener, but she could ask
sudden questions too! Among others she inquired what
was the religion which was to replace the Christianity
upon which her husband had pronounced sentence of
death; and his answer does not seem to have been either
complete or ready. She was very eager for her husband

to be happy, but she could make reflections as well upon her own need of happiness—and they were sometimes most bitter: "I have just come home from making my calls as a bride. My heart is heavy. These too frequent storms break one's heart or subject it to an anguish that is very cruel." Her reverence for her learned and renowned husband was very real but she found the constant watchfulness which it imposed could have its hardships:

10 April, 1849.
Another blunder on my part and a fresh separation from his affection. I thoughtlessly said something which I meant as a mere pleasantry and he was deeply wounded. I went into his study to excuse myself. He said many things which cut my heart. Mon Dieu! I am near despair. [5]

This young wife desired to be, on the whole, just what her husband desired her to be, but she was also accustomed to being very much herself. Her father, whom she had seen crowned by a halo of romance, because of the wonderful tales he could tell of his wanderings in San Domingo and in Louisiana, was the hero of her childhood. He had found her resistant personality amusing. He encouraged it, and called her his "little princess." Michelet for twenty odd years had held undisputed sway not only over princesses, but over the greatest potentates and all the powers of the long past, and he was imperative, quick, and passionate. The emotional drama which the adjustment of two such personalities created was rendered more stormy still, perhaps, by the coolness and opposition which such a marriage with an unknown young woman created among some members of his family, opposition that ended finally in several sad estrangements.[6] The adjustment

[6] Cf. introductions, and prefaces to all publications of her husband's work by Mme. Michelet; R. V. d. Elst, *op. cit.*, pp. 15–41. This author has undertaken to solve the problem of the collaboration of Mme. Michelet. He takes no account in this discussion of a work on which she was engaged during Michelet's last sojourn in Italy and

between husband and wife was accomplished, however, and it was complete.

It was undoubtedly from the heart of these experiences of his married life that Michelet's books on marriage were written. The problems of marriage which he studied are, on the whole, those peculiar to his own class. They are addressed to an intellectual aristocracy. Later he said: "I took them from my own fireside," and in his diary, under date of June, 1849, he wrote that his lecture on "The woman according to the heart of God" had been modeled on his wife. "Woman, growing in the grace of God through the sadness of age, the sorrow of widowhood, and of the loss of children." Other earlier associations must have played their part in this composite picture of the woman pleasing in the sight of the Lord. Memories of his daughter, of the little princesses he had taught, of his mother, his austere aunts in the Ardennes and scores of others, must have fed his inclination to over-idealize and reverence woman, and to understand and misunderstand her. In the Bible too and in all the Oriental legends, he had studied her. His doubts in regard to her had found nourishment in the warnings of history, in his own experience, in all literature and life; but most of all, in his prejudices, grounded and ungrounded.

Michelet's books on women are full of the experience

which appeared in English translation under the title *The Beauties of the Earth and Sky*. (Cf. Bibliography, and G. Monod, *Un épisode dans la vie de M. Michelet en 1871*). A study of this production could only add to whatever evidence one might use in proving that Michelet's work is his own. This fact has been complicated but perhaps never seriously obscured, by the fact that the matter of Mme. Michelet's collaboration became eventually a question of litigation, and was bound up with the question of her rights and authority over the MSS. of her husband. Cf. V. d. Elst, *op. cit.*, p. 25. The one production in which through sheer force of indignation Michelet's widow attains to real sincerity of style is in her *Mort et funérailles de Michelet*.

of his later life. His sense of the importance of what he
had to say, and the purport of his message, are already to
be found, however, in the autobiographical notes of his
youth.   There are literary associations of a lifetime in
his picture of woman. Distinct reminiscences of the
Julie of *La nouvelle Héloïse* presiding over the vintage
festival [7] are to be found in the woman pictured as the
Lady Bountiful whose every glance carried a joy and a
blessing with it, lightening the hearts of all who labor
about her.   Even in the naturalistic mysticism of the
portrayal of womanhood, there are faint but distorted
suggestions of the bliss that a smile of Beatrice might
bring.   The picture bears the mark of many influences.
The "Jewish Encyclopedia" had contributed the *Song of
Songs*, and a shade of the exaggerations of the pronouncements of the Saint-Simonists is probably lurking in the
proclamations of perfect faith in the divine power of love,
and of its dynamic as a social force.   In its strange mix-
ture of mystic rapture, exalted idealism and stark ma-
terialism, all the characteristic manifestations of Michelet's genius find full and unrestrained expression.   The
mingling of all these elements serves partially to explain
the lack, unusual even with Michelet, of proportion and
balance in these books.   He himself wrote of his book
La femme, "it all seems stifled," [8] and this is quite true
in spite of its exuberance.

Michelet's homily on marriage is interwoven with every
imaginable variety of theme.   The main purport of it all
is: a man's duty in marriage is to understand woman and
to adore her, to understand and worship life and share
this worship with her.   It is also to understand women
and beware of them; to understand above all one woman,
the wife, and to adore, reverence, and beware of her.
These books are composite idyls, symbolic poems in prose;

[7] *La nouvelle Héloïse*, part V, lettre vi.
[8] Mme. Quinet, *op. cit.*, pp. 307 ff.

they are also tracts on sanitation, dietetics, and hygiene. We are told in quick succession that woman is a religion, that she must sweat a little every day, that she should eat but little meat,[9] that she is worthy of all worship and never quite to be trusted. Is it enough to say that however different the source of one's amazement, Balzac's outrageous flippancy in his trivially modernized Pantagruelistic treatment of marriage hardly startles one more than the strange mingling of sober fact, real psychological penetration, pseudo-science, poetic tenderness, practical masculinity, sensuality, and religious mysticism in Michelet's picture of it? Balzac had frankly admitted that his book was a temptation of the devil.[10] It was indeed such; and his particular devil was full of the old "esprit gaulois" and of its cynical cruelty.

Michelet's was also a temptation, but it was a temptation of Michelet's own "Satan," his transmuted "Satan." This spirit of persistent denial of the "sterile" religion of saints and ascetics, this champion of life triumphant, this glorified Satan had led our quite too human prophet up to a high mountain-top of idealism and showed him from there all the kingdoms of the world, and all these kingdoms were to be found—in the heart of a woman! There man's heart might be remade. This vast domain he would find was not only one of glory, but one of tremendous responsibility, which would be revealed by the fulness of woman's vision and by her sense of pity, for love would show her the world's great need and she would demand the satisfaction for it. Her cry would be for a remade world:

A harmonious world of order, of sweetness and of peace, a city of happiness where I shall not have to weep, where the

<hr>

[9] *L'amour*, livre II, chap. vi; livre IV, chaps. vi–viii.

[10] H. Balzac, Introduction to the *Physiologie du mariage*. Any one interested in verbal "sources" could find matter of comment in comparing certain phrases of this introduction and the opening pages of *L'amour*.

felicity of all may crown my own, for, tell me, what peace could
I find in this sweet nest if I should suffer there from the need to
pity? I would almost hate my happiness.

Whereupon the proclamation goes forth:

In the name of woman, sovereign of all the earth, man
is commanded to change the earth. To make of it a place of
justice, of peace, of happiness, and bring heaven down to
dwell therein! [11]

But it is soon apparent that this feminine " sovereign of
the earth" reigns through her incapacity to reign. The
sovereignty of woman, Michelet seemed to show, like
that of the people, sprang from her combined weakness
and strength; therefore man's self-protection depended
upon his protection of her. The social life and the married life were not to be the "association des égoismes"
save in the sense that they should be the association of
needs for guidance, and of the necessity to guide. The
force of woman's demands must be met, her influence must
be reckoned with, history had shown it; each man must
make it his personal affair and it was in the family that
this influence must be exercised. Love set to woman's
service was love set to the service of humanity.

So fundamental a truth could not be set forth as simply
as this, however. Michelet considered that it would have
to be carefully hedged about with reservations. For him,
as for the Saint-Simonists of the beginning of the century,
the formula (although he had not stated it in so many
words) "the social individual is the man and the woman,"[12]
was absolutely true. "A woman who lives alone, has not,
morally speaking, any life." But where other interpreters
of the formula had found in it the demand of some political
and social independence for woman, Michelet interpreted
it as a formula which defined clearly and definitely the

[11] *L'amour*, pp. 64–65.   [12] H. Louvancour, *op. cit.*, p. 255.

interdependence of man and woman. Marriage must become. a relation so exclusive, a state where the mutual
intellectual and moral demands of husband and wife
would be so great, that the individuality of each would
be strained to the utmost in order to meet these demands.
Marriage would ultimately take on a sanctity which
would make of it the transforming force of the entire
social life—"If I were a woman, I would know how to
make myself loved—by asking much." [13]

So much of love and sacrifice this ideal woman demands: so much this ideal husband is ready to give, that
one has to make a vast imaginative effort in order to
picture what the great common social life would be with
such closely organized units as its basis. "The social
individual is a couple," the Saint-Simonists had said;
Michelet seemed rather to put it: "The couple is a social
individual." So it was! chained together by very imperative demands of mutual sacrifice and service.

Michelet's interpretation of love had already been con-
cisely given by La Rochefoucauld: "Love is in the soul a
passion to rule: in the mind, sympathy: and in the body
a hidden and delicate desire to possess what one loves." [14]
.Meredith's *Egoist*, whose dream it was to shut out for
once and always "the world" from his own life and from
that of the woman he marries, holds an ideal not more
exclusive than the mutual devotion which Michelet's two
ideal beings would be forced to impose upon themselves
in order to lend to marriage its full meaning. Such marriage would seem in the nature of things to prevent all
sharing in outside life. This, however, was not Michelet's
thought. Marriage was to teach sacrifice, and then to
put it to general service. He so represents it in his letter
of the 20th of January, 1849, to Mlle. Miarlet: "Yes, *la
grande amitié* can only embrace all humanity if it has

[13] *La femme*, p. 243.
[14] Maxime LXVIII (cited by E. Seillière in articles on Michelet).

been first born in the heart of man. Let the spark of sacred fire which will be handed on be first kindled in the hidden hearth, it will but glow the more warmly." Therefore, having closely drawn this charmed circle of intimate service, Michelet suddenly breaks it, and signals a "loud knocking at the gate" of the carefully guarded domain of married life. "Who knocks?" "The struggle of life!" [15] One might ask how, with hands so manacled by the chains of constant service and with feet grown, through domestic devotion, so unaccustomed to walk the public ways, it would be possible to meet the demands of this intruder, the wider life! This Michelet did not explain—taking it for granted that the mere learning of the lesson of love and sacrifice in marriage would be the lesson that was needed for the larger social life,—the lesson that would encompass all.

In the pictures that he drew of the family in other countries, he considered that the English wife had learned her lesson best and that the English Protestant home, for the moment, was the most nearly perfect. Protestantism was in his eyes a "mere matter of transition"; it held, nevertheless, for the family, the secret which gave it its real unchangeable nature. Michelet found this secret in the fact that the Protestant marriage was based upon the "union of two," with no intervention from without. "God," he said, "may have been mistaken in thus founding it, many will deny that he ever did so found it, and will defend the family of three, in which the intruder is authority itself, creating a discord justified by law; it is systematized divorce. In "the family of three" the hearthstone was "hung in mid air, with nothing to give it surety and support." There could exist then, in a society with a family so organized, no real unity, no peace, no national security.

Where the family included the third member (the

[15] *L'amour*, pp. 262–263.

priest), such understanding as existed in the English family was impossible. In the English family also, wives were trained to respond quickly to any demand, to be ready for any adventure, for any need of life.[16] When the call for instant flight across two continents came, it found the English wife quite prepared: "Just a moment, my dear, I must put on my hat," was the only comment on the call. It was thus that England had made her great colonial conquests, and thus she had held them. The German wife's obedience was admirable, but too passive. The absence of passivity in the French woman, her "resiliency" could make of her the perfect wife in the family organized as it should be. In the "family of three" it was a menace.

"The French woman is a person, very strong both for good and bad," wrote Michelet. She was such by nature, by breeding and by training, such by the French laws of inheritance which gave her economic independence. All this could have made the abdication of all of her personal demands, the giving of herself, a very precious thing; but what had really happened was that it had made such abdication very rare. The French marriage would have been the perfect one if the French woman had only been trained to understand it. But the past, Michelet insisted, laid grappling hands upon her. She did not bring to her husband undivided allegiance. "French mothers are terrible," was the historian's conclusion.[17] Their demands for continued authority, their insistence upon exclusive affection, their desire to hold all the economic reins of the family organization, drew the French wife back into the family she was supposed to have left, her

---

[16] *La femme*, p. 340. At other moments Michelet refused to the English family the same unity which he found in the French family, because of the relegation of English children to their "nurseries."

[17] *L'amour*, p. 89.

sympathies and her interests held her there, while her husband was forced to go on towards the future and fuller life alone; unless he too, in discouragement, sank back into the quiet of non-resistance.

A curious thing in France, contradictory in appearance, but not really so, is this,—marriage is a very weak tie, and the spirit of the family is very strong. It happens especially that in the provincial bourgeoisie, a woman who has been married for some time divides her soul in half, giving one half to her children, the other to her parents. What does the husband keep? Nothing. Here the spirit of the family annuls marriage.

One can hardly imagine how tiresome the woman is, sinking back into the dead past, imbued with old ideas. The husband lives calmly, but he quickly changes for the worse. He will lose whatever ideas he had gained by study and comradeship that might have helped him forward toward the future. [18]

The only true marriage, Michelet claimed, was the one in which the husband could catch up and carry away the woman he loved. The wife, in order to live the life which was the "new life," illumined by science and by new social hopes, would have to be as clay in the hands of her Promethean husband in order that he might remake her for the changing world, transformed from day to day by wider knowledge and by higher hopes.[19] The French woman did not lend herself easily to this process of re-modeling. And Michelet was divided between his admiration for her resistance and the problem that it offered.[20] He found no other solution than to advise that marriage should be quite freed from all economic complications, that it should cease to be either a quickly made or a hard fought bargain. In order to be sure that his wife was quite his own, the French husband might best take her

[18] *La femme*, p. 12.
[19] *L'amour*, pp. 93–97.
[20] *La femme*, pp. 224, 229.

with no fortune and with no family.[21] The lack of fortune is a requirement that is easily met in almost any state of life, for the historian hesitated to counsel the venturing outside the established social lines, but the difficulty of assuring freedom from all family entanglements is greater. As someone has pointed out, "it is not given to everyone to be born an orphan!"

As I have just remarked, Michelet did not easily admit that the ideal marriage might overstep recognized social lines. This would risk its ideal happiness. But for the great rôle that marriage might play in forming national character and in bringing the world over to the French ideal there were no bounds he would not overstep. As he saw the France of the Revolution instinctively reaching out toward all the nations of Europe to bestow on them her newly formed social and political ideals, so he foresaw the France of succeeding ages carrying French life to the uttermost parts of the earth. He still conceived of her, as he had seen her in her origins, as the great Gallic cauldron into which the life of the world is poured, and out of which it flowed; by which the life of every race was bound to be renewed and which was to send out life to remake the world. The white man's burden might, he seemed to think, be reduced to a simple question of mating, undeterred by sensitiveness in regard to race feeling.[22]

Indeed more than once he pointed out how race prejudice had caused the English to be strangers in their own colonies and had created a hostile India; how America, which might have been the land of a great new composite race, "a vigorous mulatto people," had become a vast caravansary subject to chance and hazard, unguided by purpose or understanding; where any safe assurance of future life was impossible because there was no future race there

[21] La femme, pp. 12–13, 68–69; Le peuple, pp. 232–240.
[22] La femme, 205–218.

in the making. The huge dream that he suggested of marriage as Loti has painted it, infinitely multiplied over all the surface of the earth, is one which no one but he could have seen so transformed and idealized as he was able to idealize it, by pity and "understanding." "All Frenchmen are born a Paul or a René," [23] ready to protect and pity—to love and to make one's own, as a matter of course—a woman of any color or of any climate. The men of other nations had left behind them wherever they have gone the hatred engendered by slavery and oppression, while René could leave behind him only affection and an infinite regret!

This remarkable manner of pleading the cause of pacific colonization and world conquest, was characteristic of the Michelet who was the champion of life,—it was but the crowning proof of his boundless respect for life. The sudden opening of the closely guarded walls of idealism in which he had enclosed his poetic picture of the perfect marriage, to let all the winds of heaven and of the underworld blow through, is the most curious example of how his sense of the triumphant force of universal life, came in the end to take ascendancy over every judgment, prejudice or reservation that would otherwise have seemed to him inviolable.

Life, he maintained, was sacred in all forms. Through all the universe one great impulse ran, and it was divine. That Christianity should have laid it under a heavy curse and then redeemed it, was the double proof of the injustice and presumption of the Church. In his unbounded unreserved reverence for this great impulse of life, of which he felt the throb and beat within himself and which he thought made him akin even to the farthest stars, the assumption of an authority which could judge and condemn life seemed to him a sacrilege. It was the domina-

[23] *La Régence*, pp. 167–172.

tion of something purposely malignant setting itself up in authority over the divine.[24]

It was this adoration of life which led him to condemn Christianity and all its works. And he directed his attacks, naturally, at its dogma of original sin. Psychology had not taught him what it is supposed to have learned since about instincts and emotions, and therefore Michelet could fight the dogma in the name of "human justice" itself. He chose to look upon it as a formula designed to hoodwink humanity, and most of all, as a malignant attack upon the dignity of woman—a curse, it seemed to him, which had been laid on her, which must rob her in her own sight of all sense of human worth, of all respect for life and thus of the courage which could help her to ennoble life. It could but take from her all initiative, all desire to associate herself with the universal social impulse of a world in the constantly renewed effort of creative social life. The dogma was for him a morally paralyzing and deadening spell which priests had used to get human life within their power or put it under ban.

It was Michelet's joy to predict what a transformation the lifting of the ban would bring and to show that it was the mission of the hero-husband to free woman from such bondage; to show her that all life was a joyous struggle against a lifeless submission to spiritual domination.[25] He was to be the Perseus who should snatch the captive Andromeda away from all the forces armed to destroy her. But by this rescuer the greatest dangers were to be met after the bold act of rescue had been accomplished. Nothing could be harder to destroy than memories of the past, haunting fears, and terrors of captivity, and these still would continue to beset the woman. He must conquer them and strengthen himself by his resistance, and

[24] *Le peuple,* 170–177; *Nos fils,* Introduction; *L'amour,* pp. 111 ff.; and notes 3 and 4, pp. 439 ff.
[25] *L'amour,* pp. 394–395.

lend this strength to her. Her weakness itself was a force which would overcome him unless he made it his. Eternal vigilance was the price of the happiness that he would find himself forced to guard constantly and well.[26]

A woman takes possession of a man when he least is conscious of it. "At first it is like a thread that a spider casts out to float loosely in the wind, but which may catch and closely cling: then the tendrils of a vine from whose close little fingers it is hard to break away, and in the end it may come to be as the vine itself which sends its roots deep down into the very heart of the tree; to cut it out you must dig out the heart itself." If, however, man could make this strength his, it was a force by which his own could be continually renewed. "The poor child, alas! is all ignorance. She has learned only what it is necessary to forget. Her heart, her charm would only avail to ruin both of you, and your child and your future, if from the very first day you should not take upon yourself the authority that learning and knowledge give." [27]

This ideal of the "heroic marriage" was indeed heroic. It would mean a hard fight to dominate an influence which had made and unmade the destinies of the world. For woman, so Michelet stated, had always been man's judge in the end. Man's victory must be complete and final or he would discover that she had passed condemnatory sentence upon him: and that would mean for him just infinite despair and the hopeless confusion of all life. Conquer and dominate then, both the weakness and the strength of woman! [28]

This is an old tale, many times told. Here Michelet retold it, in a new way it must be admitted, but still it is an old tale. Shakespeare's Katherine tells it too in her own way; but however differently she comes to it, she

[26] *L'amour*, pp. 168–182.
[27] *Ibid.*, pp. 156–157; livre II, chap. viii.
[28] *L'amour*, pp. 94–95.

ends with much the same warning, and her admonitions
are Michelet's own:

" Thy husband is thy lord, thy life, thy keeper
Thy head, thy sovereign, one that cares for thee
And for thy maintenance commits his body
To painful labor, both by sea and land,
And craves no other tribute at thy hands
But love, fair looks, and true obedience.
Why are our bodies soft, and weak, and smooth—
Unapt to toil and trouble in the world,
But that our soft condition and our hearts
Should well agree with our external parts? "

It is with no desire to mock at Michelet that I suggest
how simply Shakespeare saw the thing done for which the
French writer had recruited all the forces of heaven, of
earth. It is to show how fundamentally the historian's conception had transformed the old tradition of "true obedience" and had freed it from all trace of the traditional
cynical banter; his insistence upon the duty of the husband
—the duty of assuring himself an unquestioned authority
—is untouched by it. Petruchio's use of other means than
"knowledge" and "understanding" quite in the spirit of
the old fabliaux and of all popular tradition, was a solution which could not for a moment be admissible to
Michelet's idealistic interpretation of the necessity of
woman's glad and wholehearted submission to education
in sacrifice and love.

But this submission, however glad it might be, must
be complete. Michelet's theory of marriage was built not
only upon respect for human personality, but also upon
reverence for what he believed was woman's capacity for
service and sacrifice. "Every woman's folly is a result of
man's stupidity." By this formula Michelet carried the
responsibility of Katherine's waywardness back to the
neglect and carelessness of man, who had been too content

to be either browbeaten or a woman-beater! Such logical and inevitable stubbornness as hers would naturally necessitate in its turn a continuance of the outworn Petruchio type. Some other way would have to be found to real understanding, and it was man's duty to find it.

Michelet's respect for woman's personality was in proportion to her willingness to sacrifice it. Man must teach therefore to woman the value of sacrifice, and life should be so organized as to make the sacrifice seem easy. The modern hero, face to face with the woman fashioned by him, was to realize that "whoever strikes a woman, even if it be only with a flower," was guilty of unpardonable violence (unless, added Michelet, she herself should feel the need of a husband's churlishness to free her from womanish weakness, and from obsessions: then she might be granted a gentle blow or two).[29] Her only discipline was to be found in love and understanding and, if need be, in infinite forgiveness. That the tyranny of such exalted reverence for woman might find subtle means of fastening upon her an intellectual and moral inferiority which she might perhaps find as hard to bear as the imputation of a physical one,[30] would in no wise have dismayed Michelet. For he regarded the relations of men and women from the man's point of view. A pitying reverence for woman could only ennoble the devotion and service of the husband for the wife, and through the husband's added dignity, exalt the institution of marriage.

[29] *L'amour*, pp. 327, 508.

[30] Michelet's pity for the negro had undoubtedly been deepened by the reading of *Uncle Tom's Cabin*, which he mentions at the beginning of *L'amour*. Michelet's ardor for the faith in the universal brotherhood of man led him to seek encouragement in all evidence that could help him believe in the possibility of the modification of races and of physical characteristics: cf. *La femme*, pp. 206–217.—At the Williams College Institute of Politics, on August 13, 1922, Dr. Manuel de Oliveira Lima is reported to have announced the success in Brazil of the miscegenation of races.

This conquest of woman's perfect obedience, however, was but the beginning of a discipline which would insure her full participation in a life made up of aspirations and of untiring effort. All life and effort were in Michelet's eyes a religion, and for the married life there were to be rituals and sacraments which should mark its holiness. "Marriage is confession—the conjugal confession (a sacrament of the future) is the essence of marriage; one will feel that marriage has for its object to pour out into another soul every day without reserve, one's ideas, one's feeling, the telling of all one's affairs, so that one keeps nothing to oneself." This ideal of marriage, fed by a reverence for life, a reverence for man's own power to love, full of the sense of his love as a manifestation of God himself, was the one according to which Michelet seems to have endeavored to live; an ideal which, he believed, would bring to man and woman a sense of the sacredness of their mission as arbiters of human destiny.[31]

Confession as the discipline of marriage, so he said, he had taken from the "shadowed mysterious half lights" of the confessional and had installed it by the fireside. But confession was only one of many rites by which the spiritual life of woman should be formed and guided. The husband must take upon himself the oversight of the reading and of all the intellectual activities of his wife. The husband and wife must pray together, drawing their prayers from their own hearts. They must meditate together in a common endeavor to find their way to a common belief and to a worship of the God whose life was their own life and the life of all. That such worship could not find expression in great public ceremonials was a source of continued regret to Michelet. Until the "temple" for this worship had been built out of universal

---

[31] *La femme*, p. 347. Michelet disapproved of divorce, but admits that great unhappiness might justify it.

understandings and aspirations,[32] the fireside would have
to be the only altar:

> In this eclipse between the old and the new, let each man
> every day make for himself his own religion.
> The world is looking for prayers. It cannot find them.
> God is willing that it should not find them in order that it
> may make them. He wishes that the torn heart should be its
> own remedy. The modern man in his necessity has the habit
> of imploring himself first of all, of appealing to his own energy,
> he no longer waits idly for material help to come from on
> high. He is right and he is wrong. Right, as acting; wrong in
> not looking upward. Prayer is still the great necessity of the
> world, as a harmonization of man with God. It reconstitutes
> our unity with him.[33]

Michelet wrote these lines two days after the death of
the child born of his second marriage. At the mother's
anxious request the boy had been baptized. The comments which follow show how all his aspirations were set
toward stamping out forever all doubts as to the innocence
of life. He felt that only the knowledge of its scientific
laws could bring this assurance and establish the sanctity
of life and love. Woman then must be led to study life
and to know that wherever life was found, it was but the
manifestation of the love of God. Such discovery would
lead her, as he believed that it had led him, to stand at
last before the very face of God.

Thus guided, she would learn that every child born of
a love so enlightened, was born to be a saviour of the
great common life: and she would attain to real respect
for the courage that makes of living the effort to fulfill the
great tasks which are the realization of God's power. By
her understanding she would be able to impart courage
and strength to all life about her. How could a woman
but hail as a saviour the man that should bring her such

---

[32] *La femme*, 362–366.   [33] G. Monod, *J. M.*, 289.

revelation, freeing her from superstitions and from all degraded scorn of herself!

But, to be the saviour born for such a mission of enlightenment, men would find it necessary to have the strength to fight all the battles of life, of which one of the most difficult was woman's battle against herself and against a world still in bondage to tradition. If he came armed with youth and all the authority that his own victories brought with them, then all the victories of the modern life would ennoble the love that he received:

She loves you because of Linnaeus and the mystery of flowers, she loves you for the diamonds of heaven that Galileo first saw, she loves in you even the sciences of death which have taught us the profound secret of love, and which, against the barbarous impiety of barbarous times have said, Woman is pure! [34]

Of such love God was ever born anew, said Michelet. The old Jewish traditional hope of a saviour might, if people would, receive its daily realization. Every child born of noble love and nourished in such love would be a Messiah, come to save.

If the child were not God, if the relation between his mother and himself were not a religion, he would not live, if there were not in this mother the marvelous idolatry that renders him divine! What is magnificent and really divine is that he is so rich in life, that he lends it liberally to all objects. He is a creator! [35]

And so the living chain of life would be wrought. God being constantly revealed by this triumph of life which in its triumph was tender and full of the noble impulse to set itself to the humble task of service, to reveal the joy of sacrifice. To plant this instinct in the hearts of children would become the glory and duty of man and

[34] *L'amour*, pp. 96–97.   [35] *La femme*, p. 81.

woman. It was by seeing daily sacrifice that children might learn their lessons of sacrifice and of duty; it was for this that the family existed.

Family life lived thus would be a means of strengthening what is nobler than anything else in human nature: "the noble temptation of subordinating nature herself, of dominating liberty by a liberty that is higher still, that of willing effort and sacrifice."

The will, then, to work in love was, according to Michelet, the lesson to be learned in every hero-household, the learning of this lesson was God in the process of self-revelation. Mankind might learn thus to know itself—to be divine; to know that the sum of human effort could work harmoniously, in so far as it worked in love and sympathy with nature, and could thus give renewed strength to the Godhead which was the source of life. Man filled with this sense that existence was the supremely divine gift, would know when he saw a smile play on his child's lips in answer to the smile on the mother's face bent over him, that this was a light which came direct from God, he would know that his child and God were one; "He did not know that a God would be born to him. There is nothing left for him but to fall upon his knees." The study of the mysterious life of his child would teach him the beginnings of those things that he would have to learn from the study of the universe itself.

He would come thus at last to learn that the universal Providence was a mother of infinitely protective gentleness. "Providence is a mother, she is afraid of being too strong. Her infinite force, instead of over-riding weakness, wills that weakness shall be a force." [36] It was the necessity of protecting the weakness of the mother and child which had put power into the aspirations and ideals of the social world. The necessity for the protection of weakness had made a social force of weakness itself.

Every mother the source of divine life, every child the

direct expression of God himself! Such was the burden
of this dithyrambic defense and this mystical glorification
of motherhood. It was the heart of Michelet's message.
It was, so to speak, a democratization of "Messianism,"
making of life everywhere an incarnation of the divine.
The world must be trained to see that each new life born
of understanding and love brought the revelation of the
God in expectation of which the world had always lived.

The recognition of this fact would bring to the world
its salvation. As the importance of this message grows
in Michelet's imagination, he seems to take on for the
reader's imagination the aspect of a Michelet-Ezekiel; the
Ezekiel of Michael-Angelo as Michelet himself described
him in his *Renaissance*, shaken by a great zeal, aglow with
an intense fervor.[36] The prophet is "casting defiance in
the teeth of all those who have said that the sources of
life are not all infinitely pure!"

Such was the revelation of Michelet's mission as he saw
it. It shows the over-emphasis of the polemic orator who
attacks all accepted religions, the zeal of the reformer who
attacks unintelligent tradition, and the enthusiasm of the
idealist who would make of life a thing of beauty and
dignity.

This once admitted, the judgment that one feels oneself
called to render is already largely implied. There are
several comments, however, that may be made. First,
it might be noted that what more than anything else
may have contributed to give a certain air of ambiguity
to Michelet's treatment of woman and marriage is the
uncritical use which he makes of the word love.[37] It has
already been noted that certain sects of Michelet's period
(as has happened in almost all ages) had been led to bizarre

---

[36] Also in *Nos fils*, Introduction. "Dieu est une mère," etc. *Les
Jésuites*, p. 336.

[37] This may perhaps be best studied in the "Notes et éclaircissements" of *L'amour*.

extremes through their contention that life was of God, and that love was the source of life. Michelet's thesis had this in common with these "reformers": the belief that the dogmas of the Church, as interpreted in its discipline, had taken hope and belief in life, and all the vigor that could be derived from them, out of the possession of the social world; they claimed that this belief was a right of which current tradition tended to defraud them. But while the more extreme of these innovators had gone further and made of this claim an attack upon the family, Michelet, on the other hand, tried to use it as a means of ennobling the conception of marriage and the institution of the family. The discipline of passion he found not in disbelief in passion and in disrepect for woman, but in respect for life and in a reverential pity for woman; both of which attitudes he believed might be inculcated by a study of the sciences of life. And his contention was that the knowledge derived from such study should be made a part of an intelligent preparation for life.

There is nothing to be gained by trying to determine what ground of truth or falsity there may have been in Michelet's claim that the Church had diminished the dignity of life. The chief interest to be found in his polemic is that it makes a consistent chapter in the exposition of his belief that the disciplinary power of human energy and impulse was to be sought in a lofty conception of all human relationships, indeed in all relationships in which life is a factor. There is, however, it must be confessed, an unpleasantly false note to be found in his presentation of this belief. His picture of the family based upon a religion of sacrifice and service, finding its dignity in the intelligent compromises and in the self discipline that human relationship inevitably imposes, would have carried more authority if it had been content to paint just this. His presentation of it as a picture of sheer delight showed at moments errors in taste and was misleading in a degree by far too apparent. That he should have met protests from those who found that the rôle of "hero-husband" was beyond them, is not surprising. They might more easily have believed in the reality of duty than in the promise of a life compact of exalted beauty. Hesitation might well have lurked in the mind of any woman before she would consent to confide unquestioningly all her moral and intellectual destinies to an unyielding authority, just for the joy that there might be found in such surrender! Or if there were no preliminary hesitation, there might well have ensued subsequent disappointment. Michelet's manuals on woman and marriage strike one as being neither entirely frank nor strictly honest, although sometimes curiously indiscreet. Therefore, they ran the risk sometimes of making an appeal by what was least noble in them.

But there was much that was uplifting in them. The family ideal that they present, stripped of some of its trappings, is a conception which has probably been that of all decent folk who have tried to make of marriage a part of right living, without necessarily consenting, however, to make of service and sacrifice a mutual tyranny. But such folk have always found it possible to live in all the relations of life *with* religion, without making of any of these relationships *a* religion. Michelet has the air of preaching human love as *a* religion.

In his pictures of life as it existed and of life as he hoped that it might become, he showed all the contradictions that a man is bound to show when he insists that all should be changed in spirit, and yet has not attempted to divine all that might logically result from such change. In his theories in regard to the family, as elsewhere, he shows evidence of having been an unquestioning revolutionary lodged in the same personality as an uncompromising conservative. He could not conceive of a highly

developed individuality save as set to ennobling service.
But he refused to relinquish any of the nobility and aus-
terity of the French tradition of unquestioned patriarchal
authority. He clung to this tradition with the more ardor
in that he found in it a powerful auxiliary for the realization of a future in which all priestly authority might be
suppressed. He insisted on it the more strongly because
he knew that in France the tradition had weakened, having yielded to many potent influences. As the result of
various causes—of which he emphasized among others
the economic factor—the French woman had become "a
person" and had to be reckoned with.

In his insistence upon the necessity of a husband's authority, there were perhaps reasons less worthy than the
demand that affection should be its basis, and the absolute contention that it would insure community of
sympathy and belief. There lurked in it, seemingly, the
instinctive jealousy of the male, as well as the jealousy
which a highly wrought sensibility can render so acute
when intensified, as it was in his case, by an imperative
sense of the need for an immediate response to sentiment
and emotion. All of this, plus the practical reason, which
made him consider that the husband's authority should
be absolute (thus leaving no access to the domination of
the director) received in his eyes its supreme justification
through his sympathy with what the French call the
"Germanic" idealization of woman. This is the apotheosis
of womanhood which consists in attributing to woman a

superhuman dignity, since she is the instrument of man's self-exaltation and self-perpetuation, even while she is denied the ordinary personal, intellectual and moral independence which might be supposed to be the right of any human being. Therefore, as he himself said, he was accused (might he not well be?) of having "chained her to the altar that he had erected for her worship."

Thus Michelet may be said to have ended by refusing to woman as an individual just that which he had demanded for her with such eloquence: the indefeasible right of unrestricted personal dignity. The tyranny of sentiment, moreover, compromised not only the ideal that he framed, but the beauty of the picture which he drew of that ideal.

The historian had put a characteristic emphasis upon the importance of the rôle of sex. He naturally discussed it as a determining element in every detail and phase of the organization and development of the family. In his poetically symbolical and mythical interpretation of life, religion and nationalism it lent him often the figurative language which he seemed to find most full of meaning. In the relations between nations he detected "the hatred which there is in love." Religions he defined as "masculine" and "feminine." The religion of the Church being in his eyes "feminine,"—a "religion of grace"—he strove to replace it by a "masculine" faith founded on "justice."[38]

It has been noted that in the *History of France* he had represented the family, religion and society as having been, in a certain sense, woman-ridden, and that he had tried to show that throughout the whole course of history woman had been denied that respect and regard which could justify and safeguard her influence,—a respect

---

[38] Michelet's characterization of Christianity as a religion which owes "nothing to man," is to be found in his *Bible*, pp. 431–458. For his prediction that the future cult would restore the "pontificat domestique," *ibid.*, p. 382, note.

based upon an intelligent understanding of life which alone might ennoble her as it would ennoble man to bestow this respect upon her. He wrote in his *Bible de l'humanité:* "But how vague and obscure is this word Love without justice. The love of caprice and favor may become the scourge of the City!" Man alone seemed to him strong enough to hold with steady hand the scales of "Justice!"

In considering the accusation that the historian allowed his imagination to be unduly swayed by his recognition of the importance of the influence of sex, it must be remembered that he lived in an epoch in which all sciences of life had taken on for many serious minds an exalted rôle not only because they gave wisdom and knowledge, but because they were supposed to promise revelations and hopes which they have not wholly realized. Michelet's interest in physiological matters and pathological problems had been increased by association with men who sought lofty revelation in the sciences of the forces of life. In his consideration of life in all of its phases his earnestness and nobility seem equally apparent in spite of possible exaggerations and errors of taste and

[39] Cf. *La femme*, pp. 207–218. In the notes to *L'amour* it emerges that this book was written with certain preoccupations occasioned by the decline of the French birth rate. Cf. pp. 433 ff.

Exaggerations, possibly errors of judgment, surely errors of taste abound in Michelet's interpretations. But they seem to arise from excess of zeal rather from a lack of nobility of feeling. One is sometimes inclined to ask oneself whether one would find proof of greater or less nobility in the conviction that some of his rhapsodies were spontaneous rather than intentional. They were undoubtedly written with the belief that the appeal to emotions of pity could only touch the noblest chords of human feeling. Stirred by the reading of *Uncle Tom's Cabin* or by reports of difficulties in efforts in colonization, he wrote pages which seem variants of Chateaubriand's exotic pictures. They are evidence of the writer's tendency to have recourse to appeals that are over-done rather than indications of his capacity for emotions that are over-wrought.

judgment.[39] His optimistic belief that all human feeling had evinced a continuously developed self-disciplinary power which had set it to the tasks of service and had taught it the value of voluntary sacrifice, made it easy for him to lend to his celebration of life and of love—in *La mer* for instance,—a note of fervid enthusiasm. He had carried this note into his study of human love and marriage.

These are some of the considerations which in Michelet's Ideas upon Marriage gave rise to various contradictions and exaggerations. It has been seen that underlying them all, one can trace the fundamental thought which we have had constant occasion to study. It comes to the surface in the end, however great the confusion which obscures it, and it does the historian honor.

The Michelet-Ezekiel, thunderous with his admonitions about the sacredness of "the forces of life and generation" over-emphasized certain accents and dwelt too long on certain notes. Michelet the artist drew pictures of family life which, although full of charm, do not seem at first glance to express in its full beauty the sacredness of life which the historian cherished with a mystic's exaltation. The mingling of a Correggio's delicate grace, with the banal loveliness of Greuze, or with the humble beauty of the commonplace which it was sometimes Chardin's gift to render, suggests intermittently something much less real, at any rate much less noble, than Michelet's earnestness. The woman who moves through his pages,—a being who appears from time to time wearing the sophisticated grace of a Devéria portrait, seems perhaps not just the woman who could lift to its loftiest heights a family religion and hold it there.

They may not present the most convincing support for his arguments concerning racial intermixture, but they do reveal his belief that such intermixture should be based upon the respect for the human person rather than upon scorn of it.

Such discrepancy is due probably not only to the inter-mixture of biographical data and of poetical idealization which is constantly to be found in Michelet's work. It was due as well to his conviction that life in any manifestation was worthy of all the idealization which one could lend it. There was no accepted phase of family relationships as humanity had developed them, incapable of being invested with a reverence compact of religiosity.

It was not only the sway exercised over him in the last half of his life by a "fine et pétulante personne" through the adoration she evoked, which can explain the conviction that Michelet put into his insistence upon the supreme importance of investing the husband's mission with a lofty authoritativeness and a protective tenderness, although it may well explain the fervor of the idealist who, after having often abdicated his idealism, found himself at last in possession of much which corresponded to his ideal. Nor yet can the polemic anticlericalism of the historian wholly account for the emphasis which he put upon the necessity of clothing the husband's rôle with a pontifical dignity which could lend to all the rites of daily life a potent and peculiar grace. It sprang from his fundamental belief that the full recognition of the dignity of the individual could impart to that sacrifice of individualism which life imposes, a significance which properly understood would afford the needed understanding of social life as mutual service and sacrifice gladly rendered.

This thesis that life must be respected, that the individual must be accorded all the consideration that individual and social dignity demands, is everywhere to be found (albeit somewhat unevenly defended) in the poetical and vaguely mythical flights of fancy in which Michelet's social homilies were often dissolved, obscured and sometimes, seemingly, lost. Such respect was the basis of his demand for scientific and enlightened education in regard to sex, for his protest against an easy dismissal of the problem which prostitution offered, and against the light acceptance of social conventions and individual ideals which could diminish social and individual dignity. It suggested to him methods such as are actually used in what is known in charity organizations as "case work,"— a patient personal study of each individual case of mental or moral suffering. It formed the basis of his plea that social regeneration should be inaugurated by the only means he found for its accomplishment, by individual regeneration.

But if one reads the historian's pronouncements on marriage as a consideration of the means of ordering society in a way best fitted to insure the happiness and well being of man and woman as individuals, one is left with a sense of lack of steadfastness, despite the flashes of psychological insight which they display, despite the wisdom and thoughtfulness which they often evince. They translate loftiness of aspiration, but the man who is offered as an example seems to have torn much of his dignity into tatters in order to dress out woman in a disordered bravery which becomes her less perhaps than garments she might have fashioned from her own self-respect.

There is, however, another approach to Michelet's insistence upon absolute community of sympathy and thought between husband and wife which brings one to a more vital sense of what its meaning implied to him. His emphasis upon the need of perfect conformity of an intelligent will and purpose in the "social individual" is more intelligible when one realizes that it was the expression of his belief that such conformity alone could insure "a world of harmony" where childhood might receive proper protection and well-being. Viewed in this light whatever may be one's opinion of the premises upon which the historian based his contentions, one respects them—even to the passion with which he urged them.

When one recalls Michelet's hunger for some faith which would be sustaining in that it would give him assurance that all the past of humanity had not been lived in vain, and would satisfy him as a pledge that the present and the future demanded man's best effort; and when one reflects that he found it in the faith that all forms of service, sacrifice and all noble human self-expression entered into the fabric of human life and enduringly ennobled it, one can fathom somewhat the religious reverence which he felt for childhood, the profound importance which he lent to his consideration of parenthood, and the significance which the family assumed in his eyes as the school of service and sacrifice where the ideals of national and international relations are first glimpsed in the homely acts of every day life.

What he had to say upon the need of care concerning all prenatal education and of the rôle which sincerity and nobility of feeling played as beneficent influences upon the life of children born and unborn, had been said before him and has been often said since. His speculations seemed to touch on matters with which the new born science of eugenics is said to be concerned. They were perforce vague and fragmentary but the importance of all considerations which could benefit life as a whole was necessarily a preoccupation with him. The recognition of the helplessness and sensitiveness of childhood as constituting an appeal of which the social rôle had been great and was destined to become greater, had been as whole-heartedly admitted by others as by himself. But it had been admitted with a significance somewhat other than that which he seems to have lent it. For him its significance was supreme.

Michelet's regard for human life held the profound reverence which the Christian puts into his reverence for God. It held all the steadfastness and exaltation which the Christian may derive from his faith in immortality.

Therefore, as has been noted, he saw the existence of each individual as full of a pathetic grace because as the individual expression of an infinite and universal aspiration, it was brief and incomplete, but full of beauty and promise because it was. The life of each child implied therefore a responsibility of incalculable importance. It demanded to be studied reverently and with all possible understanding.

The *Oiseau* translated poetically this religious respect for life and for the forces by which it was maintained and transmitted from individual to individual, imparting to the whole scheme of existence an infinite hope:

"J'aime à tire d'aile du nid au nid, de l'œuf à l'œuf, de l'amour à l'amour de Dieu!"

Michelet's version of his conception of the holiness of life one may name, as I have named it, the "democratization of Messianism," or, if you will, a mystical belief in life as the expression of the divine. It lends in any case a very special interest to any study of a personality whose boundless aspirations for the future led him to the belief that a boundless faith would find its justification in the knowledge and understanding of life. Such understanding would make of love, service and sacrifice the laws of life. But for the resolution of the fundamental problems of social life this prophet of the future had final recourse to the means suggested in that simple and very ancient prayer: Create in me a clean heart oh Lord, and renew a right spirit within me!

The sincerity with which Michelet seems to have proffered such prayers as this, gives dignity and a certain authoritativeness to the "message" which he brought to those who no longer found consolation in long accepted beliefs,—the message that there still remained for them the consolation, ancient, but ever new, to be found in "faith in faith," and that this faith might be woven solidly into the very fabric of daily life.

BIBLIOGRAPHY [1]

I

MICHELET'S WORKS

Précis de l'histoire moderne, 1827.—*Principes de la philosophie de l'histoire*, traduits de la *Scienza nuova* de J. B. Vico, précedés d'un discours sur le système et la vie de l'auteur, 1827.—*Discours d'ouverture* (dated in later editions 1830, but published as having been delivered in 1834).—*Introduction à l'histoire universelle*, 1831 (written 1830).—*Histoire Romaine*, 1ᵉ partie, *République*, 1831.—Luther, *Mémoires* (with preface), 1835.—*Œuvres choisies de Vico*, 2 vol., 1835.—*Origines du droit français*, cherchées dans les symbols et formules du droit universel, 1837.—*Fragment d'un mémoire sur l'éducation des femmes du moyen âge*, 1838 (published with *L'introduction à l'histoire universelle*, ed. 1843).—*Procès des Templiers*, 1841-1851.—*Des jésuites*, 1843.—*Du prêtre, de la femme, de la famille*, 1845.—*Le peuple*, 1846.—*L'étudiant*, 1847-1848.—*La Po-*

[1] The present bibliography makes no claim to being complete. It has been compiled with the purpose of presenting a fairly representative showing of the comment and interest which the historian's writings have evoked. It comprises most of those works by Michelet and of those works about him which have been consulted or utilized for this present study of the historian (for those portions of it as well which are not herewith published). Much of the criticism of avowedly controversial content has been excluded. On the other hand certain works by Mme. Michelet, Mickiewicz, Quinet and Mme. Quinet, not bearing directly on Michelet's output but more or less closely related to it, have been included in the list. The abreviations used in the bibliography, which may need explanation, are *R. D. M.* for *Revue des Deux Mondes*, *Rev. bl.* for *Revue bleue*, and *J. M.* for Monod's *Jules Michelet* (1905).

logne et la Russie, la légende de Kosciusko, 1851; Les martyrs de la Russie, 1852; Principautés danubiennes, 1853 (published together in 1854 as Les légendes démocratiques du nord, with a life of Madame Rosetti).—Les femmes de la Révolution, 1854.—L'oiseau, 1856.—L'insecte, 1857.— L'amour, 1858.—La femme, 1859.[2]—La mer, 1861.[2]—La sorcière, 1862.—La bible de l'humanité, 1864.—La montagne, 1868.— Nos fils, 1869.[2]—La France devant l'Europe, 1871.— Soldats de la Révolution, 1878.

L'Histoire de France, 19 vols. (8 vols. 1833–1844; 11 vols. 1855– 1867). The edition here cited is that of Calmann-Lévy, 1898–1899.—Important prefaces, introductions, etc., of the Histoire de France: General preface of 1869, vol. 1; " Eclaircissements," vol. 3, dated 1833; Preface of 1847, vol. 4; Introduction of La Renaissance, written in 1842, and a note " Sur la méthode," vol. 8; Preface, vol. 14; Preface dated 1863, vol. 17; Preface of 1866, vol. 18; preface of 1868, vol. 19.

L'Histoire de la Révolution française, 9 vols., 1847–1853.— Prefaces, etc.: Prefaces of 1847 and 1868, vol. 1; Appendix, " De la méthode et de l'esprit de ce livre," dated 1847, vol. 3; Preface of 1868, letters from Béranger and P.-J. Proudhon, vol. 4; Preface of 1869, vol. 7. (The edition cited is that of 1879.) L'Histoire de la Rév. is supplemented by L'Histoire du XIXme siècle, 1875–1876.

SOME OF THE WORKS PUBLISHED BY MADAME MICHELET UNDER THE NAME OF JULES MICHELET

Le banquet (Un hiver en Italie), papiers intimes, 1879.—Ma jeunesse, 1884 (with appendix, " La maison de Sedaine ""). —Mon journal, 1888.—Rome, 1891.—Sur les chemins de l'Europe, 1893. (Of these publications Le banquet may be possibly considered as Michelet's work, the Journal surely is such, according to G. Monod.)—Lettres inédites adressées à Mlle. Miarlet, 1899 (edited by Mme. M.) con-

---

[2] Unless otherwise indicated the edition of La femme here cited is that of 1885; of La mer, that of 1885; of L'amour, that of 1859 (The edition of 1920 has the same pagination); of Nos fils, 1870.

tains her replies; is preceded by preface by her, and interspersed with extracts from Michelet's *Journal intime.*

Works of Madame Athenaïs Miarlet-Michelet

Mémoires d'une enfant, 1866.— *Nature,* or the poetry of the earth and sea, 1872.— *La tombe de Michelet,* 1875.— *La mort et les funérailles de Michelet,* 1876.— *Ma collaboration à* L'oiseau, L'insecte, La mer, La montagne; *mes droits à la moitié de leurs produits,* 1876.— *Jules Michelet et sa famille,* 1878.— *Le centenaire de J. Michelet,* 1898.— *Les chats,* 1905.

II

Books and Articles by Other Writers

A. Albalat, " Michelet artiste," *La nouvelle Rev.,* 1899, pp. 276–285.

P. Albert, *La littérature au XIXme siècle,* 1885 (cours de 1876), pp. 61–78.

A. Alison, *Miscellaneous Essays,* " Michelet's France," 1878, pp. 184–195. Pub. in *Foreign and Quarterly Review,* April, 1844.

Ch. Aubertin, " L'histoire de Louis XV selon M. Michelet," *R. D. M.* 1866, 1er oct., vol. LXX, pp. 655–683.

G. Avenel, *Lundis révolutionnaires* (1871–1876), " M. Michelet" (1875), pp. 50–60.

J. Barbey d'Aurevilly, *Des philosophes et les écrivains religieux,* 1887, pp. 167–205 *Les historiens,* 1888, pp. 259–274.

F. Baudry, " Les frères Grimm leur vie et leurs travaux," *la Rev. germanique et française,* 1er fév. 1864, pp. 307 ff.

P. E. Bersot, *Littérature et morale,* 1861, " M. Michelet—La Mer," pp. 335–353.— *Discours de M. Bersot, président de l'Académie des sci. mor. et polit., prononcé aux funérailles de M. Michelet le 18 mai 1876.*

E. Biré, "*La Vendée* de M. Michelet," *Causeries littéraires,* 1887, pp. 122–164.—" Un chapitre de l'histoire de la presse royale sous la monarchie de juillet," *Le Correspondant,* 1899, vol. 194 (n. s., vol. 158) 10 janv., pp. 146–166.

H. Bordeaux, *Les écrivains et les mœurs*, 1900.

P. Bourget, " L'enfance de Michelet," *Rev. critique des idées et des livres*, 1912, 10 avril, tome 17, pp. 5–17.

M. Bréal, " La politique étrangère de Michelet," *Rev. de Paris*, 1898, 15 nov., v. VI, pp. 319–330. (Preface of *Les légendes démocratiques*, etc.)

M. de Brahm, *Les curiosités de Carnavalet*, 1920.

A. de Broglie, " De la civilisation au XVIme siècle," *Le Correspondant*, 1858, janv., pp. 1 ff.

J. Brunhês, *Michelet, prix d'éloquence*, 1898.

Centenaire de la naissance de Michelet, Compte rendu officiel des fêtes, 1899.

E. Charavay, " Lettres inédites de Michelet," *Rev. bl.* 1898, 28 mai, pp. 702 ff.

C. Chassin, *Edgar Quinet, sa vie et son œuvre*, 1859.

A. Cim, " La seconde femme de Michelet," *La Rev.*, v. 120, 1918, déc., pp. 403 ff.

J. Corcelle, " Michelet géographe," *Rev. de géographie*, 1898, juin; pp. 152 ff.

F. Corréard, *Michelet*, 1892 (first ed. 1886).

E. Des Essarts, *Portraits des maîtres*, 1888, " Michelet," pp. 157–189.—*Portraits des maîtres*, 1888, " Edgar Quinet," pp. 238–289.

T. De Quincy (Ed. Masson), vol. 5; " Joan of Arc," pp. 384–416. Appeared in *Tait's Magazine*, March and Aug., 1847.

A. Dorchain, *Ode à Michelet, dite au théâtre national de l'Odéon par Mme. Segond-Wéber*, 1898.

R. Doumic, *Etudes sur la littérature française* (4me série), " Amours de tête," 1901, pp. 77–98.

L. Drapeyron, " Comment Michelet est devenu historien et géographe," *Rev. de géographie*, 1898, vols. 42–44; sept., pp. 188 ff.; oct., pp. 264 ff.

E. Drumont, *Les tréteaux de succès; figures de bronze et figures de neige*, 1901, pp. 57–68.

L. Dufougeray, " Michelet royaliste et Catholique," *Le Correspondant*, 1891, 10 mai, pp. 430–461.

J. Duparc, " Michelet et la guerre actuelle," *La Réforme sociale;* 1916, t. 71; série 8, t. 1; 1er–16 mai, pp. 415 ff.

E. Estève, " Vico, Michelet et Vigny," *Rev. universitaire,*
1919, pp. 191–198, 259–269.

E. Fage, *Michelet et Mgr. Berteaud,* 1905.

E. Faguet, *Etudes littéraires du XIXme siècle,* 1887 (republished as *La littérature du dix-neuvième siècle,* 1900).—
Politiques et moralistes du XIXme siècle, 1891–1899.

A. Fouillée, " La psychologie religieuse dans Michelet," *Rev.
philosophique,* vol. 47, 1899, mars, pp. 259–275 (Introd.
to *Du prêtre, de la femme, etc.* and *Les Jésuites*).

V. Fournel, " Les fantaisies historiques de M. Michelet,
Correspondant, 1860, mars–avril, pp. 445 ff.

L. Gautier, " Michelet," *Portraits du XIXme Siècle,* 1894, vol.
II, pp. 343–353.

T. Gautier, *Histoire de l'art dramatique en France,* 1859, vol. iv,
pp. 228–229; vol. vi, p. 158.

E. Gebhart, " Michelet et le moyen âge français, *Institut de
'rance, acad. des sci. mor. et polit.,* 1900, n. s., v. 54, pp.
345–359.

E. Gilbert, *Michelet, écrivain naturaliste,* 1898.

J. Giraud, "Michelet inspirateur de Musset," *Rev. bl.* 1910,
10 déc.

Göttingische gelehrte Anzeigen, "J. Michelet, Histoire de France
au XVIIIme siècle," 1864, vol. 2, pp. 950 ff.

J. Gourdault, "*Nos fils,* par M. Michelet," *R. D. M.,* 1869, 15
déc., pp. 1024 ff.

M. Gréard, "Michelet et l'éducation nationale," *Institut de
France,* etc., 1903, pp. 393–419.

D. Halévy, "Le mariage de Michelet," *Rev. de Paris,* 1902, v. 4,
pp. 557–579.

H. Hauser, "Michelet en voyage," *Rev. bl.,* 1893, 26 août, pp.
374 ff.—"Michelet naturaliste et l'âme française d'aujour-
d'hui," *Rev. du mois,* 10 janv. 1919, vol. 19, pp. 151 ff.

O. d'Haussonville, *Etudes biographiques et littéraires,* 1876. (Cf.
R. D. M., 1876.)

H. Heine, "Französische Zustände," *Lutetia,* 1843, LIII.

K. Hillebrand "Jules Michelet," *Wälsches und Deutsches,* 1875,
pp. 137–147.

J. Hitier, *Annales de l'Université de Grenoble,* 1898, vol. 10, pp.
429–444.

Grace King, "An old French teacher of New Orleans," *The Yale Review*, Jan. 1922, p. 393.

G. H. L., "Modern French Historians," *Westminster Rev.*, July-Oct. 1841, pp. 211 ff.

R. Laborde, *Bulletin de la société sci. etc. de la Corréze*, t. 20, 1898, pp. 399–418.

C. Langlois, *Questions d'histoire et d'enseignement*, 2me série, pp. 93 ff (Lecture of 1904 at the University of Pennsylvania).

G. Lanson, *Hist. de la littérature française* (paragraphs on Michelet).—*Mélanges de philologie offerte à M. Wilmotte, 1910*, "Les itinéraires de Michelet."—*Le tableau de France de Michelet, notes sur le texte de 1833*.—"The Historic Method of Michelet," *International Quarterly*, 1905–1906, vol. vii, pp. 71–101. (Published also in *La Rev. d'histoire*, 1905–1906, vol. vii, pp. 5–31, under the title "La formation de la méthode historique de Michelet.")

P. Lasserre, *Le Romantisme*, 1905.—"Les idées de Michelet," *La Rev. critique des idées et des livres*, 1909, v. 7, oct.-déc., pp. 209 ff.

E. Lavisse, "L'étudiant de Michelet, "*Rev. de Paris*, 1899, 15 fév., pp. 326 ff. (preface of *L'étudiant*).

Ch. de Goffic, "Un héros de Renan et de Michelet," *Rev. bl.*, 1908, 17 oct., pp. 499 ff.

J. Lemaître, "L'amour selon Michelet," *Rev. de Paris*, 1898, 15 oct., pp. 732 ff.; année 5, vol. 5 (preface of *L'amour*).

C. Leymarie, "Michelet et Géricault," *L'Artiste*, 1897, n. s., v. 13, pp. 434–445.

J.-L.-E. Lerminier, "L'Eglise et la philosophie," *R. D. M.* 1843, n. s., v. 4, pp. 169–196.

J. Levallois, "Milieu du siècle," *Rev. bl.*, 1894, 8 déc., 11 août, pp. 167 ff., 769 ff.; 1899, 21 oct., pp. 530 ff.

London Quarterly Review, 1845, sept., art. 1 of "Religious Controversy in France," pp. 163 ff.

P. Loti, "Après une lecture de Michelet (Reflêts sur la sombre route), in *Œuvres complètes* (Calmann-Lévy), vol. viii, pp. 642–651.

F. de Mahy, "Michelet et Quinet," *La nouvelle Rev.*, n. s., vol. 5, 1905, pp. 485–500.

X. Marmier, "*Histoire de France* de J. M. Michelet," *R. D. M.*, 1835, janv. 15, série 4, vol. i, pp. 207–221.

C. Maurras, *Trois idées politiques*, 1898, "Michelet et la démocratie," pp. 18–27.

C. de Mazade, "Les rêveries bibliques de M. Michelet, à propos de *la Bible de l'humanité*," *R. D. M.*, 1865, 10 fév., pp. 698 ff., n. s., vol. v.

G. Merlet, *Portraits d'hier et d'aujourd'hui*, 1878, "L'amour et la femme selon M. Michelet," pp. 305–324.

C. Meunier, "Pourquoi on ne lit plus Michelet," *Rev. bl.*, 1898, v. 40, sér. 4, v. 9, pp. 786–790.

H. Michel, "Le centenaire d'Edgar Quinet," *Rev. bl.*, 20 déc. 1902, pp. 769–774.

A. Mickiewicz, *Chefs-d'œuvres poétiques* traduits par lui-même et par ses fils, 1882, in *Œuvres poétiques complètes*, traduction par Christien Ostrowski, 1859.—*Les Slaves*, Cours professé au Collège de France (1842–1844), 1914.

J. S. Mill, "Michelet's History of France," *Dissertations and Discussions*, pp. 198, 259. Published in the *Edinborough Rev.*, Jan., 1844.

H. H. Milman, *Erasmus and Other Essays*, 1870, pp. 357 ff.

J. Milsand, "De l'imagination dans l'histoire, M. Michelet et le moyen âge," *R. D. M.*, 1863, 2nd period, s. 43, pp. 631–654.

E. de Mirecourt, *Les Contemporains*, Michelet, 1857.

H. Monin, "La rupture de Michelet et Quinet," *Rev. d'histoire lit.*, 1912, année 19, pp. 818–841.

G. Monod, "Jules Michelet," *Bibliotêque universelle et Rev. suisse*, 1874.—*Jules Michelet*, 1875.—*Les maîtres de l'histoire*, 1894. —*Portraits et souvenirs*, 1897, pp. 15–59, "Michelet à l'école normale."—"La première œuvre de Michelet," *Institut de France, acad. des sci. mor. et polit.*, 1900, n. s., v. 54, pp. 37–58.—"Cuvillier-Fleury et Jules Michelet," *Rev. historique*, 1903, sep.–déc., v. 83, pp. 77–79.—"Le centenaire de Quinet," *Ibid.*, mai–juin, 75–80.—"Michelet et l'Italie," *Cong. Internazionale di scienze storiche*, Atti, v. iii, pp. 131–146. (Cf. also *Revista d'Italia*, 1903, anno 6, marzo–aprile), reprinted in *J. M.*—"Michelet et les mémoires de Madame Adam," *Rev. historique*, 1904, v. 85, pp. 299–305.—"Miche-

let en 1842," *Rev. bl.*, 1904, série 5, v. 1, pp. 225–230, 263–
269, 289–293, 321–325. Reprinted in *J. M.*—"Jules Michelet et son père," *Ibid.*, 1905, série 5, v. 3, pp. 225–227,
260–262, reprinted in *J. M.*—"Michelet et George Sand
d'après le journal inédit et leur correspondance," *Institut
de France*, etc., 1905, n. s., v. 63, pp. 271–317. (Cf. also *J. M.*
and *Rev. de Paris*, 1904, v. 6, pp. 531–564.)—*Jules Michelet
1905.*—"Michelet et l'Allemagne," *Rev. germanique*, 1905,
1me année, pp. 129–142. (Reprinted in *J. M.*)—"Michelet
et Madame Michelet en 1871," *Rev. bl.*, 1905, série 5, v. 4,
pp. 582–584.—"Un épisode de la vie de Michelet en 1871,"
Institut de France, acad. des sci. mor. et polit., 1906, pp. 619–
635. (Note, Michelet, J. et A., L'expiation," pp. 628–635.)
—"Une élection au Collège de France en 1830," *Rev. bl.*,
1906, pp. 673–676, 713–717. (Cf. *Institut de Fr.*, t. XLVI).—
"Jules Michelet et Alexandre Herzen d'après leur correspondance intime (1851–1869), *Rev. des rev.*, 1907, mai–juin,
série 4, vol. 68; pp. 146–164, 307–321. (Cf. *Rev. bl.*, 1905,
4 nov.)—"Paul Huet et Michelet," *Rev. bl.*, 1908, 27 juin,
pp. 801–803.—"La place de Michelet dans l'histoire de son
temps," *Bibliothèque universelle et Rev. suisse*, 1910, déc., v.
60, pp. 449–470.—"La place de Michelet parmi les historiens du XIXme siècle," *Ibid.*, 1911; tome 62, pp. 449–482.—
"Isidore Geoffroy de Saint-Hilaire et Michelet," *Rev. bl.*,
1911, pp. 481–484.

E. Montégut, "La Renaissance et la Réforme, Michelet, ses
œuvres récentes, *R. D. M.*, 1857, t. vii, pp. 643 ff.—"De
l'amour et du mariage selon M. Michelet," *R. D. M.*, 15
déc., 1858, pp. 931–951, t. 18.—"Les fantaisies d'histoire naturelle de M. Michelet," *R. D. M.*, 1861, 2me période, v. 31,
pp. 719 ff.—"La poésie des montagnes à propos du nouveau
livre de M. Michelet," *R. D. M.*, 1868, 1er mars, pp. 217 ff.,
2me period, v. 74.

A. Nettement, *Histoire de la littérature française sous le gouvern-
ment de juillet*, 1854, t. II, pp. 406–431, 452–473.

E. Noël, *J. Michelet et ses enfants*, 1878.—"L'opinion de
Michelet sur Jésus en 1854, *Rev. bl.*, 1895, 1er juin,
pp. 731 ff.

North American Review, Oct., 1846, "Michelet's Life of Luther,"

pp. 466 ff.; July, 1859, "Contemporary French Literature,"
pp. 217–221.

Nuova Antologia, "Jules Michelet, la sua vedova e i loro amici
italiani," 1916, maggio-giugno, sesta serie, v. 183 (v. 267),
pp. 273 ff.

J. Watts de Peyster, Introduction and supplement to *Prussia,
its Position and its Destiny*, by N. H. Loring, 1887.

G. Planche, "Une nouvelle Histoire de la Révolution française
de M. Michelet," *R. D. M.*, 1850, nouvelle période, v. 5,
pp. 343 ff.

A. de Pontmartin, *Dernières causeries de samedi*, 1860, vol. 1,
pp. 387–399.—*Nouveaux samedis*, "La Régence," 1872, pp.
14 ff.—*Nouveaux samedis*, "M. Michelet," 1878, pp. 62 ff.—
Nouvelles semaines littéraires, 1883 (art. dated 1863), "M.
Michelet," pp. 333 ff.

Sully Prudhomme, "La Bible de l'humanité," *Rev. de Paris*,
1898, 1er sep., pp. 5–30 (used as preface to same).

Quarterly Review, "Michelet as an Historian," 1901, v. 193,
pp. 130–150.

E. Quinet, *Idées sur la philosophie de l'histoire* (traduit de Herder), 1827.—*De l'Allemagne et de la Révolution*, 1832.—*Ahasvérus*, 1833.—*Napoléon*, 1836.—*Prométhée*, 1838.—*Le génie
des religions*, 1842.—*Le Christianisme et la Révolution française*, 1845.—*L'Enseignement du peuple*, 1850.—*Histoire de
mes idées*, 1858.—*La révolution religieuse au XIXme siècle*,
1857.—*Merlin l'enchanteur*, 1860.—*La Révolution*, 1865.—
La Critique de la Révolution, 1867.—*Lettres d'exile*, 1884–
1888.

Mme. E. Quinet, *E. Quinet, avant l'exile*, 1887.—*E. Quinet,
depuis l'exile*, 1889.—*Cinquante ans d'amitié*, 1899.

H. de Régnier, "Michelet," *Rev. de Paris*, 1898, v. 4, pp. 225–246.

E. Renan, *Discours et conférences*, 1887, "Discours prononcé au
collège de France, pour l'inauguration du médaillon de
MM. Michelet, Quinet, Mickiewicz, le 13 avril 1884" (p.
253).

Revue des Deux Mondes, "David, Géricault, souvenirs du Collège de France," 1896, 15 nov., pp. 433 ff.

L. de Ronchaud, Chronique littéraire, *Rev. germanique et française*, déc., 1863, pp. 194–197.

L. Salembier, "Michelet, sa vie, sa méthode, ses idées, son style," *Rev. de Lille*, 1906, année 17, pp. 221–239.

Sante-Beuve. For short allusions *Causeries de lundi*, i, p. 283, iii, pp. 16, 108; xii, 92; xiii, 276.—*Nouveaux lundis*, t. ii, 1880, pp. 111–15, "Louis XIX et le duc de Bourgogne par M. Michelet."

E. Saisset, "La renaissance du voltairianisme," *R. D. M.*, 1845, n. s., v. 9, pp. 377 ff.

G. Séailles, "Etude," preface of *la Sorcière*. (Ed. Calmann-Lévy.)

E. Seillière, "Jules Michelet," *La Réforme sociale*, 1919, série 8, t. 8, pp. 285–308, 377–390; t. 9, pp. 36–48, 95–111.— "Edgar Quinet," *ibid.*, 1919, série 8, vols. 7–8; pp. 256–307, 376–404, 471–513.

E. Schérer, *Etudes sur la littérature contemporaine*, 1891, v. 1, pp. 29 ff. (published first in 1863).

E. Schuré, *L'âme celtique à travers les âges*, 1921, pp. 210, 211.

J. Simon, *Mignet, Michelet, H. Martin*, 1890.

F. Spielhagen, *Vermischte Schriften*, erster Band, 1868, "*Die Liebe*, von J. Michelet," pp. 259–274.

A. Sorel, "Etude," Introduction to *Jules Michelet, Histoire et Philosophie*, 1900.

F. Strowski, "Le Messianisme en France sous Louis-Philippe," *Rev. des cours et conférences*, janv. 20, 1913.—"Michelet," *ibid.*, 5 déc., 1913.

H. Taine, *Essais de critique et d'histoire*, 1882, pp. 97–154.

R. Van der Elst, *Michelet naturaliste*, 1914.

A. Vincent, *Michelet et une nouvelle forme de religion naturelle*, 1899.

A. Vinet, "Michelet, Histoire de France," pp. 399–476; *Etudes sur la littérature française au XIXme siècle*, 1849–1851, t. III.

Westminster Review, July, 1847, pp. 198 ff.

INDEX OF PROPER NAMES

ANALYTICAL INDEX

208, 209, 210; each, realization of Messianic hope, 208–209

Children, Pity for, partial inspiration of Michelet's polemic, 59; their nervous energy, 167; education of, 168; to be taught respect for themselves, 168–169

Christ, judged by Michelet in 1833, 89; found beautiful in 1850, 89; repudiated by Michelet later, 90; as model for future " City," 90–91

Christian sentiment, Influence of, on Michelet, resistance to, 13

Christian tradition, Compromise with, considered by Michelet to jeopardize civilization, 59, 101–104; where attacked by Michelet before 1852, 59; accused by Michelet of being in league with worldliness, 55; types of heroes offered by, refused by Michelet, 92

Christianity, Michelet enemy to and borrower from, 14

Church, The, Michelet's farewell to, 67; types of human experience admired by, 90; judged by Michelet, 139–140; indictment of, by Michelet, 61–62

Citizenship, Conception of, offered by Vergil, 33

' City,' The Vision of, xxix; construction by Michelet of, xxxi; France as, 138–139; to be gathered in common worship, 159; " of Providence," July Revolution preparation for, 50; France to be, 99

Civilization, Achieved through struggle, 85; modern, a failure through distrust of life, 86; admirableness of non-Christian, 92

Civilizing force found by Michelet in Rebelliousness, 94

Class distinctions, Promoted by pity, 6; both respected and disregarded by Michelet, 160–200

Clubs, Origins of Woman's Revolutionary, 157

Colonization, To be pacific and effected by suppression of race prejudice, 200–201

Communion, Absolute, demanded

by Michelet in marriage, 128, 196, 197

Community, The Great, 29

Compassion, Multiple uses of, by Michelet, 10–11; evidence of continuity of life, 11–12; produced strong reactions in Michelet, 46

Confessional, Danger and condemnation of, 176–177; duties of part of husband's pontificate, 206

Conscience, " Divine fruit of every religion," 86

Contradictions, In Michelet's pronouncements on woman, 159, 160

Creed, making of, layman's task, xxvii, cf. Michelet, Part II

Criticism, Of Michelet's ideas on woman and marriage, 212–218

Curiosity, Michelet's, masked by pity, 24; aroused by new social systems, 113

Death, Not to be overcome, 85

Degradation, Picture of, used by Michelet as plea for education and dignity of human impulse, 63–65

Democracy, Foreseen by Michelet as a social order created and unified by social pity, 23

Democratic, Spirit contrasted with aristocratic *belle âme*, 46

Dignity of social life, 23, 104; woman's, how preserved, 107–109; of human person in national tradition; man's in relation to woman, 108–109; of marriage, how preserved, 118; desired by Michelet for all women, 165

Divinity of humanity, 93

Divorce, Social, rôle of Jesuits in, studied by Michelet, 119; caused by ignorance of life, 120

Dogma, Christian, repudiated in name of human pity, 16

Don des larmes, Le, 3

Dowry, 199–200

" Droit de Cité " bestowed according to capacity for sentiment, 28